# WHEN THE JONQUILS BLOOM AGAIN:

*Book One*

*An Enema,
A Birthday spanking,
A Love Story*

by
J G Knox

*AuthorHouse™*
*1663 Liberty Drive, Suite 200*
*Bloomington, IN 47403*
*www.authorhouse.com*
*Phone: 1-800-839-8640*

© *2008 J G Knox. All rights reserved.*

*No part of this book may be reproduced or transmitted in any form or by any means, electronic or mechanical, including photocopying, recording, or by any information storage and retrieval system, without permission in writing from the Publisher except of brief passages quoted in newspaper, magazine, radio, television or Internet reviews..*

*First published by AuthorHouse 1/16/2008*
*ISBN: 978-1-4343-3907-2 (sc)*

*Printed in the United States of America*
*Bloomington, Indiana*

*This work is fictional. The types of experiences in it were common and many may have been experienced by most people living in America during the 1930s through the 1960s. These sharings may bring back memories of loving and caring real events for these people. However any resemblance to any person or event is coincidental.*

## Table of Contents

Chapter 1  THE FRENCH CURE ................................................ 1
Chapter 2  JONQUILS PRESENT ............................................. 17
Chapter 3  JONQUILS PAST..................................................... 31
Chapter 4  BIRTHDAY SPANKINGS ....................................... 43
Chapter 5  GROWN UP BIRTHDAY SPANKINGS ................ 51
Chapter 6  RECOLLECTIONS OF CORRECTIONS ............. 63
Chapter 7  READING AND WRITING .................................... 75
Chapter 8  BRUSSELS' SPROUTS............................................ 87
Chapter 9  DADDY .................................................................... 97
Chapter 10  SEX, BAD SEX ..................................................... 109
Chapter 11  LOVING AMBER NOT BRUSSEL'S SPROUTS ... 123
Chapter 12  THE ENGAGEMENT............................................ 143
Chapter 13  ALBERT'S ARMY ................................................. 161
Chapter 14  THE PREACHER'S GOD ..................................... 173
Chapter 15  MY AUNT MINDY................................................ 187
Chapter 16  GOOD GIRLS DON'T GET PREGNANT........... 203
Chapter 17  A TALE OF TWO FARMS ................................... 213
Chapter 18  THE OLD PADDLE .............................................. 233
Chapter 19  NURSE MINDY..................................................... 253
Chapter 20  NEVER SAYING GOOD BY ............................... 271
Chapter 21  PEARL HARBOR .................................................. 281
About the Author........................................................................ 293

## Chapter 1
# THE FRENCH CURE

*Present day*

Every extraordinary day of living is a lifetime of every days. Jonquils live every day of late spring, summer, fall and winter ordinary, blending with grass. A few weeks in early spring they bloom, dance the ballet of life, live their extraordinary days.

First flora, winter's last pirouette, delicate blooms sweep and dip. Life on ice, flowers in snow, blossoms in six petal tutus with matching trumpet leotards, jonquils, also known as daffodils, dance in cold wind. Sun lights a backdrop of blue sky and pink clouds behind a black stage. A night scene ends. Twirling shadow-gray ballerinas turn yellow, ray by solar ray. The dance, an extraordinary day, emerges from darkness.

A special day, my first visit to my Grandparent's home in 30 years I am excited. My colon rumbles, wakes me with a familiar tune. I dance short quick steps and stop. Holding on I squeeze back a rumble. It passes. More quick steps, the throne, I make it! I have Irritable Bowel

Syndrome (IBS). Two days of runs and irritability following three of constipation and irritability, then more diarrhea, more irritability is that why they call it Irritable Bowel Syndrome? Release relieves constipation, but with IBS relief, acidic diarrhea, burns the colon, makes it worse. Stress, excitement makes it worse.

Sick, I need help, my husband's help. Returning to bed I slide under our blanket cuddle close to him and feel his warmth. I want my cold feet on his warm ones, but I don't want to wake him. He is my warmth in winter, my danseur, the one that holds my hand, spins me, tosses me toward the sun and catches me in his arms. He is my partner, the sun in my sky. He is the source of extraordinary days, the one that will wake with a startle if I plant icy feet on his.

He needs rest. Old, up every few hours to urinate, he sleeps under a winter blanket, not in the best of health. I won't wake him, nor will I stop wishing him awake caring for me. When we are young I wake him. I put cold feet on his when I need him. He wakes, takes care of me, when we are young. I am lucky. IBS is a disorder of men, but mostly women. Ninety percent of IBS patients are women. Other women suffer, pace the floor, scurry to the toilet, alone. He wakes, takes care of me. He has taken care of me for 54 years.

Can we bloom one more year like jonquils, dancing, springing, leaping? Can we be young--- not old, have another spring, another summer, another fall? Awake, I remember the decades: is he dreaming of our seasons, our lives?

They are seasons to remember, decades to dream about. Dreams bring them back as they were, could have been and are. Green grass, budding trees, fields of flowers, shy lover's glances, life is spring light. Hot days, bare arms, warm nights and sizzling kisses, life is summer touch. Walking together hand warming hand, leaves of gold, sheaths of grain, life is fall harvest. Long nights, cold feet, warm fires, watching him sleep, life is love under a winter blanket. Life is days, seasons, years, ages, life spans, a flower dancing at sunrise, a dream.

We have our springs, summers, falls and winters, dances with jonquils, our days in sun, nights loving and hands held through years of joy--- memories, and grand leaps to come. Snow and gray, our hair promises a season of reflection. Winter, bulbs in ground, swell with life, prepare for living new in spring. We have lived it, spring of promise, summer of action, fall of harvest and now, winter of remembrance.

We rise en pointe on children's feet and live through other's dances. Sitting rather than spinning our toes point in rhythm with the music. We watch. Once young and in love we are old, and in love.

Young jonquils from old bulbs dance around our home. Our youth dancing in the yard is a memory, as it was. Youth of our children, their children and now a fourth generation… youth eternal toddles, watches old feet move to old dances, ads a new step to a new day. Two old bulbs we live to dance with young flowers. Humans change. Jonquils don't. They flower in spring, disappear in summer and fall, die in winter, and are born new in spring, never sharing a step with their children.

We live beyond winters cold. Bulbs, cloves split off, grow in my belly, are born and grow as I watch. My great grandmother loves jonquils. I, as a child, come to love jonquils. Lizzy, my great granddaughter loves jonquils. She will love them when old, as her great granddaughter comes to love them.

I watch my great granddaughter grow, dance a slow dance with her among the jonquils and then hurry to the bathroom, my intestines rumbling. Okra for supper, and flax seed easing, yet churning in my gut, I will go again. I wish he would wake up, give me enemas and ease my spastic colon.

Knowing leaving home will do this to me why are we going? I want to go. I want to stay close to our bathroom. After all these years, does my love have sympathy for a woman that doesn't like to travel with diarrhea or does he have empathy? He understands that stress causes IBS and travel, change, a break in routine, can ease it. He cares for me, helps me. He takes my hand, husbands me, dances with me and moves me on days I sit and need to move.

Today, an extraordinary day, a day to remember, a day of visiting special days long passed, is to a place once home, my ancestral home, familiar. Other times he takes me to places ancient, unfamiliar.

### *24 years earlier*

Once upon a time there were enchanted castles, France for a month. Danny, our youngest child, causes that bout of IBS, as he does the present one. After graduating from high school he enlists in the Army.

"Bye, Momma!"
*How can he do this?*

His going leaves me alone, an alone that never ends in our childless home. It is the greatest stress I endure. Having constipation followed by diarrhea for weeks I have my worst attack of IBS since I am thirteen. He escapes me. I can't escape him. Every room in our house, every street, passing the school, everything reminds me of him. He is everywhere familiar--- not France.

France fulfills dreams of knights, ladies, parapets and castles. Being there realizes a fantasy, adds to the problem. Irritable Bowel Syndrome, once activated by stress, all stress, good or bad, worsens. Airborne, over the Artic, others sleep. I am perpetually in line for the toilet.

"Pardon, Madame et Monsieur, I have an urgent need!" I say nine times on the plane. The wild, pleading look in my eyes added to broken French is sufficient to convince, to let me go ahead of others less distressed.

Traveling by train, first class with a private room, we have a toilet, small and needed. Versailles, there is a place, beautiful, an extreme shortage of toilets. French kings value self, bladder and bowel control. Will I make it? Will I please the Sun King, earn his respect, or will I, brown stained, humiliated, give him a laugh. Several times it is close. I understand the French revolution. IBS, constipation followed by diarrhea in repeating bouts, helps me understand. The masses, deprived of dignity and toilets, deprive the royals of life itself when the suppression of constipation turns to the diarrhea of revolution.

This lesson comes home in an ancient French fortress. Tiny yellow flowers grow between old steps once new. My colon rumbles. Waves of diarrhea call. An echo, the same urges grip a woman ascending these stairs 600 years ago. My condition is ancient passed down from some long distant ancestor born before France or England exists.

The tower, a defensive position, a dozen conscript peasants, made soldiers the week before stand on the parapet looking over an army of English invaders. Gleaming axes threatening, promising, they will attack. Undermanned, the tower is a place of extreme stress. The wife of one of the conscripts, her only child another, she dresses as a man, goes with the father to the fortress. Her son, 13, drinks his first grog from his mother's hand celebrating his manhood, his becoming a soldier. He wakes with a hangover in his mother's dress, her long hair laying on the cottage floor beside him.

An English rapist moving through the village with the first wave of invaders puts down his helmet and axe expecting sport. The beardless boy in a dress grabs his axe, finishes him and runs away. The boy will grow, will fight another day in another forgotten war. He will love and be a father.

Is some of his blood, his mother's blood, mine? Do they live in me? Is that why I am drawn to this spot, this ancient time? I feel her presence, feel a breath of a breeze wafting through my hair. She is close. Does she feel me? Does she know I have come to join her on this wall?

This wall, on this wall she fights as no man fights that day, her husband bleeding, dying, she pulls him behind her. Grabbing an attacker's axe she holds the place by the parapet with a ferocity admired by those that kill her. Stormed and taken in 1358 A.D., every conscript of their village dies on this wall, their first and last military assignment.

Diarrhea, frequent during their week of service, is a common response to fear. My problem, not new, curses soldiers of every time. The problem results in reeking latrines near every battlefield from times before the first fortifications are constructed. A solution is built in stone. The guide points out two round holes cut in a bench on the stone parapet, toilets, 1000-AD-toilets. Fascinated, drawn, I look at them as no other in the group slipping behind an exposed wall. The other tourists make their way to another toiletless area of the fortress. I sit beside the memory of my ancestor spilling our guts on the wall below. Relief! Comfortable at last, I catch up with the group at the grand hall.

All is forgotten until passing under the parapet.

The guide stops. "Monsieurs, I must speak to the Madames. Ladies, while the toilets of the parapet may have outlasted many nations, their use, under local code, has not. Toilets require sanitary drains. You can see, looking up, the openings empty onto the wall--- and the workers restoring the wall." He points out one workman.

The man holds a brown splotched hat no longer on his head. It dangles pinched between two fingers from one unbrown spot.

"Our workmen, peasants, are accustomed to being defecated upon by the elite of our society, less so foreign tourists," the guide says.

The gray-haired man with the hat fumes with a foul smelling indignation. Can revolutions occur against tourists?

"Of course this is a misdemeanor with a small fine. Not that anyone will be prosecuted, none of the laborers have seen her face. Nevertheless, I suggest the guilty party not moon any of the witnesses, displaying recognizable features. This also is a misdemeanor, one with a fine." With a patrician gesture the guide directs us to the bus.

My guilt is undeniable. Dignity gone, red faced, I flee, as would have the twelve soldiers had they had a bus running and waiting. Dragging my husband we arrive at the bus first. My husband having obtained front seat reservations our position is overrun by the English speaking horde hiding axes in smiles. Passing to seats farther back each smile is different, some hide contempt, others don't. The one resembling King Louis XIV is amused.

The most painful blow comes not from strength. It comes from warmth turned cold. From the beginning of the tour a young school teacher from Wyoming befriends me, makes me feel part of the group. From the rural west, unacquainted with our people, she sees me, my mind, my accomplishments, not the stereotype. Others see differences, not her. Changing, she glares at me with revulsion.

*Why? I had diarrhea, couldn't wait. I'm Sorry! Doesn't she understand necessity? I didn't want to go. I had to go!*

I think it. My husband says it.

My love, my defender, my knight says, "I'm sorry, she has spastic colitis!" as each one of them passes nodding in recognition.

This is his defense of his lady in distress? Sir Walter Raleigh threw his coat in the mud to prevent Queen Elizabeth from soiling her feet.

*Why doesn't he take off his blazer and throw it over my head?*

Slinking in my seat I smile at no one. Each of their smiles hides an axe. Unconvinced eyes climb over the wall hacking another gash in my dignity.

I dig my fingers into his knee thinking, telegraphing, *Please stop! Don't say anymore*!

He is confused. He is trying to help, saying the wrong thing, when saying nothing is the only correct response. I know that look in his eyes.

"I think the Yankees will win the series again this year. Don't you?" he says, to an elderly Englishman man entering the bus.

The man passes by looking at my husband without an answer. He knows the Yankees beat them in the revolutionary war, and helped win the last one. *What series is America embarking on this time?*

I squeeze his knee. He looks more confused.

"Feynman's lectures, have you read Feynman's lectures? Wonderful job, a wonderful job," he says to the next person.

*Who is Feynman?* I see in their eyes.

He is succeeding. Forgetting my sins other passengers are looking at him. *Is he crazy? What is he talking about?*

I kiss him. That is the only way to stop him. Everyone is looking at us.

Stopping talking he pecks me with a kiss, a sheepish look and says, "I love you."

"I love you, too," blushing I whisper in his ear.

Silence settles.

I want to ask the driver, *Could we have other seats, in the back of the bus. I am used to sitting in the back of the bus, or better yet, let my husband sit up front. I'll be more comfortable under the bus with the luggage.*

Extra room exists down there, a compartment unused. Dark, rumbling, transported alone I visualize being drawn from under the bus after a suit case. The workman waits his browned hat discarded, a black hood over his head and a large axe in his hand. I see the block.

"Pardon moi, Monsieur!" I say as Marie Antoinette says before losing her head. She only steps on the executioner's foot, my error more odious will the workman accept my apology before I die for my sins?

Saying nothing, I sit. The last person passes and smiles. My husband squeezes my hand. The coach moves. I have used a 1000 year old toilet, a once in a life time experience--- never to be repeated, never!

Disobeying Mr. Ensley, the high school principal, once, I didn't do it twice. This time my face glows red. No glowing bottom, tears flowing, or severed head held high for onlookers to witness, today there will be no axe, no paddle, no fine. Embarrassment is sufficient, most sufficient.

At every stop thereafter, at least two ladies, trying to help, point out public toilets.

My husband helps. 4 PM, we arrive at our hotel. "We need ten liters of boiled water," he says, tipping the bell hop.

"Ten liters of boiled water," the puzzled young man questions?

Seeking okra my husband finds ochre, black ink. So much for French culinary acumen! Fried okra is a required vegetable for fine dining. Planning ahead I have eight bottles of slippery elm tablets and a pound of flax seeds in my suit case. Not joining the others for dinner, I sip a soothing herbal tea as my husband finishes his brought-in dinner. Water boils in our coffee maker.

Finished filling his innards, it is time to fill mine. He dilutes hot with cold water. Testing with the bath thermometer we carry my husband adds baking soda. Our world-traveling beaker fills. The sound of water pouring in the container soothes me, is a welcome sound from home.

"Thank you." I hug my beloved from behind.

He finishes the preparations.

Our beaker travels the world empty. Never more than ¾ full it makes short working trips, and one of those per enema. From counter to bed I carry it. Sitting on the bed, his back against the headboard a towel over his knees my husband is ready for me. Handing him the water, climbing over his knees as a child to be spanked I grasp the beaker, this time gripping it between my knees.

"Thank you for helping me." I relax bottom up over his thighs.

*Why doesn't my husband talk to me when I am having an enema?* He gives me instructions after the doctor teaches him how to do it. Now he does it without a word. Is there nothing to say after thousands of times over his knee? Is it because he knows how I feel? Is he leaving me time to go within myself, feel the love, as the water goes within me?

Having an enema is always exciting, emotional, a rush, an intimacy unequaled for the patient. A novelty when we are first married, my submission, controlling me, my struggling to hold it for him, the enema excites us both. It is a part of exploration, learning each other. Now for him it is routine as exciting as sharing the sink when we brush our teeth.

An ordinary, simple procedure made Freudian powerful for the patient. It is no more than an internal bath--- if it weren't for toilet training. There is shame, the pelvis, hidden smelly things. An enema exposes the inner workings of the receiver as no other medical procedure.

Others never this open, exposed, with their husbands, fear revealing too much. I reveal my soul, my mind, my bare bottom and have his love. He loves me in ways other women dream of being loved.

I stroke his knee. The touch of his body on mine, the connection is electric. The hair of his leg on my fingers are live wires tingling my fingertips. I want him giving me the enema, filling me with warm water, electric surges tingling within me, quivering with the holding of it, the taking of it. An enema is never routine to this receiver. Is it to anyone being given enema?

If done often it becomes routine for the giver. Is my husband exposed? Does he hold it, feel it? My buttock in his hand, stroking my hip, he lingers, he senses my excitement. Lying still, quiet, I await ecstasy, dancing, my calves quivering. I will look into his eyes with the pleading of a two-year-old wanting to go potty, with the love of a wife cared for intimately. He feels it.

Downstairs the band plays. The music floats through the open doors on our balcony. Ladies take the hands of their gentle men, waltz. Upstairs his hands on me, I rub my fingers under his knee, this time gently, caressing, water surging within me. The syringe does the box step, filling then emptying, filling then emptying. Downstairs the dance goes on cherished women following in the steps of their lovers' feet. Upstairs the dance internal, I follow my love my toes tracing in air a primeval dance step.

My buttocks soften, relax let the warm glow in my abdomen spread. I melt with warmth. I float in a dream state. The enema creates a warm upwelling waltzing within in me. Soothing, surging in my rectum, relaxing, swirling and gurgling I take bulb after bulb from our adult syringe. Each move takes me closer to a point of being completely full, unable to dance another squeeze of the syringe.

"I don't think I can take any more," I say.

He fills the bulb.

Pouting, tense my buttocks don't relax. His hand caressing the small of my back eases me, helps. Giving up in bits, I go limp over his knee. I feel the enema tip. It glides into me.

My husband holds the bulb gently keeping up the pressure. As I breathe out a shallow breath he squeezes. Surge meets surge. My calves quiver in time with the music down stairs. My colon is full. An enema is done, over. He climbs from underneath me, stretches beside me. I snuggle in his arms.

A jonquil blossoming, my petals quiver in the warm wind of his breath. He holds me. I open to him. Our cheeks meet. Our heads on one pillow we talk.

"You are a good girl," he says.

"I am a good girl," I say

"You are a good woman."

"I am a good woman."

"God loves you."

"God loves me."

"You are loved," He says.

"I love you!" I say after a pause, an intimate surge pressing his words deep in me.

Nuzzling my ear, hugging me, not saying another word, he loves me!

We are one.

As I kiss him on the bus to quiet him, soothe him, he kisses me. The surging, the urgency, the submission eases me into ecstasy. Care passes between us. Unmoving contact of our stomachs together without arousal, without tension, yet more sensual than sex, we warm in love. Physical gurgles within me mix with coos of harmony between us. I am love. He is love. We are love!

He makes me a mother and keeps me having babies, often without a word spoken. He makes me what I dream to be, what I want to be, what I think my whole life will be. In 19 years I have not conceived a child. In 19 years every child is gone. Is my purpose, my life, gone?

"Sharon, I love you." He senses the thought without me saying it.

"I love you."

"I need you to take care of me," he says.

"That is all I live to do!"

"It's not enough." He kisses my forehead.

*What!* My world dissolves into sludge.

The four words hurt. A rumble pours through me. A twinge, a cramp, I have trouble holding it. The hurt is too much.

"It's not enough. You must have a life too. Your life is not me. It's not the children. It's more than that. I am here and need you now. Danny and his brothers and sisters love you, need you, are grown and gone. Some day I will be gone too."

"You can't leave me. You can never leave me! I can't live without you!" I wrap my arm around his neck hugging him to me.

*Why is he interrupting this tender moment with this? Why now as I trust him with the childlike adoration of a toddler being lovingly toilet trained by her mother?*

His plan, something that must be introduced when I am open deep, he shows me. He warms me, prepares me, now he takes me as a virgin to a world outside then inside my life as it is. I hold the enema and every word; each syllable floods a cellar storing the canning jars of my life. Thoughts and beliefs held since childhood float off shelves, float in the muddy water within me. Left on my own I will pick them up, wipe them clean and restore them to their place after the water goes. His plan, a lid unscrews, with a cramp the contents empty into the muddy flow. Squeezing my buttocks together I hold this, preparing to release what can not be held.

"Sharon, I'm well. I'll be with you a long, long time. I'll be your husband every day of the rest of my life. It's just--- you have to be you, have to be more than a woman having babies, more than a mother, more than a wife now. You must make your life around other things as well as me or our children, around things immortal, God, purpose, service beyond family, things that lasts, eternal things." He kisses my cheek. He kisses his way to my eyes and forehead. "What about church? Do you want to teach the adult class? Nothing will stop your studying or preparing. You can focus on that."

*Is that what this is about? Does he want me to teach the adult class?* "I like teaching the early teens."

"I like teaching them too."

"You said teaching them restored your faith in capital punishment," I strike back, trying to divert the deep erosion of this purge.

"Not for all of them, Sharon, only a few!"

"George Jr., the preacher's son?"

"The death penalty was not even considered with him, honey. He has another parole hearing next month. I'm testifying for him."

"How many witnesses refused to testify because they were afraid of George Jr., dear husband? How many of the witnesses that did testify appeared at his last parole hearing pleading in fear of their lives if he gets out?"

"Three testified, and those same three were at the parole hearing. But he's changing. Every time I visit him he is a perfect gentleman."

"Wasn't it you that convinced me to vote for Richard Nixon because you believed him to be honest?" I raise my eyebrows and continue, "If George Jr. gets parole is he going to attend church, the adult class?"

"Yes, of course."

"I don't want to teach the adult class!"

"Ok, you don't want to teach another class at church. Do you want to work? Do you want to go to college now, maybe be a school teacher?"

"Aren't there more George Juniors in public schools than church classes?"

"What do you want to do? It is time you have a life of your own. Think about it, OK?" He kisses me.

"Ok," I hold him tighter. I don't want to change, have a life beyond him, beyond my children. At home, I feel pain being in an empty house alone all day. I want my babies back; dream of life as it has been. Can I see this, this solution, this life change? Trying to fluff it off with Nixon's honesty another jar opens, dissolves, I have another cramp. I change. In this foreign land away from all I know he brings me putting distance between me and our life as it is for thirty four years. He understands, guides; he husbands me.

"I think George Jr. will get out this year."

*Will I have George Jr. watching me, scheming, as I teach the adult class?*

My husband leads me.

Fear fills me, a fear of not being able holding on, a fear of not letting go.

"Hold me!" A quiver rips through me.

Holding me tighter, he slides one hand down my back comforting me, stroking the goose bumps on my bottom. "Let the children and I be as important in your life as we have been, but with more room for you to explore your self. It's the time in your life you have the freedom to be you, to explore your mind, your soul. Dream, new dreams." He kisses me.

"You are my dream, my dreams. All I want to take care of you, be your wife, be a mother!" I shiver. "Please!" The cold comes from inside me. "I've never worked outside our home. Everywhere I go you take me, except a few school events, or to get groceries or something else for the family. Now you want me to become someone else! I don't want to be someone else!"

My husband knows me. The light rubbing over my goose bumps soothes the depth of my soul, draws me to him.

"What do you want me to do? It is not my role to be a decision maker. It's yours. I am a decision critic. You make decisions. I critique them." I snuggle deeper into his arms.

An obedient wife I always do what he tells me to do, when it is what I want to do. What if it isn't? I listen, critique in my mind, watch his eyes and wait for a moment of openness to influence his thinking.

Before we marry he is afraid for me to have children.

"It is dangerous, and hurts," he says. "Let's wait a few years, be together first."

I listen. *Is he afraid for me to have a baby? Will he not make love to me, rather than risk me having a baby?* I can see it in his eyes, the fear, the love. I want children. I want a baby. I want a baby since Daddy gives me my doll, Samantha, when I am five. His greatest fear, losing me in childbirth; my greatest fear losing him, barren, without childbirth, we have a conflict. I want children. He wants me.

We are wedding in two days, and there is no birth control in common use in 1949 except the rhythm method.

"When did your last period start?" He asks.

"A lady doesn't answer questions like that!" I blush.

"Ok, but if you are in midcycle it's dangerous to have sex. Are we OK?"

"What is midcycle?" I having the standard sex education girls have in 1949? We are told girls have periods; if we have sex, we stop having periods; we have babies, nothing else.

"14 days after your period starts."

"We are OK."

On our wedding day it will be the 13th day after my period, not the 14th.

Listening, I obey, a good wife I tell him when it is my 14th day on our honeymoon. *Should I have told him before we made love three times?* It is his fault, his decision. We could stop. He doesn't want too. I am sure that 4th time causes it. I don't feel pregnant the first three times.

It is lust, new lust. His father tells him he will like sex. At 20 he listens to his father, a twenty year old listening, he has to know for himself. By the second day of our honeymoon his father is a wise man. The day before, a boy, he knows what he is told, what he reads. He knows fantasies unexplored, a mystery in panties. Today, a man, he knows new passion. He knows its feel and its source. He knows me.

After three times this morning he touches me again. A little sore, I will stop if he wants too, only if he wants too. In his mind he is ready. His body, quivering, a man, he pushes his limits. It shows. A perfect moment to alter his thinking, a virgin the night before, I know what I can do to him. I chose that moment to stop, talk to him, to tell him it is my 14th day.

"I am a woman. I want to have your babies." I kiss him. "I'll never leave you. I won't die and I'm not afraid of pain as long as you hold my hand; you know that. Make love to me!" I give him my first order, my first decision in conflict with his. I want him. I want part of him inside me growing. I want part of him nursing me when he is at work. I want him.

He tries to respond, can't. "I love you! I don't want you to die having a baby!" Quivering his body is shaking cold with fear, not a rational fear, the fear of a childhood ghost haunts him. "You could be pregnant already!" Gripping my waist in a vice grip he nuzzles his head to my chest.

Understanding I kiss him. "I love you."

I play with his hair stroking it, running my fingers through it, rubbing a breast against his face I reach over him for the hair brush. Holding him to me I brush his hair sliding my hands over his back down to his buttocks. His grip relaxes. I work the brush through his hair for an hour. Finishing I slip beside him kissing his lips. Feeling him ready, I roll on my back my fingers penetrating deep in his hair. His head lifts. My hair spreads out on the pillow. My arms slide down his back.

"Make love to me," I say.

"Don't ever leave me, don't die having our baby!"

He worries for the whole nine months, until the birth is over, then is ecstatic over our girl. Drifting to sleep holding me am I a mist, a dream that can be lost with the slightest stir of air? Is it possible for my husband to love me this much? I watch him sleep.

This time he is not going to give me a 14th day to avoid. Always kissing, loving, brushing his hair and massaging him on 14th days, the days I want sex most, I am a mother, want to be a mother. *Am I a decision maker?* Having babies is my decision, not having them is his. We have eight.

Back in France the enema surges within me. *How long have I been holding this enema?*

"Are you ready to go to the bathroom?" he says.

I climb over him heading for the toilet.

In the restroom water cascades out, waste from the past flows with it. Tension eases. The euphoria that follows the flushing of a good enema purges my mind. My mind washed, empty, I am ready to conceive. Am I too old to have a baby? Babies aren't the only births of a good marriage. He keeps me pregnant mentally and spiritually too.

Expelling what is, was and should be gone, enemas purge, evacuate, create vacuums. Does nature abhorring a vacuum, fill it? Ready for his filling, I return to my husband's husbandry. My irritability gone I am ready to learn, ready to change, ready for new life to grow in me.

"OK, what do you want me to do?" I ask.

He smiles kissing me, this time with passion. I know what we want.

Later I ask him, "OK, now what do you want me to do?"

His mother brushes his hair. Brushing his hair brings out the boy in him, brings out every hidden thought in his child mind. Later, for me it is sex that teases out his innermost thoughts. Brush his hair, give him sex, work him until he is sated, warm, at peace and he opens up to me as to a mother.

"Sleep maybe, sleeping is good," he says.

"I mean about my life, what do you want me to do?"

"Something. You need a new motivation. Of course you can still have dinner at 6 PM, my shirts ironed and the house clean."

I will be 90 years old, creeping to the ironing board to iron another shirt. That is my future. I see that.

"Think about it. There must be something calling you. What do you want to do? Let me know what you come up with," he pecks me and rolls over to go to sleep.

"But, I want to know what you want---"

"I want what you want. I have always wanted what you want. Don't you know that?" Turning back to me he kisses me, this time covering my mouth for a long lingering smooch, then says, "Bon soir."

*Isn't he going to give me a 14th day to avoid?*

He snores.

An extraordinary night, a jonquil bulb below the surface, deep in the depth of its being, splits conceives another clove of life.

## *Chapter 2*
# JONQUILS PRESENT

*Back to the present*

Other trips, not as embarrassing or as filled with potty stops as our trip to France, I remember with love. When will my husband take me to our honeymoon hotel in the city? Going there for a long weekend at least once a year we make love, sleep, eat, take in an occasional show, maybe a tour. We relax. We live. We love. These are my favorite trips.

Always seeking women's rest rooms on other vacations, schedules to keep, people waiting, adventures to places unknown and unfamiliar, these are the vacations we take pictures, make movies and talk about with friends, not the ones I long to remember.

I adventure far, a traveler. Born to a people untraveled, living their days rooted in one place this is new. My grandfather lives in two counties, travels through a third and never sees the state line. My great grandfather and back another four generations live out their lives in the county of their birth never seeing flat land, the sea or a building taller than three floors. People born to work the earth don't move. Their feet as deep rooted in the earth they grow as the crops they grow, in one spot. Travel is unthinkable.

Women follow men: men follow mules. Smooth brown backsides, swishing tails, pooping as they go mules lead. Generation after generation they plow, feeding civilizations they never see, furrow by furrow. Scholars in cities write history. Farmers in fields make history. Cities flourish when harvests exceed demand, wane when crops falter. Civilizations disappear when crops fail, grow when fed by fertile soil and favorable climate.

During my lifetime a revolution occurs, not one with guns, a real one, with plows. Agricultural productivity becomes greater than ever imaginable to any previous generation. We eat as never before in history. From 90% of people being employed in producing food farmers dwindle to less than 10% of the population. We go to town.

I am born to farm people, made a city girl. My father trades dirt for steel, cuts the tap root to work in a plant, crosses the state line to another state, another world. He puts down a new steel tap root inside the plant's gates with release bolts. He can leave his machines for weeks on vacation then with a wrench reattach his roots. Daddy gives us mobility on ribbons of steel with a steam engine ahead. At nine years old I see the Empire State building and more states than any of my ancestors before my Daddy.

I marry a man of books, little squiggly lines penned on paper, formulas from France, Germany, the sands of Arabia, any place thought occurs. Our tap root in the soil of minds and imaginations the earth is not large enough to hold him. We travel.

My husband insists on taking vacations afar: Charleston--- "Y'all know where the toilets are?" The Grand Canyon--- "Where is the bathroom!" echo, echo, echo. Wyoming--- "What do you mean, 'Get off the horse and squat!' I can't do it with a cow watching at me." I panic-search for bathrooms in 24 states and five foreign nations.

Is it better after my king buys the motor home? Happiness to a queen in her 23 foot castle is a throne with a privacy door less than five steps away! Why aren't we taking the motor home? It's Danny's idea. Danny again! He says we need to sleep in the ancestral bed where five generations of my family slept. He says we need to feel the soil under our bare feet, let our toes grow into the earth, feel the roots with our blood, be with the place as it was and is, our tap root.

"There are no motor homes in 1849." Danny says, "and your room has a private bath."

"A month, how can I leave for a month? What about Lizzy? It will be her fifth birthday. I have to be home for her birthday," I say.

"We will have you home two days before Lizzy's birthday, Momma."

"Rustic toilets? Did you say rustic toilets? I don't know if I can do rustic toilets! Natural and historic are different. Rustic toilets are old, have spiders, corn cobs and smell bad. I have to have a regular toilet, Danny."

Did we take Danny and his brothers and sisters on constant camping trips? He remembers that. I answer the call behind more bushes than B'rer Rabbit. He remembers that. Does he know anything about my experience with medieval toilets? My knight in rusty armor protecting me, only he and I know about that.

"The house has regular toilets, Momma. They only have rustic doors. Hiding behind the rock outcrop is a modern kitchen, dining room, men and women's bathrooms and showers. 1840s clothes, plowing with mules, eating by lamp light, this people will do. They won't give up modern toilets, toilet paper or running water. We account for that," my son, the retired Sergeant Major, says as if I am a green recruit.

What can I say, *yes sir*? I won't say, *yes sir*, not to my baby boy. I potty trained him. "Danny, the bathroom had better be modern or I am catching the next train home!" Mommas do not say, *Yes sir, or Yes Sergeant Major*, to use proper military jargon, to sons, even if they are sergeant majors.

I look through the window. Along the driveway jonquils are dancing, beautiful. The sight of them brings a smile, eases me, stops the rumbling in my gut. *How can I leave my Jonquils when they are blooming? What if we have a delay coming home? Will Lizzy celebrate her birthday without me? Will she cry if I am not here or worse, not cry?*

My husband awake, slipping up behind me as quiet as his Grandfather slipping up on an unsuspecting settler to scalp her, hears what I didn't say.

"We will be home before Lizzy's birthday," he says.

*How can he know what I am thinking? Is he like his grandfather?*

His grandfather, a medicine man, knows things, sees what others do not see, hears what others do not hear. Moving silently in this and other worlds, watching, listening in his brown skin and long black hair he frightens others, white others.

An honor student, would he have learned more, or at least longer at school, had he not been a big Indian? 1880's students and staff, afraid of Indians, are more afraid when it is a big Indian. A big Indian that slips up on the Latin instructor grabbing the small man's wig, whoops and does a war dance. The college kicks him out after that incident ending his grandfather's formal education.

Home he tells his father, "I didn't like school. I didn't like the way they treated me. They treated me different."

His father helps him hook up the mule and points him to the field.

"I didn't dislike college this much!"

An opening at the Indian school for a teacher comes open. Half a college education saves him from following brown backsides down furrows for the rest of his life. He marries another teacher, a white woman, and is a fanatic about educating their children. Every one of their children hear the call of knowledge, the wind whispering in the oaks, the voices in the heads of others and the school bell every morning. Every one of their decendents finish school are nurses, doctors or teachers.

*Or is it my husband's sleeping next to me, his arm ever around me holding my thoughts, that lets him hear the voices in my head?*

"How are you doing? Do you need an enema before we go?" He says.

"There isn't time," I say, "I'll be OK."

Nestling back into his arms he engulfs me. I am always all right with him holding me. Besides it takes at least two enemas, one to wash out the acid. Holding a second baking soda one for thirty minutes soothes the irritation. My bowel easing I relax after the enemas. Is there enough time to do that and catch the train? Maybe he will treat me tonight after we get settled, depending on how rustic the toilets really are, not now. Now I am irritable, edgy, holding in emotions.

"The jonquils are pretty this morning," he says, "and so are you!" He squeezes me.

Having two hours before we go, is there time? There is, but not for an enema!

Wiggling around I face him. In the silence of early morning, without saying a word, I kiss him, entice him, nibble one of the wrinkles on his chin. Marry a vegan. Vegans keep good arteries longer than meat eaters. Not only are they more likely to be there in the morning hugging you after 54 years, they are more likely to be in your bed doing more than hug you.

On time, two hours later we are in the driveway. A jonquil kisses my ankle. A faint touch in the silence, is my flower kissing me goodbye or wishing me a happy journey, a journey into the past?

Is going back to that glen, to the place of my origin, a stress? What is there? What memories frighten me, take me out of my comfort zone? Why do I have diarrhea before going home? Am I afraid of a flood of memories, missing Momma and Daddy, my family?

"Sharon, it's OK." My husband holds my hand in the back seat of Donald's Blazer.

It's time to leave.

Not enough room in our Toyota-hybrid for us and our luggage, my grand-son-in-law's four-wheel drive has the room, and is better today with snow and ice spots on the roads. He and Sandy, my granddaughter, sit in the front with the baby. In the back beside us yawns Lizzy. Of the things I will miss, I will miss Lizzy most.

"See the flowers, GrrGrandma?" She says slurring with sleepiness, "They are so pretty. I like flowers!" Yawning she watches them dozing off. GrrGrandma, equaling Great Grandma, is a Lizzyism.

A young girl, ancient flowers, I will tell her about them when we come home. Aunt Mindy and I plant them in beds by the porch more than sixty years ago. Digging the bulbs on the farm, moving them to her house, then ours as more bulbs grow Aunt Mindy is the Johnny Apple-Seed of Jonquils. Momma and I transfer part of them along the driveway the year before Daddy trades his Knox automobile for a new power-glide Oldsmobile, the first car manufactured with an automatic transmission. Six of my husband's new cars sit in that drive, growing old, as will Donald's Blazer, going the way of the Knox.

Each spring the Jonquils come young, never old. I read somewhere that they find a bulb in a Mummy's hand in Egypt and plant it. It grows producing a flower. Is it a jonquil? Watching my flowers bobbing, unfrozen in the winter landscape, I love Jonquils.

"When we get back to GrrGrandma and GrrGrandpa's house do you want to make a snowman, Lizzy?" Her father looks in the rear view mirror at my great granddaughter.

I touch her knee, warm with life, asleep, dead to the world. She doesn't answer.

"Grrgrandma, I'm going to build a huge snowman when Lizzy wakes up," Donald says.

Finishing piling snow into a big snowman he is going to have one excited little girl. Out of their apartment, their first time with a snow covered yard of their own Donald and Sandra are house-sitting for the month, until we return from the farm. Would I love to see Lizzy's expression as she watches her father shoveling snow, helping with her wagon and spade? By the time Sandy feeds Lizzy and they begin the snowman, we will be half way to the Mason-Dixon Line. A few hours later and Danny will be waiting at the station.

Snow decreasing as we go south, the storm doesn't hit as solidly here as at home. Green shows through in every open area.

Waiting alone on the platform, standing at attention, the sergeant major looks like he is about to order the band to start playing "Hail to the Chief." His hand popping from his side as if to salute, the boy in him moves his head and body forward waving as we get down from the train.

He waves like that the first time we pick him up from band camp his sophomore year of high school. Excited to see us, our high school sophomore in uniform, speaks two words, hugs me over his tuba and plays "Hail to the Chief," the new piece he learns in camp. Danny has that same excitement, a gray haired boy with a new tune to play, something to show his Momma and Daddy.

Why does the conductor fuss over me? Am I old or disabled? I get down from the train with white hair and no wheel chair. I move as fast as a middle-age mom seeing her youngest child for the first time in two weeks. Breaking free from the conductor's support I rush headlong, arms extending to my son.

Danny hugs me then Daddy, then loads our luggage into his new car. Watching giddy dancing in the sparkles of my boy's eyes on seeing us I am glad to be on the last ride of the day. We power onto the main highway.

"When did you get a gold Cadillac, Danny," I say?

"I bought it in town about a month ago. I thought you would like it, Momma."

I do, Uncle Jim always drove a gold Cadillac. My first visit to the farm, I ride in Uncle Jim's new gold 370B, Phaeton. My first ride on the farm after four decades in a gold Escalade is appropriate. In my instructions to my children my last ride on earth is to be in a gold Landau hearse, not a black one, or white one, a gold one.

"There is a new dealership, Honest Jim's. They made me a good deal," Danny says.

*Honest Jim's? Can it be?*

So many years ago I and my siblings look for a gold Cadillac. Walking home from school, seeing it in our drive, we start running, "Aunt Mindy, Uncle Jim!" Hugging and kissing starts. For a moment I see her, Aunt Mindy. She is in my mind.

Riding in a gold Escalade going to Momma's home, back in time, years fade. Looking over the hood the creek rolls brown with spring run off as it rolls color coordinated with another Cadillac, another time.

The last leg of our trip, a small paved one-lane road, we are almost there. Before I can ask him, Danny stops. His Cadillac SUV with the tag frame "US Army Retired" crunches gravel on the edge of pavement going silent.

"Momma, see the Jonquils," he points. "Did you know they are 140 years old?"

I smile. I know.

My son, my youngest child, starts the story, "Your great, great grand aunt planted them---"

I listen. My husband, holding my arm, squeezes it, winks at me.

Letting my arm drop he waves.

"Who are you waving at?" I say.

"The girl. Don't you see her? The girl in blue standing in the middle of flowers."

"You see her?" I say.

"I don't see anything, Daddy!"

"She is there, Danny, always there, whether we see her or not," my husband says.

I swat his shoulder, "You old teaser. You know I have seen her." I think, *Now he learns to tease at 74 years old. Why couldn't he have been better at this when we are young, when I was in prime wrestling form. We could have had fun wrestling matches after such teases.*

"I know, I believe you, or at least believe you believe you have seen her," my husband says.

"I take it you know the story?" Danny says.

"Not your version, son. Tell it to us. I will keep this old geezer from interrupting you," I pat my husband's cheek.

"Dad, Do you think the president would have used you as an advisor if he had known you see ghosts?"

"Your mother sees things, things I don't. Without her to advise me, show me what I can't see, I would never have been considered by the president. She is and always was my most important source. I believe in her. If she sees the girl, I do."

I go quiet. What can I say? A life time and he is still the man I married, the man I love.

Danny finishes in about twenty minutes. A long story, it's a good one.

Aunt Mindy's version I hear my first day on this sacred soil when I am going on two years old, one of three new babies seeing our grandparents for the first time. Too far away to come for short visits, to far to come until an important event, we come for her wedding. Aunt Mindy tells it best until Danny.

He polishes and makes this speech to every spring visitor or group of visitors when the Jonquils are blooming. If they come to the farm in his Caddy, he stops and gives them the lecture on the road. 70 years earlier my brother stops at that spot in his rusted T-Model. He stops for me too, a car sick baby, crying and practicing my projectile vomiting.

It isn't here I first heard the story. Aunt Mindy waits for us at the house, not on the road.

If visitors don't see the jonquils from Danny's car looking across the creek, he walks them to the field from the house and gives the lecture to them in that square of grass surrounded by Jonquils. This is where Aunt Mindy tells it to us.

No one walks to the flowers the day of my first visit. Uncle Jim's new Caddy goes places no new Cadillac now goes. A high ground clearance, spoke gold-trimmed wheels, tall with narrow tread for following ruts, things are different in 1933. Cars are different. Roads are different. I am different.

Danny tells his version seven decades after Aunt Mindy tells me hers. Of those hearing Aunt Mindy tell us about the girl, only I am alive, and I am a baby. Danny hears it first as a baby. I tell it, Aunt Mindy's version, to my youngest son, his brothers and sisters the first, and only, time we bring Danny to the farm. My mother walks with us to the jonquils, listening as I tell it. My husband carries Danny.

Hearing it as a baby soothed by the sound of his mother's voice, not understanding the words, Danny is two, learning more deeply and permanently than he ever learn in his life again, remembering no details. I am eighteen months old listening to Aunt Mindy. Neither Danny nor I remember the words, we both listen to the sound, absorb it and come to it later in life with an emotion best understood when you know we make it part of our lives as babies.

Does a story heard only by a baby exist? Is it gone? The words are gone. The sound goes on. Babies have no permanent memory of specific events. Neither I nor Danny recall a single word of the story we heard. How much of an impression was made that day by my Aunt, that field and those flowers? A memory below the surface of an ocean of thought rising with the tide of spring flowers, pulled by the moon's gravity, its origins are lost in the vale of forgetfulness of those early years. It floods estuaries, wetlands creates tide plains of life, leaving me to question why? Momma tells me it, the why. My Aunt Mindy tells the story even if I can't remember the details, the day. The story exists more powerfully in my infant mind than if I learn it when older. I am there. I have it in my being, as does Danny.

Momma tells me Aunt Mindy's version of the story after I see the girl in blue when I am eight. Unconscious memory meeting conscious, Aunt Mindy retelling her Aunt Constance's version is influential in my life. I don't remember telling Danny the story at an age he can remember it. The next time he sees the farm and hears the story he is

42 years old. His baby fingers reach through the years grasping it to his adult mind.

My mother and her brother have a falling out over something silly the year before my grandfather passes. Unwelcome, we never visit the farm after Uncle Randolph takes over. Being younger Momma expects to outlive him, go to the farm again. Aren't older people supposed to die first? My uncle lives to be 106. I am a great grandmother when he passes. Never seeing the flowers in the field again my mother lies under a bouquet of jonquils I place on her and Daddy's graves yesterday.

Uncle Randolph inherits a trust, a farm, a place that can not be sold, can never be his. It is our family's home under my Uncle's absolute control. My distant grandfather's brother sets it up that way cutting it off from the main mountain estate, creating the farm for his beloved brother, a perpetual trust. His, not his, it is a trust for his family and their descendants. The farm will never leave the control of our bloodline as long as one of us sleeps under its trees, can bend down and take its soil in hand letting it run through fingers with love, and then plow its furrows with sweat. A gift of love to one who loves this earth with a passion that others love a woman, marriage is a requirement. To hold it, keep it, it must be lived with, wedded to.

The farm lies vacant for two years when my uncle dies.

A lawyer smiles and says, "Occupy or vacate!"

If no one moves onto the farm from our family within six months, the trust dissolves and the land goes to the state.

An aging cousin, too old to relocate, young enough to write, sends a hundred and two letters to family members scattered over the nation and eight foreign countries. Make it a heritage farm. Operate it as it is in the 1840s when my people first break soil tilling it. Have a rotation of managers, volunteers to live on the land at the pleasure of a board of family members then pass it on to other volunteers.

"It's better this way. Better than it going to one person without any say by others," my cousin, the legitimate sole heir to hold the estate, says and signs creating a historic farm.

The second manager, serving a one year enlistment that becomes four, is my son, Danny. A lifetime leader, he organizes. Bringing in others he makes it a collective work involving family from seven states and a summer work program for dozens of teens. His orders, take the hill. With his army he attacks with armored plows, a cavalry of two mules and infantry with hoes.

Hammering alone, breaking the silence after the rooster quiets, the sergeant works.

"How does it look, Momma."

I walk up the steps to the new boys' barracks, moving slower than when last on the farm. Two new buildings will be ready for the teens by summer break, one for boys and one for girls.

"It looks good, Danny." What am I supposed to say? Plain wood finish, no paneling or other niceties, it is a barracks, room for six boys with bunk beds, desks and a common area. A summer only residence unless the wood stove fires up it will be empty most of the year. It is basic housing. Alive with boys in their underwear in June it will be a home.

For now his army, cavalry in old cars, infantry with books under their arms, is in school till June. Coming first, yellow Jonquils, white haired people in the main bedroom, those of us who cover this hilltop during weddings, funerals and yearly family gatherings into the 1960s, come home. My husband and I, his first guest of the season, come to stay in the farm house for the first time since my childhood.

I sit warming by the fireplace built by my great, great, great grandfather and see the Jonquils bloom in the field. So true to detail I expect to hear the screen door creak and my grandfather, in overalls, come in from the barn, my grandmother carrying plates and pots come out of the kitchen to the dinner table.

Arriving second, snow and Jonquils gone, the young soldiers of Danny's army come to work. A horde of cousins, first cousins, second cousins and third cousins, plow with mules, work the land as those of their blood do long ago. A different energy comes in summer. Now energy is old. Not clearing land or planting crops, seeing shadows, looking to long ago, what was we remember.

Only electric lights made to look like oil lamps, and indoor plumbing behind hand-hewn doors, betray the reality of a modern world, two miles and one freeway exit away. Restoration in constant progress, farm equipment, tools and clothes from the era of John Brown taking Harper's Ferry make it look real, make life as it was. A chimney, a few wall-logs of the house and the jonquils remain from that time. The only living thing identifiable from the first inhabitants is in the field, the Jonquils.

Alive then as now, if those yellow trumpets talk what stories will they tell, what stories do they wordless remember? Growing from nothing, appearing where no people live, each spring they welcome us home, to who we are, to where we began. Blooming when the world is brown, dead, they promise life to come every spring since 1857. Different, timed early, their extraordinary days are when others lay dormant. Is that why they are noticed when blooms competing in summer heat live in profusion and mass, and die off at first winter frost not marked by anticipation or future promise?

Am I a Jonquil, a different flower, delicate yet tough enough to withstand snow, ice and years with no human nurture? Am I a woman, different, coming from roots deep and bulbs planted on this farm long ago? Am I loved of God, or am I hated of God for flaws, imperfections, errors--- sins?

I come to this farm after Amber, my sister, goes away. Returning North to home, nothing is the same after Amber leaving. Changing everything, my mother changes. Teaching me to repent, see my sin, see and feel God's wrath momma is different. I lose something very important, God, my mother and my sister's love on a sunny afternoon. Did Amber love me? Did my mother love me? Does God love me?

A cloud, white and shining, one unlike any cloud ever before, floats by. Blue sky with a clear view of heaven, I feel love. Love lights the interior of Danny's Cadillac. My husband, love in his eyes, as there is it is in my son's eyes they glow. The sun of God's love shines. Time brings. Time takes. I feel Aunt Mindy, Amber, Momma in that blue sky, gone, ever present. Looking across the creek, pasture, cows, jonquils blooming, some things time leaves unchanged.

Life is and has been a dream, a wonderful dream with some nightmares along the way. I lift my husband's hand, kissing it.

"Why are you crying, Momma?"

"Danny, your father, he is my life. I advise him. He leads. 'His rod and staff comfort me, make me to lie down in green pastures,'" I quote the 23rd Psalm. "No he isn't God, just a god to me, my husband. Without him you wouldn't be. I wouldn't be me."

Drifting into silence, it is my husband that as an adult shapes me, husbands me. There are others. Most of the people that make me, me, lived and worked this farm, this piece of earth and are waiting for me at the house. They are here. Are their sound, their words, and their stories in my mind? It is long ago, another time, an old tin Lizzy, another Cadillac, my mother young, and I, a baby. The Jonquils are blooming.

## Chapter 3
# JONQUILS PAST

*Spring 1933*

 *I am a baby, without intelligible speech. I see. I listen. I learn. I watch Momma. I know all, never telling, never asking why, what, when, where, who or how. When I learn to speak, it is Da Da, Ma Ma and--- why? Babies learn far more than adults can ever learn, saying nothing, remembering patterns, values, a world of life, then grow and ask why. I ask my Momma, why, what, when, where, who and how. This is the story. This is what she said. What I saw, I say I saw with a baby lisp and a septuagenarian lips.*

 Sammy's Model T rolling to a halt, gravel crunching in ruts of the road he looks at me. Is that the look of a loving brother? I am a good baby! I don't mean too! Only a few hundred yards from the house, earping on Momma, and his car, I almost make it! A Model T, an old road, a car rocking more than a fishing boat in a gale, what does he expect? I throw up again. Bouncing in Momma's arms I head to the creek.

Standing in remnants of snow, a small ice shelf extending over running water, Momma reaches down retrieving a hand full. Cold water splashing on my face freezes the part of my brain that is thinking about throwing up again.

*Momma, that's cold!* I want to say and would if I knew how. Instead I inhale hard. It is freezing!

"Let me help, Momma!" My sister Amber says, taking me from my mother.

Momma starts cleaning her coat. Amber cleans me. Sammy using a wet rag cleans his car. Being a two car family by necessity, there are too many of us for one Model T. Daddy, ahead in the other Model T, keeps going. He is too close to our destination to stop. Parking on the hill by the house he looks back. Do we need help?

My brother yells after him, "It's still running, Daddy. Sharon's sick."

Sammy should be able to get his Tin Lizzy up the hill without needing to push it. If he needs help Daddy will come back. Car two, Sammy's car, is Momma's car filled with a baby, a toddler, a pint size teenage girl, a little Momma and only one person with the legs to push anything, Sammy.

Washing my new dress Amber scrubs. It looks better, doesn't smell better.

"Sharon, you naughty girl," Amber pats me on my diaper, the closest to a real spanking I will have for the next two years.

Feeling better I coo at her grabbing her nose.

"Grrrrr!" Amber snaps nibbling my fingers.

Squealing I pull my fingers free wrapping my arms around her neck. Who is that? I notice a girl across the creek. In a blue bonnet and dress standing in the middle of yellow flowers, what is she doing? Am I the only one that notices her?

"Guffawpffpff!" I say waving at the girl.

She waves back. The jonquils flutter in a breeze.

I look again, she is gone. Normal to a baby, people disappear, stop existing, all the time. Walk around a corner out of sight and they are gone to me. What is different about doing it in a field?

On top of the hill, I see a new person, a pretty young woman in a blue sweater, Aunt Mindy, Momma's sister, the bride-to-be. Her Jim, standing by her, holds her by the waist. Two days till the wedding, he can still see her and is not run off by the women folk.

Aunt Mindy lugs me on her hip the entire day. Amber, my sister, abandoning me, joining other teens to chatter, misses the trip. Why am I in a car again? Uncle Jim cranks. It starts. Resting on Momma's lap I find my thumb, sucking it. Where are we going, and why? Snuggling close to her husband-to-be in the front seat Aunt Mindy is purring like his engine. I feel rocking. I grunt at Momma. She pats my back.

Uncle Jim drives us to see the jonquils. Rolling and rocking slowly through the field his new gold Cadillac is quiet, not as noisy as my brother's car. A special car, not like other cars, sparkling gold and yellow, white wall tires, everyone notices Uncle Jim's car.

Special only to Sammy his car would be ordinary, but it is old. My brother's car is black, the color of death. Every Model T comes from the factory black. Henry Ford says, "You can have it any color you want, so long as it's black!" Time changing my brother's car, no longer black, is black and brown, rust brown with black spots remaining. It has a death rattle, a noisy-rusty-black death rattle.

I pat Uncle Jim's Cadillac, yellow, yellow-gold I liked yellow things, especially his car. It is pretty and stopped. I like stopped cars, not rocking cars, not roaring motion-sickness causing cars. I like stopped cars!

Over the unmoving golden trunk I see brown, not rust, water, rolling brown water. At flood stage the creek is high enough to make everyone drive the back road to the farm. Water stretches over fifty feet wide, a river licking to within ten feet of the jonquils, not unlike the last flood with the cabin standing in the field.

Jonquils, pretty, bright, delicate, what attracts me to that particular flower? Of all flowers, jonquils draw me magnet-like to their beauty. I experience the same wonder each spring, with each blooming of the jonquils. Having no way to consciously block the repeating the loop of seeing flowers in snow then smiling, the only change is the number of wrinkles in my smile as I go from baby to old woman.

A baby, I am sitting in a square space of grass surrounded by yellow bobbing heads; a creek runs by; cows munch grass. Cooing I grab one, a yellow chewy. Put in this place by Momma. Is it my choice? Is this flower tasty? No and No! Yuck! Sptpfspuffl!

"What has that baby got in her mouth," Momma chases me.

Crawling fast, can I escape? No, try as I might. Aunt Mindy grabs me as I head for the creek. If she hadn't put me there as a baby, my eyes tasting their sweet beauty, and learning that all things yellow are not apple sauce, would I love jonquils? OK, what is bad about loving jonquils? Well, nothing, but it is Momma's, Aunt Mindy's or maybe the girl's fault, the one that planted them.

Aunt Mindy smiles, snuggles under soon-to-be husband Jim's shoulder. Starting to talk, she shares. The importance of family, the importance of love, the importance of sharing with him, she is his: her family and her history are his. A side of Aunt Mindy new to him, he loves it. As she talks her eyes sparkle, her words sing, her husband-to-be's eyes coaxing a flood of loving words from her. Each person in the family that lives on the farm has a different story of the jonquils. That one told to Uncle Jim from the depths of Aunt Mindy's heart has a life only love can give.

Aunt Mindy tells a story, a history of love, loss, faith, hope, years and jonquils.

### *Summer, 1849, the land*

It isn't always a field, where the jonquils bloom, a meadow maybe, part of the Great Eastern Forest certainly. In 1849 Americans walk from Washington, DC, to Chicago never leaving the shade of the Eastern Forest. Men like fields and pastures more than trees. It isn't a field until the trees are cleared. The first land in America anyone in my family ever has, my distant grandfather clears. He builds a cabin from trees cleared on soft woods-dirt, letting the soil run through his fingers.

"My land," he says turning to his wife, "It is ours, our land!"

He has it even though he can never own it. This makes him free, a man. People call him Mister: a man favored by his brother. His wife rides to town her head held high, the free wife of a land holder. His brother's boy the first part of his life he serves the man he loves. In 1849 he has a trust deed. This brother, not the pale little boy that played in the creek beside him, is now governor. A special bill, a trust, a way around restrictive laws, his brother succeeds in giving my ancestor the land they love, the land where as boys, they play, chase birds and become men.

It is here in the mountains far from the main house that they do what my ancestor loves best. Pulling a school reader from his pocket the future governor and he sit in the shade of a huge oak reading. Peering over his shoulder, then sitting beside him, my great-great-great grandfather sounds out letters and words, learns to read. Eyes bright, laughing together, learning, he reads each of his wealthy brother's books. Fascinated, a new world open, my ancestor loves to learn, sees the unseen in words, imagines, goes far beyond the mountains and the piedmont in his mind, never free to travel in his body.

His brother's travels are more exciting to Samuel than anyone else, after each return from Richmond, Washington or overseas, Samuel runs beside his brother's horse to the main house. He waits. Rounds of kisses and visits in the mansion over, it is the mountains for the boys. Willing to share with one that loves him as no other ever will, his fine clothes in the closet, his riding clothes on and horses mounted brother in boots rides with bare foot brother. Listening, wanting to know every detail, Samuel's thirst to live through his brother's experience, life, stirs. The boy in boots thinks of the brother in calloused feet as his best friend, and his best servant. They discuss books, things boys discuss, things men discuss. Things the future governor ponders, he ponders with Sam.

A respect for skill, insight and a friendship deepens between the siblings, one born in the mansion two months before the other is born in a shanty down the hill. More than custom, or duty binds the brothers. They have friendship. They have respect. Their love is overlooked by the father of both boys, knowing they are brothers, much the same in body and mind, and overlooked by locals knowing the wisdom of keeping criticisms of a family that owns most of three counties to a minimum.

It is as with President Jefferson and the woman, Sally Hemmings. She loves him. The president loves her. She bares him four sons. It is known, and tolerated because he is Mister Jefferson. It is tolerated of a boy that one day will be a man and rule.

Both born and bred to the land they love they look beyond fences, caste and time. They look to the earth, the rocks, the trees, the soil of all that ever was or will be. A huge estate extending from the rolling hills of the piedmont into the mountains it will come to the legitimate brother, the sole heir. To these sons it's the mountains. Land less valued by others, it is their special place, the place they can ride, hunt and fish together. Alone, far from prying eyes, sitting under an oak tree reading fewer than fifty feet from where Mister Sam will build his cabin and where the older brother will spend his better days visiting, they read. They talk, boys cut from the same cloth, then men, friends from birth.

Looking at his brother Sam, the future governor thinks, *No one will ever love this land as Sam and I do, and but for a different mother, it would be his.* Looking over the glen and the creek, he says, "Someday, when this is mine and I have the power, I will make this land yours, and you free on this land, Samuel!" The young man, the heir to all they can see promises and fulfills when lesser men renege, forgetting youthful oaths given to servants, those not of proper class or color.

Bounded by the creek and a straight line due north from the tall rock over the hill to where the creek doubles back going east it is our land, our farm. Mostly rock, cliffs and trees, of five hundred acres, one hundred are flat enough to farm. Year-round water makes up for 400 acres of steep rock hillside making those farmable acres a family feeder, a special place.

Mister Samuel likes the sound of his creek gurgling steadily in late summer even in the driest years. Building their cabin close to the water he never thinks the gurgle can roar with spring runoff or when a warm winter rain melts snow in the mountains beyond. Roar it does. Is that the reason they move? Too close to the creek, spring floods cover them in brown rushing torrents twice during the first ten years my family occupies this land.

### *Fall 1857, the Jonquils*

Finding a man's purse in town he gives the young girl a dime.

"A full bag of jonquil bulbs, please!" Sarah says to the store keeper.

My great great grand aunt, is thinking, *Momma will love these flowers!*

A blue heaven above, one growing ever closer to her, smiling, she asks, "Please God, let Momma love these flowers and remember how much I love her, when she sees them!"

Lifting a sod of grass with a small spade she slides the last bulb into the earth. Going to play in the field, stopping to say good morning to their milk cow near the creek, she looks back loving her family. The cow moos. Sarah leaves the flowers a surprise for her mother. The surprise comes in spring after the flood, after two dozen floods and more than a hundred and forty nine springs, the jonquils continue surprising.

Floods make a mess, sometimes kill. The second flood drowns one of the girls, the one who plants the bulbs. Trying to reach the milk cow she disappears in a brown swirl of water. Refusing to live near the creek, her mother sleeps with her other babies under a great oak. On a flat rocky outcrop in a lean-to overlooking their cabin she wakes, looks over the creek to be sure it is not rising then goes down to stoke the fire and prepare breakfast for her family. Relenting, Mister Sam hitches a mule to the door lintel and pulls. By afternoon the cabin is in a pile with only an adobe chimney and fireplace standing.

Writing "Sarah," her birth and death dates in chalk on a shaved board they lean it against the old fire place.

It lasts a few weeks till the overseer sees it.

"Sam, who wrote this for you?" the man says.

"A traveling man. I paid him," Sam says.

Not believing, the overseer throws it in the creek.

A month later, hearing of the incident, grandpa's brother and the new overseer ride to the cabin. He holds Mister Sam as he cries and sends a tombstone with the words and dates that won't wash away. Standing today in a small church cemetery by her mother and father's stones, chipped by time and frost, "Sarah," is not forgotten.

Further back, 500 yards away from the creek, the cabin is rebuilt. Dragging logs up the hill they disassemble the first cabin log by log. Protected from sun by the great oaks, protected from water by elevation, forty feet higher, it never floods. The old cabin is one room with an adobe fireplace. The dirt chimney and fireplace melt to a puddle before spring leaving a small rectangular rise of poorer soil with less grass, a good place to set the tombstone.

The new cabin, unchanged that year, grows in other winters, grows when time comes to leave the fields and do construction. It becomes what it is today with five generations adding to it.

"Sarah!" Her mother cries the rest of that winter.

She never stops missing her baby, going back again and again to the old house site until everything is picked clean. The only thing they don't move is the jonquils. They forever belong to the girl, to that place, to that cabin. Nothing removes the pain of what happened there. Others go to the old house site for water or work, her mother goes for her. Sitting by her daughter's tombstone among her flowers her mother sees her playing in the field, talks to her girl.

It is there they find her mother, sixty years after her daughter's death. The old woman comes every year, tottering slowly down the hill on her cane. Sitting in the grass box made by her daughter's flowers, she feels her, sees her with an aging mind. A little girl plays near the porch; her high pitched voice sings above the clatter of the creek. Do the old stop loving? Does time make the old woman stop missing her child? They say being old, her heart goes silent, stops, fills with the still-deep sound of love. A clear blue-sky day they are together, a mother, a loved daughter, their flowers, their love, alive.

After her mother dies they move Sarah's tombstone to the church cemetery placing it by her mother, her father in what becomes a yard of family stones. The field becomes a field, a field of jonquils in spring, a field with a presence, a love, a peace, a girl unfound. Do others see a girl walking among the jonquils when they bloom in spring?

Is she seen in her blue dress by the creek? Is this a family legend of our Mecca? One we want to see, one of a girl, an angel that protects us. Her jonquils are a magnet, a pull, drawing us back to our roots. Mecca, a starting point, a returning place, Muslims go there to walk the earth of the beginnings of their faith. Everything mortal has a Mecca, a Jerusalem, a shrine, a Holy place of history--- a beginning. The place our family's history began, the point to which our pilgrims return in spring, is marked by a yellow box of flowers saying, *This is the spot where the jonquils bloom, where life begins.*

Is that why Aunt Mindy brings me, my mother and her husband-to-be to this spot? She wants to show him, wants to give him everything she is, has: her life, her memories, her family, and her family's memories.

Two days before their wedding six generations of us, three still living, feel the soft rich earth give under our feet on this spot. Memories of a fall morning, a wooden digger digging, planting, creating life that will go on forever around a single-room house that will not, this is our Mecca.

Neither the jonquils or the story end here, they begin. Aunt Mindy, sharing our history, talks. Momma and Jim remember, both telling me different versions of Aunt Mindy's history long afterward. I absorb it.

### *Spring 1863, the first sighting*

Thicker, more solid each year, leaving more and more questions as to why they exist, why they bloom every spring in a pasture. She is gone. The cabin is gone without a trace. Cows remain. Her flowers remain.

A Civil War soldier dismounts, walking among them. Asking his captain, wondering, "Why are daffodils here, and a tombstone, but no grave?"

Why does anyone plant daffodils, jonquils to us, around a square piece of grass in the middle of a pasture? Never knowing, no one there to tell him the story, he wonders. They find the house nearby, recently abandoned, rugs still on the floor and enough food to make a meal for them. Eating, soiling the rugs with muddy boots, they rest turn North.

Riding away, trampling through the jonquils, the soldiers go, never hurting the mother, daughter or the bulbs. Protected by briars, the horses don't come close to the woman and her child hidden under the pine needles. The bulbs, the part hidden in the earth too deep for hooves to cut, the trampled flowers bloom the next spring as if the war has not been.

A middle aged woman and a child watch, hiding in the briars. The woman could tell him about the little girl who planted them, her daughter. The Yankees are killing slaves the next county over. Unsafe to be found, a sick daughter unable to run away with the others, trapped, the mother and daughter hide. Covering her and the girl with a blanket, putting pine needles over them in a shallow hole at the edge of a briar patch her husband kisses her before he and the rest of the rest of the family run deeper into the mountains hiding. The rabbit hole working, she and the girl are never seen.

Hidden, watching, remaining absolutely still her mother protects another daughter, praying she and the girl won't die on the bank of the creek. Resting in the pit, never moving for two days, she watches the Yankees ride out. Looking back toward where their cabin once stood, her mother is the first to see the ghost of her beloved daughter by the creek. Only a flash, she is there, a little girl in blue standing in the middle of trampled flowers. Looking down the valley her mother listens to be sure the Yankees are gone.

Climbing from under her pine blanket, running, falling among the tatters of the flowers she kneels calling, crying, "Sarah! Sarah! SARAH!"

Quiet fills the field. Sarah is gone.

Decades pass, the sightings of Sarah continue. Aunt Mindy sees her when she is six and several more times, always among her flowers, always she waves, always looking after our family.

Our farm's location far from navigable water or road makes it, in 1849, of little value. Until after 1900 it is accessible only by horse. Steep ravines block every possible wagon trail. During the Civil War both Union and Confederates do not bother with the arduous climb after the one Union patrol.

Greater danger exists in peace than war. A place safe from war by lack of strategic value and less commercial value. Being rock cliff mountain land without agricultural significance, others ignore it. If valuable others would take it, trust or not, as my ancestor's brother foresees. While he lives, until the 1870s, he protects us. After his death, the main estate dwindles, holdings are lost, the way is open to more dangerous predators.

The Klan comes, in the 1880's. Something frightens the old overseer's horse near the Jonquils. He falls landing on a rattlesnake, dying from the bite some days later. Two other Klansmen see the girl. Did the girl, or was it the snake that spooked the stallion? Having seen her, fearing her they don't come back.

Others, members of our family, see her. I talk to her. She is no more than a friendly ten year old. I like her, our angel in blue. Liking her too, Aunt Mindy believes she is there for a purpose, a good purpose.

Looking at our flowers, soon-to-be Uncle Jim hugs her. Aunt Mindy is happy, has a glow that never fades as long as Uncle Jim's image reflects in her eyes.

"She loves you so much!" Aunt Constance says patting Jim on the arm.

There is something in Mindy's intensity and devotion to this man that worries her Aunt. Why? It is good for a woman to love her man this deeply, isn't it? It is true, though. Others love their husbands, but not like Aunt Mindy. Beautiful, smart and educated, she can choose among men, if she looks. Does she look? Once, and then she looks only at one man. Uncle Jim is her first beau, the love of her life, a man thirteen years older than she, everything she will ever want.

"You and our children will be like these Jonquils, ever living, ever growing, ever in my heart," Jim says.

"Only as you live, will I live, my love. You are my life. Our children, yes they will go on forever, not me, not without you. I never want to live without you, Jim," Aunt Mindy kisses his hand.

Her aunt, my grand aunt, smiles and cries both in joy and fear of Aunt Mindy's consuming love.

Two days pass. The wedding. The bouquet sailing bounces high off Amber's hand falling, fresh-mud browning white petals. Outside the circle of single young women Sammy picks it up, washes it off. A boy with a dropped wedding bouquet, it is his for life. Pressing it in a book he thinks of her, his love, the one he cannot have.

"It should have been mine!" Amber says.

## Chapter 4
# BIRTHDAY SPANKINGS

*Back to the present*

We are home from the farm.

A bouquet of Jonquils on the table Lizzy's mother, my grand daughter, lights five candles. Oblivious Lizzy squeals. Her legs kicking, over her Daddy's knee, her party dress over the small of her back, she is the center of attention.

A spanking for fun, thrilling, embarrassing, not painful like other spankings she watches a Sunday school classmate having her first birthday spanking the week before her own. From the time Lizzy is three and having little swats on the bottom for correction, she learns to come when her mother or father calls, even if it is for a spanking.

Birthday spankings different, she runs. Scampering around the table giggling she escapes three times. Her father corners her then lets her go. On the forth she is bottom up over his lap squealing.

"One, two, three, four, five," her Daddy says, "and one to grow on!"

We join in at three. Pops barely audible, they are pats until the one to grow on.

Her mouth agape in wonder, it closes, her eyes dilate. Is that is a real one, a real spank? Is her Daddy supposed to be giving a real spank? A real swat, enough to sting, not enough to bring tears it is over. Sitting on her Daddy's knee, her bottom tingles, her face is pink with embarrassment and eyes twinkling with excitement. He hugs her.

"Happy birthday, Lizzy!" Her Daddy plants a slobbery kiss on her cheek.

She hugs him, climbs down, and says the thoughts of every five year old on their birthday, "Where are my presents?"

Undeserved spankings require presents, lots of presents, appeasement.

Her mother lights the candles. Lizzy blows. Four go out, and the last one with her mother's help. Three little friends, their mothers, a few fathers, assorted grandmothers, grandfathers, her mother, her father, one great grandfather, and me, one great grandma clap. It is a fun party for all, children playing with new toys, old people watching; and young mothers dressed in their finest talking to each other having grown beyond proms and school dances where dressed, bouncy and eager they go to meet boys. Now the young women, mothers, husbands at home, have no event for which to dress except church and childhood birthday parties. Making the rounds of children's parties they hover over small children.

Beautiful young brides, now housewives, with babies, young children spreading responsibilities and bottoms, I remember that time in my own life, especially the broadening bottom part.

Momma's girl, raised by her, can I eat? Always and everything, not a problem until after my first baby, why don't they make plates not as many Brussels sprouts wide for grown, over grown, women? A simple idea, it helps, smaller plates! Figuring that out one night on the porch, it is a simple, a usable idea.

Watching the night sky with my husband, the thought comes to me. As clear as his handsome face under the full moon the thought fills my head! A fat cloud hiding it in a shadow drifts away. I see it in my mind!

I am a young mother trying to get my figure back. Will I be the skinny me, the pretty me he married? Yes! After all, I am forever a cheer leader. I keep my uniform in a trunk somewhere, to prove it.

Am I beautiful?

"Still beautiful," he says. He lies!

I kiss him.

"You are beautiful!" He holds me and kisses me every time I am nine months pregnant and fussing about being big. He always says that even though I know he likes me thin-beautiful, as I was, as I will be.

Now more than five decades after our wedding I want to be his trim, sexy, white haired vixen sitting by him on the porch under a full moon! Being big with babies is beautiful, two-beautiful. Two people in one, big bellied is the most beautiful a woman can be. Being big without a little one inside is that beautiful? It depends on the culture. In America skinny equals beautiful! My last baby born more than 40 years ago the extra five inches on my tape measure, should have gone 40 years ago.

Eating off saucers rather than plates, every portion looking bigger, is working. I lose weight. Mrs. Walinski, our neighbor, looking strangely at my saucers instead of plates, notices.

"Sharon, do you need help with the dishes?" She says.

*What? Why would I need help with the dishes? Does white hair mean a woman can't do her own dishes? White hair with a cane, maybe; I don't own a cane.*

"I mean, are you out of plates? Do you have to use saucers?" she says.

"No Miriam, I am too fat. The little plates make eating less food easier. Momma taught me to eat everything on my plate. To eat less food it helps if I use smaller plates."

Slipping on my glasses peering out the window a car turns in our driveway. Sandra, getting Lizzy out of her booster seat, comes to visit. They are back! The next day after Lizzy's birthday party, Donald, Sandra, Lizzy and her little brother Donald Jr. move back into their apartment. Missing them instantly I want them to move in with us. My husband and I live in the three rooms surrounding the kitchen. The top floor and rest of the main floor is empty, cold in winter, needs the joy of a little girl's laughter and babies crawling. Why don't they move in with us? They live in a cramped two bedroom student apartment. I find

Lizzy's doll under the bed in her own room from their stay in our house. She needs her own room, not one shared with her baby brother.

Alone, back in my routine I have gained weight on the farm. I always do that. At age five it's good. Skinny me, my grandpa says I might blow away if the cat sneezes. Now it's not.

Miriam keeps looking at my saucers. "Are you sure you don't need help, Sharon?"

"I don't need help, Miriam. I am trying to eat a little less. It is easier to do that with smaller plates."

Miriam doesn't say anymore, looking at me and my saucers in disbelief. When my neighbor is over after that I am sure to have regular plates on the table.

No more Brussels sprouts smothered in flax seed oil, lemon juice and Spike; a saucer full of celery, plain with just the crunch, yum! Yum? Is Momma here, trying to make me eat?

Gone, yet always here I hear Momma saying, "Eat what's on your plate!"

Struggling to chomp through another stalk of celery, I'm home. The beautiful new electric flat-burner stove my husband bought me disappears. Momma is there her flat-burner wood cook stove in the corner. I like mine better. It has exact temperature control. Hers, low tech, if the pot doesn't pop and sizzle when you slide it on the stove, open the fire-box door and ad more wood. The smell of Brussels sprouts simmer in the air, a pot crackles and vibrates, steam pops from its lid in bursts. A table filled with food, brothers and sisters around me, eating, talking, they are here. I feel them.

Daddy, sitting at the head of the table, smiles at me. "Good morning, Sharon."

Momma, David, Amber, Sammy, my brothers and sisters not noticing me, I slide into my place next to Daddy. It feels so real.

They vanish, Miriam's voice scattering them back to the past leaving in an instant, not one by one as they did in life. Funerals take them until I alone remain of my family. The last born, the youngest, I suppose I should be last to pass on, but there is a loneliness in it, being the last. I am alive, alone. Momma, Daddy, the brothers and sisters that shared breakfast at that table with me are dead.

Crying in my kitchen, *Come back!* I want them here again.

I want the old stove, the clamor, Amber saying, "Sharon, black berries are in down by the rail road track, let's go picking!"

Sammy covered with grease, Momma shooing him out to the garage to wash; David in his uniform and Rose Mary in her prom dress, they come to me, are here, then gone. Why are they gone?

"Please come back!" I say forgetting I have company.

"Sharon, why are you crying?" Miriam says.

"It's nothing Miriam. Something is in my eye," I lie.

Sitting down at my own table no one in the house to tell me what to do these decades later why am I hungry for Brussels sprouts? One Brussels Sprout, two Brussels Sprouts--- *Momma!* I think.

"I'll fix Brussels sprouts for supper tonight. I'll fix them for my husband."

"I'm glad you like Brussels sprouts. No one in my family will eat them." Miriam turns up her nose.

Will I eat them with flax seed oil, Spike and lemon juice? My husband likes them that way.

Doesn't he always come home to eat when we are young? He never comes home at noon to eat with me now, even though no one says he has to go into work anymore. Retiring doesn't slow him down. Now instead of going to his office he, with that long legged lope of his, goes past his old office to the Library and works there. Research he calls it, consisting of reading a few newspapers and mulling through a book, maybe two.

I don't understand the value of this research. Is there a Pulitzer Prize for newspaper reading? Over the morning a few more white haired types appear and a chess game starts in the basement, then his bridge club. The highlight of his day is when some kid recognizes him and asks a question, preferably one he can still answer. Glowing on those days, he comes home striding, loping a little less. Walking into the yard, his white hair bouncing, that contented look on his face, I know when he has had a good day.

For me there is less hope. Any kid that asks me a question now always prefaces it with "Grandma!" always considering my opinion important only when their momma or daddy isn't there to ask. I am a tertiary source to them, primarily a source of ancient history as the grand children grow up and realize my age. That being bad enough, the latest two have trouble verbalizing great grandma. A new level of authority lies between me and my descendants, my grandchildren becoming Mommas and Daddies.

"I lub you, GrrrGrandma!" Libby says.

"It's Great Grandma, Honey," her mother, Sandra, says.

"Great Big Grandma!" Libby has it, sort of, hugging my leg, looking up at me saying it over and over, "Great Big Grandma. Great Big Grandma!"

*Great Big Grandma! Heavens to Betsy!* I looked down at her over my stomach. Is it that large? She smiles up at me. Knowing she doesn't know how grown women, particularly ones that were once skinny young things, feel about being "Big!" I know she doesn't mean it negatively. She loves me. I know it shouldn't bother me, but it does. Looking in the mirror the first chance I get, *Great Big Grandma, am I great big grandma?*

"What are you doing?" Sandra asks poking her head into the kitchen.

Am I doing anything unusual? I am standing in front of the refrigerator munching on a celery stalk. OK, I guess it is unusual.

"I don't want to be Great Big Grandma!" I pout.

My granddaughter looks at me, smiles, starts laughing. "Grandma, you aren't big! You are my little grandma!"

She hugs me. It is true I am little, like my father--- at least in height! He never got fat, those powerful arms of his and that flat waist lasting all his life. I want to be like him, his girl, always being the shape I am when young.

Sandra corrects her daughter the next time Libby says it, not making a big deal about it. "Libby, call Grandma, Grandma. I think she likes that best!"

Libby goes back to GrrGrandma to differentiate me from her secondary level of information, her grandmother, a little girl that once called me Momma. All is well in Camelot. I am Grrgrandma, to Libby. The little girl forgets about the big part as we sit down at the table.

It is nice to have them for lunch. I miss having my life partner with us, he always likes the visits from Libby and her mother. I am glad he missed that comment. If he had heard it, others would have heard it and there would have been no stopping the nickname from going public.

Having the entire community knowing I am Great Big Grandma would have been a dream come true--- a nightmare. Alone, I eat too much, hear Momma's voice too much, eat more. With Lizzy's motivating new name I eat less calories. Every day at noon, two big plates of celery, plates the size of Momma's plates that is what I am eating leading up to my birthday.

Wanting something else, I don't want to be Great Big Grandma. My well filled out bottom getting fewer comments if my husband decides to chase me around the house and give me another birthday spanking. That is what I want--- fewer comments? Yes! A birthday spanking? Yes! Do I want a birthday spanking, a birthday spanking like I had when I was a little girl? Really? Really! More than anything else, that is what I want for my birthday. I know there will be a large pile of presents to open, the consequence of years spent with my belly big having babies. The present I want most, I want as naked as the day I was born, in bed with my husband--- a birthday spanking!

Looking at Libby's mother, Sandra, I remember her hiding. Trying to get away from her father she hides behind our couch. Looking around the living room he can't find her. Her giggles give her away, when other means of being sure he finds her seem to fail. I remember her squealing and kicking as he gives her the "one to grow on!" last spank. It is her eighth birthday. I remember more, this grand daughter on her seventeenth birthday dodging around the big oak in the yard running, trying to escape from a young man in his letterman jacket. Her boy friend has similar ideas.

Shouting after them, my husband encourages him, "You are making a spectacle of yourselves. When you catch her, bring her back in the house lest the neighbors get the wrong idea!"

He does, overgrown football player that he is.

Riding back into the house, bottom up bobbing along over his shoulder and pounding away as hard as she can on his bottom Sandra shouts, "You are going to get yours too!"

Does he notice? Hers is memorable. Mostly pats, with squealers sneaked in to keep her attention, that is the kind of spanking I like. I want that, even if I am old.

Does being old on the outside mean you are old on the inside? The little girl sitting at my mother's table, struggling to eat Brussels sprouts, still lives under this white hair. I want to come out and play, have a birthday spanking like my grand daughter had.

My husband and I aren't shocked to be sitting on the bride's side of the isle three years after that spanking when Sandra and her boyfriend marry.

She tells us at the reception, "I think, now that I am married, I should stop college and be a housewife. Don't you?"

My husband doesn't smile, doesn't answer. He goes straight-away taking her overgrown spouse aside, talking to him. Making it possible for both of them to complete their education, Sandra graduates three weeks before Libby is born. Now she is a housewife with a bachelor of arts in mathematics and a teaching certificate. Does she plan to begin teaching when their kids are older? Why else would she take the continuing education to keep her teaching credentials current? She is pregnant again. They are having a baby every two years planning to stop while Sandra is in her early thirties.

Lizzy, five years old, not growing and not hungry, is playing with her peas. Is my granddaughter making Libby eat her peas? Does she need those? Did I really need to eat all that food when I was little? For years it was too easy for Great Big Grandpa to catch me for my birthday spankings. She does not need to eat when she is not hungry!

## Chapter 5
# GROWN UP BIRTHDAY SPANKINGS

*Fifty four years ago*

When we are young and my husband gets that gleam in his eye, I run around the house getting back inside with barely enough time to lock the door before he reaches it. He rattling the door and yelling at me, I call Officer Clancy.

"Officer Clancy, there is an irrational, half-naked man in our yard," I hang up.

Racing over, his siren wailing, our policeman finds my husband standing red faced in his pajama bottoms hiding behind a rose bush. I smile and laugh through the living room window pointing at him. That look in Officer Clancy's eyes, why is he mad? Was sticking my tongue out at them a bad idea? I am having fun, being friendly. I wave at them. Looking demonic not the family friend he is, but an officer, he pounds on the door!

"Open up, Sharon! Open up!" His big hands rest on his hips.

Knowing that look, having seen it before, I am in trouble. Being in trouble with a parent, teacher, principal or especially a police man the rules are to be submissive, obedient and try to look innocent.

"Yes, sir!" I turn the lock.

They both enter, my husband's bare feet not creaking a board, officer Clancy's boots clomping.

"Young man," he speaks to my husband, "your wife is out of control! It is a crime, you know, to make a false police report; call an officer, causing me to be racing through town with no good cause. I could have run over a child, or a dog!" He turns his glare at me. "Did you think of that, Sharon?"

Why didn't I think of that? Why would I think of that? It is only 7 AM, too early for that kind of thinking.

"Calling a police man with a report of a prowler is serious, could have caused something serious." Officer Clancy shakes his head, no longer looking at me, he turns to my husband. "Her having called and hung up as she did, I didn't know if you were both dead!"

His Irish eyes are not smiling.

"I'm sorry!" I say.

"And you should be!" Officer Clancy says, "But this time, my dear young lady, I think I should be taking you downtown and putting you in the hoosegow, to teach you a lesson. Now what do you think of that?"

I don't think much of it, and would have answered if I had not frozen up. I giggle out as shocked as a guppy swatted out of its bowl by a cat's paw.

My husband wants to save me, puts his hand to his lip. He thinks.

He says, "She's sorry, Officer Clancy! She won't do it again. You know she is a good girl, don't you?"

"That I do. If she were a bit younger, a good blistering would be sufficient. I have seen that done with her before. It was enough and worked well. You wouldn't be having a paddle now would you?"

"I don't have a paddle. Would a good bare bottom spanking do?"

What is my husband doing? Is this how he is trying to save me?

"It would, if you have the will to do it! Be quick about it. I have real work to do. I'll wait on the porch till you finish," with that Officer Clancy walks out the door.

The officer hearing my paddling is appropriate, requisite to not arresting me, seeing it happen is not.

Startled at the sudden resolution of this confrontation, and the consequences, I blink, looking at my husband. What is he doing? Firmly, the love of my life is holding my arm. I sweep toward the couch my feet following one awkwardly over the other. Pulling me as a child where I don't want to go he spins in front of me. We stop as if to talk, face to face. Our eyes meet. I bow my head looking down. I can't talk!

Looking up at him submissively my mouth moving without sound, *It is my birthday. Aren't you supposed to be nice to me?*

Is he going to spank me, really spank me? As he sits down, his feet in my way and his hand tightly holding my arm, he pulls me. I fall forward. I bounce over his leg and land bottom up. My husband spreads my nightgown over my back. A cool breeze wafting over my bottom as the cotton flys up; he is going to spank me! The last coolness my buttocks feel that morning, I tense my bottom, expect heat.

"Wait," I say.

He lets go of my arm as I arch my back lifting my bottom up. With both hands I scoot my panties down to my mid thighs. Why am I helping him? Momma's fault. If I am to have a spanking, a real one, I am programmed to cooperate or risk more severe punishment. Feeling differently toward him than a minute ago, I know that he is my husband. He is a man with the authority to spank me, spanking me.

Relaxing into his lap I bring my arm behind my back. I grasp his forearm. He grasp mine. Ten hard licks later, sobbing, I am having the most vigorous birthday spanking I ever have! I sob. I beg. I want to kiss and make up! Why doesn't he stop? I'll be a good girl! I really will!

Never wanting him to give me a serious spanking, I want it to be a game to us, playful, not painful. Crying in a stream, I have pain, more hurt. Tears drip from self disappointment. My husband, my beloved husband, has to spank me, that hurts more than the pain.

Not a virgin to the serious side of spanking, there is a line of people who blister my bottom. Momma spanks then paddles me as I grow up. My teachers paddle me, all of them women. When a woman does it I expect to be crying, sobbing from the pain. His hands are strong enough, not as fast and intense as a paddle though. Those give tears of pain. These tears are not from pain. I have embarrassed him, failed him. That hurts.

"I'm sorry!" I blubber begging for it to stop.

I am spanked to tears by only one man, my husband. My father holds me over his knee counting out the licks of birthday spankings. I squeal in protest. Getting off his knee with dry eyes for a hug it is play, a game my siblings and I play with our Daddy. This is the first time any man has done it for punishment. He is my husband! It is his right, as it was my father's right to punish me.

A grown woman do I expect my husband to exercise that right? Fathers are known to spank, expected to spank. Husbands are not. It is a right that most men don't apply, even in the time when discipline of wives it is universally accepted. My husband, my gentle, protective husband, why would I expect a real spanking from him? This man, the man I trust like daddy is doing something I think can never happen. He is spanking me, making it painful!

Outside the porch swing is squeaking in rhythm to the pops on my bottom. Our policeman can hear me crying.

"Not to worry, just a needed spanking!" Officer Clancy says to a neighbor.

With that my husband is winding down.

"You don't have to stop on my account young man. If my wife had done such a thing, calling the law and all, I would rest a bit, if needed, then keep going!"

That is what my husband needs, encouragement! Not answering, my beloved takes that short break.

"Please stop, I'll be good," I beg.

He leans down and whispers in my ear, "Keep yelping." Then he whispers something no one says during any of my many serious spankings, "I love you!"

"I love you too!" Tears gush. "I love you so very much!" I grip his leg with my free hand.

Officer Clancy hears. "Enough of that mushy stuff. This is a spanking we are to be having!"

My husband lets go of my arm pinned behind my back. I want to slide it down to protect my bottom. I resist as I am taught to as a little girl, bringing it down in front of me, stroking his leg instead. What I want to do is turn over in his lap, sit up and start kissing him.

Feeling his hand slide down my back coming to rest on my burning bottom what is he doing? The next sharp smack doesn't hurt. He slaps his hand! My lover nudges me with his leg.

"You had better cry!" He whispers.

He doesn't have to ask, I am crying, only quietly, lovingly, an over the lap joyous, in love, stinging, tingling bottom kind of crying. He wants noise.

"Owyee! Please that hurts!" I regain my voice slipping a broad smile framed with tears back at him.

Eight more times his hand falls hard on his own hand. Then he starts to count, this time bringing his hand down on my bottom, "Nineteen, twenty and one to grow on!" The last one bounces off my bottom stinging. His hand falls back resting on my hot cheek.

I wiggle myself up in his lap, faking sniffling, really sniffling, loving him. I kiss him, and kiss him. "I love you!"

Officer Clancy says, "Happy Birthday, Sharon!" and leaves.

Sniffling, hugging him as tight as I can, my husband and I go back to bed. My lover is late for work by over an hour. I won't let him go. I start crying every time he tries to get dressed pulling him back into bed with me. Finally he kisses me so much I can't breathe and when I am catching my breath he escapes.

After he dresses, leaning back into our bed kissing me, he says, "Be good!"

"I love you!" I repeat over and over in his ear holding both arms around his neck. He pulls like our dog, Wulfie III, trying to escape from his leash. Breaking free he bounds down the stairs.

I have a new feeling for him. He is my husband, the man that I love, the one that guides me, and now disciplines me when I need it. This is a new role, one that I think will become part of us. With the feeling of being really spanked continuing after he leaves for work, I am his in a new way. He is the head our house. More than that he is my husband, the man I look to for guidance. I know he is the man I will shape to, love and follow all of my life. He saves me, yet at the same time corrects me as he thinks he must to keep me out of jail.

Wait a minute!

What did Officer Clancy say? "HAPPY BIRTHDAY, SHARON!"

That rat! He knows it is my birthday. He causes me to have a real spanking! Did he fool my husband too? Or, is my husband in on it? Am I really spanked or is it a birthday prank? I never know! Daddy never spanks me like that, nor would he fake it either. My husband, perfect man that he is, can act when he needs too. Is it real? Even if it isn't, I want it to be real! He becomes all things to me. Smiling, still feeling the tingling on my bottom and elsewhere, I snuggle back in bed. I believe it is a real spanking from a real man, really saving me. Drifting off to sleep, I live the most wonderful dream. It is one of those times I remember forever. Then the baby wakes up.

Now fifty-four years later I want another birthday like that even if I have to commit another "crime" to get it. I plan to slip a wet sheet into the refrigerator the night before my birthday. Waking up early to fix breakfast I will sneak down and get it. Easing the covers off before throwing the wet 37 degree sheet over him I will sing out "Happy Birthday to me!" Ok, maybe it will be a short song! Running, well, walking fast, out the back door, I, the skinny new me, will out run him around the house once more.

I don't dare call the police. A new officer on the beat, and everything radio controlled, such a prank can't be dealt with by a spanking. The new officer would be appalled at the prospect of a white-haired old woman being spanked, even if it is what she wants. They would arrest my husband. After taking my love to the squad car in handcuffs, he would arrest me. It would be easy to find me. I would be the one being drug across the lawn biting his ankle all the way to the car and screaming, "You can't have him!"

I will turn on the burglar alarm letting it wail for a few minutes.

I want the neighbors to see him begging to get back in the house wearing only his pajama bottoms. He looks magnificent with his shirt off. At least I think he is magnificent, a wrinkled magnificent. Is it good to remind the ladies of the neighborhood what a good looking husband I have? When I am young I think about putting a fence around him to keep other women from looking at him, wanting him for myself. I have him for myself all these years and I still want him for myself, but at our age, I want other women to know what I have in my bedroom. Is envy a sin when you cause it, but don't have it?

When Mrs. Walinski comments, and asks me how she can get her husband to do fun things like my husband does, I like it. I like this even if she always brings a cake with her and asks me if I am giving him enough to eat. OK, he is skinny. He is always skinny. I try to fatten him up, backfiring, he stays skinny. I get fat! After those comments and that envious look in her eyes it makes eating the cake she brings more delectable. Mr. Walinski never chases Miriam, but then again, she would never throw a cold wet sheet over him either. My husband and I play together and never grow out of it. That is the difference.

After that the only time I am spanked it is play, foreplay, birthday spankings from my husband. Given most often in bed, pantiless, waking me up, warming me, making me, us, feel young they are part of our special play. It reminds me of the first time he ever takes me to what is our hotel in the city. He gives me a little swat before my last enema the day our honeymoon ends. Birthday spankings are special, part of my and our children's lives. For years I wake in the dark on my birthday, my husband pulling me over his lap.

"Its 12:01 AM," he says.

"Wha---?" I say.

"Your birthday, happy birthday!" With that he starts spanking me. "One! Two!... thirty three (or some other obscene number) and one to grow on! Well, maybe not grow on this time!" Saying that as he rubs his hand over the expanse of my quivering bottom, that one always stings, sending electricity up my spine. It opens me to new ideas!

I listen warm bottomed for that last comment. "To grow on" means a little larger slice of birthday cake. "Not to grow on" means a smaller slice and more plates of celery when I eat alone.

Then he kisses me Happy Birthday. I kiss him back, blowing a noisy mouthful of air into his mouth in protest if he makes the "not to" comment. In five minutes we are making love with fervor. For decades as the children grow we only make love with this intensity in the middle of the night when the children are deep asleep.

"Momma always looks so tired on her birthday. Being 33 must be harder than being 32." Eddie, our oldest boy, says at breakfast on my birthday looking at the dark circles under my eyes and his father's.

We smile.

Isn't it curious that two of our children were born nine months after my birthday, both of them daughters? Daughters are more likely following intense repeated episodes of sex with higher pleasure and a lower sperm count.

My birthday is coming up. A new tradition, special for me and my husband, when we have our birthday parties someone has to disconnect the smoke alarms before lighting the candles.

Why hasn't he woke me up in the middle of the night to spank and make love to me for years? I had a little problem. The doctor tells him to keep me from getting too excited! The first step in getting a birthday spanking is to talk to the doctor.

"Look here, doctor, it is as possible to die from boredom as it is from anything else."

She smiles.

"My husband has not given me a birthday spanking in three years, since you told him not to get me too excited. It's your fault! Fix it! If you don't fix I am going to change doctors!"

She smiles finishing taking my pulse.

"I am better, OK! I am OK enough to have a birthday spanking! Old girls need excitement too!"

"Ok, if you want a birthday spanking, I'll tell him it is OK. Is that what you want?" she says.

"Yes!"

"And Momma, if you need to talk about you and Daddy having sex and your kinky sex habits I'll get you a referral to another doctor. That is fine with me. I thought you two were too old for that sort of thing forty years ago. I don't want to hear about it!" the doctor says.

I smile.

I remember her. Smart thing that she is, she never could elude her father when it was time for a birthday spanking. Does she still like them?

*I don't want to hear about it!*

I want to be a young girl, Daddy chasing me around the house to catch me and giving me a birthday spanking. Unlike the spankings from Momma when I run to my bedroom to finish crying alone, my husband comes with me. With no tears we always spend at least a few hours after my birthday spankings in our bedroom, nursing my burning bottom and other areas of hotness.

It gets harder and harder to get him or I really excited. Part of it is feeling. Growing old, inside the feelings are there, but sensitivity to pain, pleasure and most things fade. It is not in the mind that age comes on us: it is in the connection with life. Old fingers or bottoms do not feel with the intensity of young ones.

Body functions do not give us the warnings they do when young. Does he have wetting problems? He can control it if he knows he has to go; he doesn't feel the need to go; then all of a sudden it is on him, or more accurately, out of him. If he goes to the bathroom every few hours, urge or not, it is fine, but if he forgets, I am the one that does the laundry. Sex too, for both of us we still dream of it, can do it, and loved it. Sensitivity is less; feelings of pleasure and pain decrease with age. Is it good to increase the intensity to reawaken the past, feel the fire? Do we need to feel the fire?

Growing up with wood heat I and my husband are fire builders. Putting the kindling to ignite the flame on the bottom, letting the flames lick their way into nearby the dry wood is this the best way to build a fire? Rekindle the passion. Set ablaze the feelings. The intensity of love we had, we will have again.

Moving my bottom in the mirror is it better? Will I squirm; catch fire under his hand. Will it be to him as it is to me? Squealing and begging him to stop loud enough for the neighbors to hear they will be talking about us again.

If he blisters me I will be a little girl again, and I will make him a young man again. He will have to make it up to me--- make love to me. Then take me for a second honeymoon to the city. Our old hotel waits for us growing ever more affordable as newer more modern ones out compete it downtown. What if he doesn't offer?

I will complain, "My bottom is sore. I need a trip to help me recover!"

He WILL take me.

Looking in the mirror, a little more off right there, I will be perfect. Do backsides like faces wrinkle with age? If you spend too much time in the summer working in the garden naked they do. Most backsides wrinkle not from age, but atrophy. Hormones that maintain muscles fade with time. Maintaining curves takes time and exercise. Walking together, do I have the round fullness I have as a young woman? With exercise and a vegan diet I keep more curves than other ladies at church. I have a bottom, a woman's bottom. My husband likes it.

I want him feeling the way he does the first time I slipped my panties off for him. It is worth the dieting. It is worth the try. A few children's games and we will be young again in our hearts. A little burning of my bottom, a little burning of his hand, a little passion igniting and we will have an extraordinary day to remember.

Speaking of conscious, throwing a wet sheet over my sweet, asleep husband, is that wrong? It would be justification for using a paddle on a teen that does such a thing?

If I had thought of it when I was a teen, if I had access to him in his bed, would I have done it? Paddling or not I would have frosted his carcass, slipping in past his father's bedroom, then past his brothers' and sister's bedrooms throwing it on him. I will do it now. Me screaming, running out of our room as fast as I can, I will have a good spanking.

That makes sense! It makes too much sense! To be young, his strong smooth hands on my tender virgin bottom, pounding, spanking me, me squealing, it will be such fun!

The day before my birthday, is it time to get the sheet ready? I plan to do it before breakfast putting the sheet in the vegetable drawer. He is unlikely to see it there. I feel the wind running through my hair. I run glancing back. He catches his stride. He gains on me with that gleam in his eyes.

He is in my bed. Vulnerable, none of his brothers, sister or father will protect him. This is going to be easy! I linger. I look at my white-haired Adonis. Asleep, that little halting in his breathing, is he all right? Waking up with a startle from a wet sheet he rises. Upset, he gives me a good one, a good spanking, seventy five licks, and one NOT to grow on!

He is pale. Is he as strong as he was a few months ago? Should I do this? He hasn't given me a really good spanking for years. I am due for one, and my having one will be good for me, good for us.

I watch him sleep, his breathing more erratic than it was. Is he the young man that I married? He is. He isn't. Thinner, he is more frail this year. Should I throw a cold wet sheet over him? Can I?--- I CAN'T! Loving him, I kiss him on the cheek. He doesn't rouse. Going down stairs to fix breakfast for him, I will kiss him again when he comes down. He will kiss me.

I want him to spank me. I am craving it! Will he? Can he? What if I use an erasable marker and write 'spank here' on my bottom? How do I tell which is which the lettering is worn off? One is permanent. I will climb over his lap bottom up when I wake up. I will fake being asleep, snore, moving around, stick my bottom in his face. Will he get the idea will he read my bottom?

Tomorrow will be an extraordinary day, surrounded by more than thirty of our descendants. Will I use the leaf blower to put out the candles on my cake? Will this be enough excitement for my lover and I? Will he do it? There is hope!

## Chapter 6
# RECOLLECTIONS OF CORRECTIONS

A sunny day, leaves falling off trees, I watch children play across the street. A girl throws dirt. Another girl cries, dirt in her eyes. Will there be a spanking? I know that mother. I know that daughter. No time out, no playing in her room alone, in a short lecture the mother explains the error of her behavior. The daughter admits her wrong action. The spanking, crying time, and the girl is back playing with other children, better behaved. I like this mother. I like the way she handles things. I like their family.

"Did your Momma spank you?" the other girl asks.

"Do you want to come in and play with my dolls?" She says.

They leave me on my porch.

For a minute I am young. I get up to run upstairs and get Samantha, my doll. I want to be her friend, show her my doll and go play with her as I have thousands of times before with Helga and other young girls on that street. Thinking, I had better ask Momma if I can play. Turning, I don't move quickly. Samantha is recycled with Daddy's old work clothes sixty years ago. She is so worn there is nothing patchable left in her tattered threads.

Alone in the house, I forget, Momma died 23 years ago last winter. My husband and I buying the house from my parents when Eisenhower is president, we are the oldest residents. Our children were young. Now they are old. Looking down at my hands, the ones that carry Samantha everywhere and want to introduce her to a new friend my fingers are not as they were. Wrinkled, boney, old, spotted with age, no longer young I am not a girl. Back in the present, hearing the girl open the screen door and go in her house, she is young. I am old.

The girls gone I watch cars on the street. A new Toyota passes, a hybrid, like ours, only blue. What would Grandpa think seeing a Japanese car on our street or picking a tomato with thick skin? There are no Toyotas then, not even hybrid tomatoes, only American cars and tomatoes with thin skins growing from our own seeds in the garden. Mostly there are Fords, A models, even a few T models. Other cars, Chevrolets, Chryslers, Studebakers, Packards and close to a hundred other makes by smaller American manufacturers line the streets.

I look through my closed eyelids. I hear noises from a distant past. Time rolls back 70 years on spoke wheels. I am young. It is as it was. One of these rare old cars rounds the corner, Daddy in his Knox. Our Knox car rolls out of the factory in 1916 one of the last ones made. Its horn beeps. Daddy's home.

. Daddy drives his big Knox into the garage and reappears from the shadows, a present in his hand. Running to him, I jump him, clamping his muscular body in a leg lock.

"What did you get me?" I say.

Carrying me into the house he puts my present down. Then without warning I am bottom up over his lap.

"I got you a spanking!" He says.

It is a birthday spanking.

I remember Daddy's, and my husband's birthday spankings, given me with a loving smiles. Do I remember all my spankings with a smile? Planning the wet sheet routine is designed to get me a spanking, a fun one leaving my husband and I rolling on the bed laughing.

Contrast this to my last real spanking from Mrs. Hunter or those of my young neighbor, painful, corrective. I remember most spankings with a wince.

Continuing throughout my youth and adolescence my last spanking, a paddling, at school happens at the end of my senior year. High school seniors, none of us consider the possibility that we will be paddled. Thinking we are too grown up, too big, too mature for a paddling, we're wrong! Glad to never have that much pain from something pounding on my bottom again, I remember it and the lesson I learn. Pages from my youth turning through my mind as my birthday approaches I sit back in the porch swing, stretch my legs and rock in the autumn air. Through my closed eyes I reread that page?

I am bent over the table waiting.

"Sharon, are you going to be all right?" Mrs. Hunter says.

"Yes" I say, "Thank you for asking."

We wait. A second later pops ring out between the paddle and the boy's bottom at the other table beside me. After his tears and apology, it's my turn.

The memory brings a twinge to my bottom. Lifting up off the porch swing it feels hot to sit. Earlier that year my fiancé gives me the first birthday spanking he ever gives. I love it. I keep thinking, how can I find a reason to make him give me another one? I think that will be the only reason I will ever be spanked again, play. The one later that year is different, unexpected. At the last stage of my youth, still growing, still bendable, its pain shapes me.

Am I sorry? No! Wrong, maybe, but not that wrong, I want to say I am sorry, am ready to say I am sorry, smile, and go to my class. With a lyrical singing 'I'm sorry', a smile, a bouncing gait off to first period, with no sorrow, is that what we expect? Bending over that table, keeping my hands in place, and growing ever more sorry as my teacher blisters my bottom she instills real regret with each lick of that paddle. I am sorry sobbing out my apology after the paddling.

Our neighbor girl is sorry when the one her mother gives her is over. Spankings create sorrow. Spankings, being over, are over. No need for further punishment we are free to return to our classes or play within minutes. Reminded the next three days by an occasional twinge, I sit more gingerly. Never forgetting what I did wrong, I never do it again.

Will the neighbor girl ever throw dirt again? I don't think so. The pain, the redness, a few small bruises fade. The memory and correction don't.

Why I am thinking about this when Mrs. Walinski walks up the drive, her son in tow? Much younger than my husband and I, she has a son in high school.

"Miriam, what is Joe doing home with you. Isn't he supposed to be in school?" I say.

"Yes, but he was smoking again, suspended again!"

"So I was smoking! It is none of their business whether I smoke or not! I have rights! It's my life!" Joe rolls his eyes.

Things change! Now, paddles gone from schools, students have no tears of contrition. Notes home and suspensions are the only punishments. Isn't performance down in schools both socially and academically? Hasn't violence increased in schools? The high water mark of American education in both tested knowledge of graduates and, I believe, behavior is 1963. Every year since then there has been a decline in SAT scores. Is there is some way of testing behavior performance as well--- police blotters? That would be a good research project for my husband. Paddles are present and used in most high schools in 1963. Is the lack of discipline, real sorrow, repentance, instilled, not with anger, abuse, but the use of human, particularly child physiology, a major part of this?

"When I was in school there were no suspensions, or suspension was rare. I don't think I ever knew anyone who was suspended!" I say directly to Joe.

"OK everyone your age was really perfect then, huh, no one got in trouble!"

Is he being arrogant, or does he think I was always the old lady I am now, too senile to figure out how to get in trouble?

"No, Joe, it wasn't that. Almost every teacher had a paddle somewhere in their class. Some hung them on the wall for everyone to see, a warning. Others kept them in a drawer or under a desk. Those that didn't have them sent students needing their application to another teacher or the principal for their paddlings. If we did something wrong. It was dealt with right then and everyone, including the one punished went on with their school work." I smile at him, thinking, knowing, that would be best for him. A good paddling is precisely what he needs.

"That's wrong, letting teachers attack you and hurt you because they are mad at you! We are more civilized now. But people smoked more then. Maybe I should have been born in those olden days. I bet they would have let me smoke wouldn't they? Didn't everyone smoke?" Joe says.

"People smoked more now. Cigarette companies gave free cigarettes to service men in WWII. They came home addicted. That is when smoking really got going in America. During the war and after those companies paid Hollywood to have smoking in the movies to make it look romantic or tough. Even a President of the California Medical Association used to be on bill boards, a cigarette in his mouth, saying how cigarettes were good for you. He died from lung cancer. Some of us thought it divine justice. But no, no one smoked in school. Some kids tried though."

"I would have been a man and smoked like everyone back then!" Joe leans back trying to look like John Wayne imagining a cigarette between his lips.

Imagine, yes; listen, no; reality, no; in our house, no. No one ever smokes in our house, ever!

"You could have. Did I say all the teachers had paddles in their classes? Not all of them did, but one older teacher did, and she had a special place in her heart, and bent over her desk for smokers. The paddle was ornate, leather, a carved handle. It must have been at least fifty years old. She worked linseed oil into it every summer at the end of the school year to keep it supple. In the decades that she used that paddle, every student that experienced its use cried. Even our toughest he-men cried when she paddled them. If you had smoked in Miss Baldwin's class she would have paddled your bottom until you were crying like a baby. You wouldn't have looked much like John Wayne to the girls in your class crying like that would you? And I'll bet you wouldn't have got caught with cigarettes at school again either!"

Can he envision that? He has a good poker face. I know. He knows. A paddling from Miss Baldwin would change his behavior, if not his mind. Paddlings change mine.

If the captain of the football team had put his arm around my shoulder the day after Mrs. Hunter paddled me and said, "Let's do it again, Sharon!"

Would I do it? Would I if it were not for the paddling? After those paddlings none of us would consider it. This is Joe's third suspension for the same thing. Is he sorry? A sharp pain, a burst of heat, the first swat gets my attention. If it stops there my eyes dry no worse than a belly flop off the low board, the fun worth the pain, I would do it again like Joe with his cigarettes? Four more swats, an inferno of pain floating above the fire that engulfs my buttocks, tears stream down my face. Her and the coach's instructions, paddle until sorry. Each of us cries. The toughest man I ever knew among us that day takes ten licks. He cries. Did I ever do it again? Did he ever do it again? Not in this lifetime!

I cry, not that I want to cry or think I should cry. It is the pain. Not a hurt, a pain. My bottom is wide and fleshy enough to take the paddle without injury experiencing real pain. That pain creates artificial regret becoming real regret. Am I sorry when I am punished in school? Yes! Is a student sent home to sleep in for a day or week, watch TV and then slip out to the mall for the afternoon sorry for what they have done? Why should they be? Punishment needs to create regret, sorrow, not mini vacations!

Every child is unique and will respond to different punishments. Some benefit more from time outs, extra work or other ways of correction. Some don't! Virtually all people, small and large, avoid pain. The key is there has to be a motivation strong enough in the punishment to change behavior, if a change in thinking is needed, the punishment must create emotion. Does anything work better to ensure emotion than corporal punishment?

Laughing to myself I remember. I am in the 7th grade, Mr. Cook's history class. Do I have a problem talking too much? I do, too often in his class. Is that wise? A powerful little man having a paddle with holes drilled in it on a hook by the blackboard, he is a threat. Talking away for the third time that hour two other girls and I attract his attention. He stops the class.

"Girls, this is the third time today," he says.

We don't say anything, stopping our chatter.

He walks to his paddle.

A lump coming up in my throat, I blurt out, "I'm sorry, Mr. Cook!"

Anna Belle and Helga chimed in with their "I'm sorrys" too.

An experienced teacher, he has to do something to keep the class from going into complete squirrelldom. Why do we lead the squirrels with our chatter becoming his example? Young girl squirrels, our nature, especially before Christmas, we chatter. It is too cold to send us outside scurrying up trees and over branches chattering as we go expending youthful energy. He must quell our squirrelliness with fear for another half an hour then we become another teacher's problem. Students all squirrelly with Christmas break starting in four hours and twenty two minutes some teachers will be having an extra drink tonight, others will say a prayer of thanksgiving, another long preholiday ordeal finished.

Stopping, looking back at us, Christmas spirit in him, is he in a forgiving mood, or is it bah humbug, swat, swat? He stops. I tremble.

"All right, do you want paddled?" he says.

"No!" We say.

"All right, over the holidays write a three page paper on something important to you, about your family, a trip, Christmas, something important to you."

"Mr. Cook, 3 pages, that's awfully long," Anna Belle says.

"Would you rather have a paddling now?" Mr. Cook is being mean, and right before Christmas.

*Three days later*

Daddy talks, I listen. His early life, the death of my grandparents when he is only seven, living with his grandmother, things he has trouble talking about, I listen, taking notes. When I decide to write, I write about the man I adore, my father? Scribbling away with my pencil, Momma reads over my shoulder.

"That is really good, honey. Here use my pen, and make it neat," she says, hugging me.

Over the holidays Daddy talks. I write. Momma reads. She even does my chores for me. If dishes need to be done and I am writing, Momma does them. Dishes and chores? I would rather write. Writing is fun, I like it. My first epic, Momma asks me why I am writing it.

"Mr. Cook asked me to write a paper for him," I say.

"Over the Christmas Holiday?" Momma says.

"Uh, yes, Momma."
*She is getting too close!*
"What did you do?"
"Nothing really, Momma. Anna Belle, Helga and I were talking."
*Will that satisfy her?*
"You are being punished?"
I don't need to answer, she sees it in my eyes.

Learning it is punishment from Mr. Cook she asks herself as I listen. "I wonder if I should paddle you. If he is punishing you, I should too!"

"No, Momma," I say, "he wants me to write a three page paper. No paddling, Momma."

"I guess that's OK. Did he say three pages?" Momma asks thumbing through what I had already done. She counts eight pages. "Do you like writing? Is it fun to write about Daddy?"

"Yes Momma."

"Finish up what you are doing for me. I guess if he can make you write for punishment, I can too!" She says, "Do it if you want too. Do it if you like too. I like what you are doing. You will never buy a better Christmas present for Daddy." Momma leans down kissing me on the top of the head.

I write, ... *then Daddy met Momma...* and ask, "Momma tell me about when you and Daddy fell in love."

Back in school, Anna Belle writes three pages. Helga forgets to do hers. Me, what do I do? 37 pages of neatly penned text in a binder that is what I do.

I hand it to Mr. Cook. "Momma wants it back when you have read it, Mr. Cook."

My teacher looks at it, thumbs through the first few pages and sits down at his desk. Beginning to read he forgets he has a class in front of him. Coming to life he looks up, "Class turn to pages 106 through 138 in your history book and start reading." He continues reading my paper finishing it in about twenty-five minutes.

Turning to Helga he says, "You didn't do a paper?"

"No. I forgot!" She eyes the paddle.

"Merry Christmas," he says, passing over her.

"Anna Belle, yours is fine. It's good. You get an A on an extra circular assignment." He turns to me. "Sharon, this is something special. I read. It is very good, and very touching. It gives me a much greater understanding of your father, his life and the hardships he has suffered as well as the joys of his life. I don't think most Americans understand the hardships others like your father suffer. Your writing brings it out very well. Good job." He hands me my paper back with "Wonderful job, A+" written on it.

"Thank you," I say not knowing what the A+ means. Two weeks earlier it is a paper or a paddling, not a graded assignment.

The A+ is for the entire year's work, my final grade at the end of the year! I have an A anyway, the paper adds the +. Anna Belle's A brings her grade from a B+ to an A-, making her happy too. Momma keeps my paper with other important documents in a case in her and Daddy's room.

Did I mention I have a talking problem? I do, being a girl and all. Does it get better? No, it gets worse. Now in Mr. Cook's class he catches me chattering six times in the first week and a half of school. Am I a problem?

The first four times he walks over to my desk and says, "Stop!" The fifth he gives me a lecture. The sixth he tells me, "Come here!" He walks me to the black board. He stands me with my nose an inch away from the paddle. He has my attention.

"Sharon, should I punish you?" he says.

"I'm sorry, Mr. Cook. Can I write another paper?"

"Yes, I think that would be a good idea, but you have been talking like a Magpie for the last two weeks. Not one paper, I want one every week for the next four weeks. It doesn't have to be long, two or three pages, of fifty if you want, on other members of your family, like the one you did on your father," he says.

"Yes sir," I say.

"Is that punishment to you? Are you sorry for talking in my class?"

I look at him. *What is he talking about?*

"Is eating ice cream punishment for you, Sharon?"

I look at him. *Is Mr. Cook crazy?*

"Sharon, you love writing more than ice cream and your mother loves you and your writing. I talked to her last week at the market," he says. "It is not enough, I want a short paper every week for the rest of the school year."

Some members of the class gasp. Is that fair punishment for talking? Is it fair for me? Mr. Cook is like that if he knows a student can't do the work, he gives them less, what they can handle and diverts them to other projects. If they can do more, he gives them more. He gives me the most!

"Now, are you going to stop talking in my class?"

"Yes Sir."

"Really, Sharon. If all I do is make you write, you will be talking more and more and more. Do you see that paddle?" He rocks in on its hook.

How can I not see it; it is so close to my nose the grain patterns in the wood blur in my vision.

"Yes Sir."

"The next time you are talking in class you will be punished, five licks! Now go sit down," he begins to write something on the blackboard.

Frozen, I watch the paddle swinging back and forth in front of my nose.

"Go sit down, Sharon," he says.

That was the last time I was caught talking in his class for the rest of that year.

Do expellings work for Joe like writing for me? He likes being home. I like writing. No amount of paper or vacation punishments will stop either of us from misbehaving. My writing pleases my teacher and my Mother. Joe's being home pleases his teachers, and there is a question about his mother. That is the problem with most punishments used in schools now. Do they discourage wrong actions or encourage right actions?

There is a certainty, a child crying from a good paddling regrets having the paddling and has an emotional commitment to avoiding another! Can the same be said for most other forms of correction now in approved use? Pain, nature's punishment, is a sure way of altering behavior universal in life forms capable of experiencing it. Used where crying and deep repentance is needed it changes lives.

Joe thinking and glad he will never be paddled is restless and tires of talking to an old lady about this. His mother visiting me, while she is out is a good time for him to go home and catch a little action on the Playboy channel before lunch. After he leaves his mother and I talk.

"Miriam, if you don't do something to make him regret his actions your boy is headed for trouble. He needs a good paddling. I have a paddle here left over from our children. Do you want to use it?"

"You can't be serious! That is child abuse, beating my child to get my frustrations out! They would arrest me! Even though, I must admit, I am frustrated!" Aghast that I would even say such a thing, my neighbor, friend, is not of my age, my way of thinking.

"Miriam, a spanking is not a beating. I was spanked at home and paddled at school. Only once in my entire youth was I paddled at school in anger in a way that didn't fit the crime. That teacher did it not because of my act, but her emotions. I know there are teachers and parents that do that. I experienced it. For a time my mother was misled and punished me incorrectly, but still in love. It can be done wrong. I'm not recommending that. A paddling would help him cry and feel that his actions are wrong. If you do that and he sees his mistake, it helps him. Miriam, it helps to make a better man of him! That I know. I've seen it in school and my own family. I experienced it myself!" I look at her. Is she listening?

"No, I won't do that, abuse my boy to relieve my anger!" Her head held high Miriam answers self righteously.

No, she isn't listening!

## Chapter 7
# READING AND WRITING

I remember the last thing I offer that Miriam rejects. Is she as difficult to teach as George Junior? After five years in my adult class at church I wonder if he learns anything.

He tells the judge, quoting from the Bible, "Forgive your enemies seventy times seven."

"As a Christian, as a person, I forgive you. As a judge charged with the protection of the public I sentence you to ten years at hard labor." Then privately to the district attorney the judge says, "Thank God for separation of church and state."

Miriam's daughter, now in her twenties and still having problems, develops Irritable Bowel Syndrome as a teen. My chiropractor's treatments help me. They prevent it from ever developing with simple dietary changes and properly given large warm enemas. I am excited. I know the knowledge I have can improve her daughter's life. Does she listen?

"I never heard of such a thing. There are pills for that. Our medical doctor gave us two prescriptions for her, and told her to avoid spicy foods. We will follow HIS advice!" Sure of her programming Miriam answers and puts her daughter in the medical system completely undeterred by logic.

Does the girl ever have an enema? Only having one, a barium enema to diagnose the problem, is she ever completely well? She suffers increasingly frequent attacks through her teens. She develops colitis. I have many enemas once my chiropractor diagnoses my IBS. Do I suffer as my neighbor's daughter? I never have anything more than minor inconvenience over the next six decades. Hovering near the bathroom for half an hour to clear the first enema, then the time to take and hold a second baking soda or flax seed enema to soothe my bowel is a small price to pay for skipping the cramps, irritability, constipation and diarrhea of a spastic colon.

The other part of the treatment, the main part, eating more healthfully has a profound affect on my life. Do I expect this as a teenager? Me, super girl, like every teenager I think I am immortal, will never grow old or get sick. My body will bounce back no matter what I do to abuse it. The colon problem changes this. That too makes me, me. I am what I eat, what my mother feeds me during those years to keep me healthful.

Other kids get away with dietary sins. When young I envy them. I miss being able to eat with them and not get sick. I walk by the malt shop looking in with sadness. Sixty years later I grow old and not sick. Does a life of healthful living have its rewards? The friends I had, that are alive, eat as they did and envy my health. I take my daily walk past our high school and our old malt shop. I pass their cars in handicapped spots. I walk straight, my spine unbent. Coming home on my second mile I wave at them leaving the malt shop in their walkers.

I, the youngest child, I change my family's diet, with little affect on my grown or almost grown siblings. Continuing to live and eat a healthful vegan diet as an adult, am I a healthful 74 year old woman now? Do I have osteoporosis, heart disease, or many of the other problems common to women my age that have live on the Standard American Diet? I am healthful. Without enemas, without changes in lifestyle would I be as I am? The last of my family, I am the only vegan. I am the only one alive, alive and healthful.

Are enemas as common now as they were? No competent doctor of my era lets a patient with IBS, spastic colon then, escape without learning the value of good enemas to soothe and prevent attacks. Now, without any valid scientific research or clinical studies to justify the change, most modern medical doctors do not recommend enemas. As illustrated by Miriam's daughter's care, enemas fade in use and importance in health care as paddlings fade in schools.

In 1943 I am 13 and getting well because I have enemas frequently on the recommendation of my chiropractor. Dr. Morris Fishbein MD voices medical opposition to enemas by an authority figure. He is a long time secretary of the American Medical Association. Prior to this most colon therapy systems are in medical offices and most prominent physicians such as Dr. Otto Shellburg MD, president of the New York Medical Association, are ardent advocates of enemas and colon therapy. Dr. Fishbein recommends enemas in the treatment of colds and flu, but not during pregnancy.

Viewing enemas as risky during pregnancy is he justified? Improperly given or released enemas increase the risk of miscarriage. Doesn't staining at the stool from constipation cause the same thing? Straining, pressure, incorrect temperature or additives are the problem, not the enema itself. Teaching nurses to give large, warm, gentle enemas slowly at the proper temperature, without soap, chlorine or other deleterious additives is the solution. Teaching patients to release them slowly without straining is the solution. Prior to the 1940s properly given and released enemas were used to lessen the chance of miscarriage by physicians.

Earlier in the century laws were passed in some locales banning the driving of automobiles on city streets because they are a danger to people and horses. Laws regarding proper use of automobiles were gradually passed universally. Now people and horses stay off the road. Cars own the road and are a danger to people and horses. Enemas are given less, people suffer more and medical profits are high. Some progress is forward, some backward and some sideways.

Dr. Fishbein's opinions are being published as I am having a barium enema at my chiropractor's office diagnosing my IBS. This change occurs as the drug industry takes a stronger role in health care. Financing campaigns to eliminate natural remedies and diet in the prevention of disease drug companies succeed in replacing them with their pills. My chiropractor puts me on a proven regime of enemas and good diet to control my disorder not recommending a single pill as the "pill for every ill" is becoming the medical archetype.

Do the pills now given treating Irritable Bowel Syndrome work as well as diet and colon cleansing? Have I been free of symptoms for more than sixty years? Staying on my diet and avoiding emotional or dietary trauma prevents IBS. Stress, unavoidable, a few enemas and tender loving care from my mother, then my husband instantly corrects the episodes I have. My chiropractor's teaching me how to live rather than selling me pills prevents me from having a serious life-long problem. Now the paddle is gone from the schools; the enema bag is gone from the inside of bathroom doors. People suffer days or months with attacks of irritable bowel syndrome as pills try to do from a distance over time what enemas do in minutes applied directly to the problem.

As a student paddled I am back in class as soon as I finish crying? As an IBS patient as soon as my enemas are done, I am better. When Momma catches my problem before it does any serious irritation to my colon a single session with the enema bag, or paddle when the problem is more cerebral, and it is over. If I suffer too long with growing irritation in my bowel, like during final exams or children leaving home, it takes a few days and a series of treatments to correct it.

Leave a problem stewing too long, apply ineffective corrections and a temporary irritation becomes a festering disease. Irritable Bowel Syndrome can progress to Colitis, a frequently disabling disease. Properly treated my colon remains supple and functional for life despite having IBS. Others unsupported by proper care cripple and twist inside.

Externally, do I miss the pain of being corrected by a paddle as a youth? Paddlings hurt. Viewed after tears fade do they help? The results, the correction of social and behavioral errors which cripple more than colitis, are positive and real. The emotional side of pain as punishment relieves guilt and gives tears of absolution as well as correction. Valuable as a child, part of growing up, Momma's paddle rings less often and disappears from my life as I mature.

Enemas continuing throughout my life are different. Those I love. Properly done, intimate, caring, they feel good being given. Then there is nothing like the peaceful feel of euphoria that settles over you after expelling a large warm enema. Feeling good and making me feel good, is there anything better than a good enema? It returns me to the state of being a loved child. I never grow out the need for enemas and never want too.

The real spankings I need. They correct my actions. I change my paradigms. Grown, my life is congruent with right social laws and thinking. I have stood and stand firm under the pressures of temptation and adversity: any deformation recoiling as soon as it is brought to the court of my values. No one needs to apply any fundamental straightening to me from the outside, a little washing of the insides, maybe, but no serious flailing away on the exterior!

In my early years subject to both the paddle and enema, I am plastic, growing, becoming. I am wet concrete in the hands of Momma, Daddy, the preacher and my teachers. Values as solid as the hickory wood in Momma's paddle harden into the bones of my conscious as she works shaping the gray cement mud of my youth with her love, an enema bag and a hickory trowel.

This comes to mind with Joe and his mother, another curve comes when I talk to Sandy about Lizzy.

"Grandma, Lizzy has been getting interested in things lately, things I am not pleased about. I caught her playing with herself one night, and she has begun to notice her brother is different. Our preacher says purity starts early, and I don't want her on the wrong track. I haven't said anything or spanked her yet. What do you think I should do?" Sandra says.

*What do I think she should do? Does she know about me, about my pain, about what happened to me at Lizzy's age?*

"Sandra, what you do now will make a difference in her life. It can make a big difference. She is learning about sex. In my generation the word itself was wrong to say. Any sexual act was punished. Did that make us purer, more spiritual, more Godly?"

"Didn't it Grandma? Your generation is more spiritual than mine!"

"Your generation has more freedom than mine. As a young unmarried woman there was no birth control. If we had sex we got pregnant. Purity was a must. There was no choice!" I say.

"But wasn't it better being pure?" She looks at me.

"It's better, but the price is high. We had to marry young, and families started with no way to prevent them if we had sex as we wanted. Some other things too, the strong opposition to sex drove us to wonder, imagine, to have fantasies more than know. Sex is a powerful topic, one that can make and dominate one's whole life."

I think about my own fantasies, the years of guilt.

I say, "It's something you will need to work out. Lizzy is a little girl, forming ideas. Be sure to set an example of loving and caring for her. Don't punish her for being human. Let her see that you and your husband love each other and all you do is to give joy, pleasure and love to each other. She sees you kiss. You can't let her in the bedroom, that makes it a mystery to her, one that needs to be a loving pleasurable mystery, not a dark, evil one that thinking about it causes her to be spanked or given pain. Make it loving,"

"Grandma, you always give the best advice. You amaze me!" Sandra pats my hand.

Lizzy is playing in the living room, theoretically not hearing anything we grownups are talking about. Later she helps me do the dishes while her mother changes her brother in the bedroom.

Lizzy thinks about her birthday party remembering her first big social event. Talking about it she asks me, "What was it like GrrrGrandma, when you were five years old? Did you have lots of presents. Did your Daddy give you a birthday spanking?" Lizzy smiles up at me.

"Yes, I had lots of presents, Daddy gave me my favorite Doll, Samantha, that year. Playing with her until I was a twelve I watched Momma patch her a dozen times. Making things, or buying presents for me at the company store my brothers and sisters shared in my joy. Some gave me little bags of candy, my next older brother, David, gave me a nickel to buy what ever I wanted. It was a good birthday. And yes, Daddy gave me my first birthday spanking that day, the first of many. It was a wonderful day."

Lizzy, like my children, my grand children and now my great grand children is curious about me, who I am, my life, as I am curious about my parents and grandparents. A curiosity we all have looking at our ancestors, our origins, the fabric of our flesh, minds and who we are. It is human to question, lucky to know. I see it in Lizzy's eyes.

"GrrGrandma, you were a little girl?" she says.

"Yes, Lizzy, once I was a little girl like you,"

How do I tell Lizzy about this? I am a wrinkle faced, old woman to her. Will she ever see me otherwise? There are a few pictures. I find one and show it to her.

Taken in front of Daddy's Knox car, the car is last of its kind, one of the final limousines to roll out of the plant. Have you seen a Knox car, the big, top rated, limousine, the choice of America's elite? 20 years old when the lens flickers open a fraction of a second immortalizing it, it is no longer new, in a millionaire's service. It is a car of a large family, filling its long body with children packed in seats, not a lone man in a silk shirt.

We are on our way to church in our Sunday best. Taking the picture of us with his new camera Uncle Jim preserves the moment. Pointing at each person my finger is in the past. The yellowed picture lives. I see, I feel them. I hear the motor start. I hear Daddy.

"Let's go, let Uncle Jim get this picture and load up," Daddy says.

"Lizzy, this is my Daddy." I listen to him my finger lingering over a graying man straight-faced standing beside young men, most of them taller than him. "This is my Momma." Without this picture would I remember my Momma looking like that? She isn't young, but she, in her early forties, is pretty. "This is Sammy, my oldest brother. This is Nathan, George, Thomas, and the youngest one David, my other brothers. These are my sisters, Mary and Amber. Beside Amber, right here, Do you see him?"

Lizzy nods.

"This is Albert, Amber's boy friend. Beside him is my Aunt Mindy." My hand moves a little slower, my fingers are less straight this year. Last I point out a little girl, Aunt Mindy's hand on her shoulder, both of us standing ram-rod straight. "Lizzy, that's me. I am five years old just like you."

"That's you Grrgrandma?"

"That's me." That is still me. I am that little girl. I always will be that little girl.

Where do I start? How do I tell my life to those I carry in me, or come from those that I grow inside me? Half of what they are is me, half, my husband--- or a quarter or an eighth going down to Lizzy.

Making those that grow within me physically and mentally what they are then giving them the most important part of their environment as their mother, I have a long reach. My bony fingers bend, thinning and blending reach down the generations.

Lizzy should know, family is important, irreplaceable. Every person is no more, no less than a population of ancestors stretching back to the beginning tempered by the world around them. Where should I start--- at my beginning?

"Lizzy, I was born in the fall, the youngest of eight, and my mother's last baby. It was a special time, and my mother and daddy were special people, like your mother and daddy."

"Am I going to be the youngest too, GrrGrandma?"

"No, Lizzy, you are always going to be the oldest, like Sammy (I point to him in the picture), a special place in the order of things. You are your brother's older sister by a year, about the same as Sammy was to my sister Amber. Are you going to be a big sister again?"

"I know. Momma is going to have a baby!"

Lizzy is going to be a big sister again in about three months.

"I want a sister this time," she says.

Talking to a little girl, a time comes when she will want to know about her GrrGrandma and what my life was like in the 1930s in ways she can't imagine now. Will I be there to tell her?

I see my great great great grandfather's journal on the book shelf. Writing a few lines every few days he breaks the law, writing, something he isn't supposed to be doing. A legacy of oppression resisted by a man intended to work the fields uneducated, he reads and writes. A simple book, it is my family's most treasured heirloom.

Breath on vocal cords brings back words written by him a hundred and fifty years ago. In them he lives as no other ancestor of that or some closer generations. Years erase details, and often the essence, of everything that lives in memory, thoughts and oral tradition. Lessons learned without record, die when the student dies or at best the passing of the next two generations. Written words, preserved, live.

As I read through his little book that afternoon, what does it mean to me? The rock chimney on our farm he built stands. Rubbing my hands over the stones I know they are his, not the perfection of a master mason, the amateur finish work, rough in places, reveals a man, a farmer, who builds one chimney of which we know, few if any others. He carries round river stones in a wagon from the creek cementing them in place by hand. It is tangible, real something solid he leaves behind. Building it for heat, a pot of soup or stew warming over the hearth, a thing made by him, it warms my soul. A chimney he makes, like millions of others make chimneys for a common purpose, it is special, not unique.

Words, oral, vanish into air as said. If remembered, they change, altered by each person recollecting them. We know almost nothing of the person, the character, humor or thoughts of unlettered, unwritten ancestors after the children they rear pass. Is this true of kings, great leaders with scribes? Are important people remembered after their deaths? Why, and why are not peasants remembered? Thoughts, words written down can be recalled exactly from yellowed pages for as long as the paper lasts. Words of Jefferson, Monroe, Lincoln and others written on paper and copied in stone may last long after the nation they serve is gone.

My distant great grandfather, a great man, writes his thoughts by candle light after plowing all day in the field and leaves them on paper for us to read. Does this immortalize him and his family to those that read his words? In them is humor, wisdom, every day events a life lived and real. It lasts.

I read, "--- September 8, 1856, Today Sarah went to town to learn embroidering. She fell off the horse on the way home. Too short to get back on without help she leads him home. Her feet are sore. Momma will send her shoes with her tomorrow in case she falls off."

Government officials, bankers, lawyers, and land barons without written histories are buried in graveyards with weathering tomb stones in every community, forgotten. The paper aging, his legacy tattered on the edges lies now in a university library, each page encased in plastic preserved permanently. Modern technology, Xeroxing preserves and scatters copies over the world, some in university libraries and museum vaults; most on bookshelves of his descendents spread over America. These last. These copies last like stone edifices on buildings and outlast stone where buildings are torn down.

Gengus Khan, the greatest military mind that ever lived, conquers of 1/3 of the world, has no grave, is dust on the Siberian plain, is illiterate, the leader of an illiterate people. His history written by his enemies, those who never know him, do we know him? Do we know who he is? Do we know what he thinks? Do we know what kind of man it is that changes the world? We know him less than the most insignificant of European princes with their every act recorded, or my great great great grandfather with his simple journal.

My Grandma reads from the original copy to me when I am eight sitting in the house where much of it is written. That afternoon I wander down to the stream bank. Do I see the porch of our family's first home, the one in my maternal ancestor's book? Nodding off, I dream of words, of writing, of times passed under the shade of a small tree by the creek.

From my literate writing grandfather of long ago and his family another remains according to legend, a thought, a pale blue mist in the mind, one he writes of telling us her name--- Sarah. We know of her love and the tragedy that takes her from them. The page recounting her mother's heartbreak, the tear-wrinkled unevenness of that page writing about loosing her, is this what keeps her alive? Is this why we see her? She lives in his heart, and especially her mother's heart long after she is gone. After everyone that ever knows her is dead: she lives. She lives in Grandpa's book. Does she live outside it, a benevolent protective spirit?

A little girl, dressed in blue says to me as I sleep, "Do you want to play?"

Dreaming, I am on the porch of a simple cabin. I hear the creek. I hear the girl. Rousing, reaching for Samantha, my doll, I say, "OK!"

Where is she? There is no cabin, no porch--- no girl. Walking toward the shimmering yellow square of blooming Jonquils where the cabin once stands instinctively I know that is where she wants me. I look back. The tree tilts. The bank crumbles. Where Samantha and I were sleeping tumbles into brown rolling waters of the creek at flood stage.

Fully awake, scared, I say, "Did you see that!"

Did the girl see that? Looking around, I am totally alone except for a cow. It moos. I run home to tell Grandma.

Grandma says, "Did you see her, the girl in blue?"

I chatter away, my eyes as big as saucers, an eight year old excited. I saw her, the girl in blue.

Grandma hugs me saying, "Stay away from the creek when it is up!"

I read the copy of my distant grandfather's journal. I have read it many times. I read it to Lizzy. Loving it, she thinks it is special too. What if I write a book, one about me, and my times, my people, will Lizzy and her children value that as I do my ancestor's book? Knowing she will that night I sit down with an old type writer. I don't have a journal, but if Lizzy reads this she will know her GrrGrandma.

Pulling out that picture what will I write, about me, about my family? Every person in that picture is dead except me. What about them, what about their stories? Looking at them, are they asking me, as my teacher, Mr. Cook, asks me, as Momma asks me, "Tell my story!"

Should I write about what I am like? The jonquils are different flowers, as am I. My husband loves me as I am, fulfills my fantasies, is a true husband. If not for him, what life would I have? Taboo to talk about in our youth, more open now, it is still taboo to talk about. What if I talk about it, share my feelings about sex from a time long ago for a little girl, perhaps more than one girl, to help them accept their selves as God makes them?

My husband is coming home. I will tell him my plan, to write. I promise to tell him when I make a decision. Will he remember asking me to choose an avocation? Only 24 years since he asks me to develop an alternative plan for my life will he remember? I remember. I will write our stories.

I see the jonquils quivering in beds along our driveway. Thick, growing fuller each year bulbs are fat with life ready to transplant. This fall will be the time for digging, thinning, sharing. Will Lizzy plant them with me, listen to these stories as we dig? I will write them when she sleeps. Jonquils go on, a square patch in a field, a row on a driveway, a circle around my secret place in the woods, in a new bed at Lizzy's school and in the hearts of those who see the flowers.

## Chapter 8
# BRUSSELS' SPROUTS

*Where should I start? At the beginning?*
*October, 1931, my birth*

In spring green life from brown earth appears. Green blades, yellow blossoms, the jonquils bloom. Grass grows. People, unlike Jonquils, bloom in summer, winter and fall as well as spring. Momma swollen, full term, it is time for me to break free, emerge, come into the world. I am born in fall when plants are dying, when winter is starting.

Slipping out of Momma's pelvis I get my first look at the world, have my first spanking and I wonder what will come next, sure it will be another first. Daddy holds me, comforts me, looks at me. He talks to me with that deep voice I hear muffled by Momma's belly since I grow ears. My mother snuggles close to him in bed. They are always talking, smooching. Momma groans, coos. My world starts rocking. What are they doing?  What ever they are doing from now on I will be in another room when they are doing it. No more free rides, are they going to make me do everything for myself?

First there is breathing. Crying taking my first breath in response to pain, my bottom tingles. Why does the doctor spank me? What did I do? I keep breathing as he hands me to my father. Daddy feeds me, not with a breast, a spoon or his hand on my bottom like Momma. He feeds me through my eyes, ears and holding me. He feeds my soul and mind. Momma feeds me. No longer fed by the umbilical cord, I need food. Where is Momma? Why isn't Momma holding me, nursing me?

She would be nursing me, except--- she is dying, blood gushing from her womb. Dying without the doctor's help, paying the woman's price for giving life, she almost loses her own. The doctor working hard to save my mother, she bleeds. My father paces, holding me, worrying. He watches. Joyful at having me, joy will sour if he loses her. Praying now, Daddy's eyes and hers meet.

"I love you, Sarah!" Daddy says.

Momma smiles a weak smile, "I love you, too!"

Dr. Feinberg continues pushing putting pressure on her bleeding uterus.

"It's working!" The white haired doctor looks at my father.

A grin, a grunt, a tear falls from my father's eyes.

*What are those*? I think, salty drops splashing on my face.

"Give her the baby, Sam. Nursing will help contract the uterus," Dr Feinberg says.

Seeing Momma the first time my eyes don't focus. *What is that?* I have never seen one of those. *What is that for? Oh, I know.* Latching on with a strength I won't have in a few days I nurse her. My ear pressing to her I hear the weak heart beat that is my life, that has been my music, my world for the last nine months, my Momma. Breathing, nursed, born, I sleep. Momma sleeps.

*Years pass*

Jonquils blow in the wind, cold spring days, snow clinging to north side roots on the creek bank. A white-faced cow, chewing a lump of mixed dry old and moist young grass nearby, admires their beauty. Viewed or alone, the Jonquils grow from bulbs each year, grow as they were then, now or a thousand years before. Every year, planted in good soil and sun, they come back. Every year there are more bulbs growing from the old ones, more flowers to love.

God, smiling on my great great grand aunt's love of family, planted prayer, nurtures, waters and warms our jonquils with sunlight each year. A part of nature, God's garden, they grow never having been cared for by human hands since hers. They are, made, created, flowers in a field sustained by God alone, a feast to the soul, a message of love from a little girl that loves us from a time vanished.

First seeing her before I have language, I am too young to tell anyone or remember it happening. I wave at her. Now, age five, a long drive from our ancestral home, living in the North, I am never a southern girl. I see the jonquils, that Southern field many times. Other than summer visits to my grandparents as a child, I never live or stay longer than a few days until my son and his wife manage the family trust. We sleep in the room where my great great great grandmother and father slept, next to the room where my mother sleeps before she and Daddy marry.

My roots, my memories, my place of origin grow in another state; my voice is another voice. When I go South to our ancestral home, and the word Yankees is used, it is me and my family they are talking about. I am a Northerner, a Yankee, a child of the South. I have Southern jonquils in my yard spreading these bulbs from a Dixie farm to a Union town.

Northern flowers are fine, but a garden, that is best to pious Northerners. Food, for cold winter days and succulent summer feast--- that is what should be grown. Our preacher says and teaches that. A practical man, he preaches a utilitarian world. Beauty must serve function and have an applied purpose.

The preacher's flowers grow on stalks, thick, turning to green knots, planted, tilled with constant human care, growing in gardens created and only alive for the utility man. Are they beautiful? Gardens are beautiful, some filled with flowers in beds of blue, yellow, red, colors to feed the eye. Others, filling, very filling, their flowers are best appreciated with the mouth, not the eye.

Our preacher's view of the world is different than mine. He loves Brussels sprouts. To him they are flowers! Are they to me? Not to me when I am a little girl! Then I think Brussels sprouts are weeds among vegetables? I sit at Momma's kitchen table forced to eat those things. If I see a Brussels sprout growing near our peas, tomatoes or other vegetables

I will go after it with a hoe. It is a weed! Will Momma spank me for that? You bet! I look at them on my plate and sigh. Why didn't someone go after them with a hoe?

Our preacher breaks off stalks covered with green knots from his garden, handing six of them to Momma. Our preacher's garden--- is it a place of love, with plants he plants in love, as is the flower bed of the girl in blue? Hers goes on forever, sustained by God. Does God view the work of the preacher's hand the same as hers?

A cabbagy odd-tasting dish, he likes Brussels sprouts. Most people don't to begin with. Can they be made to develop the taste? I don't think I will ever like them. If the preacher likes them, we eat them. The preacher, a man of God, can't be wrong! Will I go to hell if I don't eat them? Am I too young to choose heaven or hell for myself? Can Momma choose for me? As a baby I eat what is stuck in my mouth. Older now I have a choice, not eat them and be spanked, then eat them, or just eat those little green yucky things in the first place. That is a choice? Momma makes me eat Brussels sprouts and other foul tasting things.

But now I am five! "Momma, I don't want to eat these Brussels sprouts. If I eat any more of them I will turn into a Brussels sprout!"

I am turning green already starting with my fingers. Why does Momma think I am playing with my food? A girl can get green fingers in other ways: grass, food coloring, some crayons, etc., things not having to do with Brussels sprouts. Unfortunately none of those ways is within reach and I am not allowed to leave the table until I am done!

Momma isn't worried, no matter how green I get. She says, "Eat them. They will make you a healthy girl."

She doesn't tell me about the laxative effect or that they help to prevent cancer. Does Momma even know that? She decides I am going to eat them because the preacher says they are good for me. That is enough for Momma. Being a five-year-old am I expected to understand these things? Am I expected to do what I am told, what is good for me? If Pastor John tells Momma eating June bugs is good for children, I eat them.

Is it lucky he gives her Brussels sprouts from his garden, not June bugs? Are there June Bugs with the preacher's Brussels sprouts?

I imagine his voice ringing out, *LUNCH, Brussels sprouts con June Bugs!*

I see them, two June bugs crawling on the table outside of church where the preacher puts the pile of Brussels sprouts. Giving them out after Sunday services he smiles. Momma looks stunning in her new pink dress, matching hat and Brussels sprouts bouquet. Six stalks a double armful can she hold my hand? Amber holds my hand, walks with me, wrinkles up her nose looking at them when Momma isn't looking. Thankfully the man of God makes no mention of the food value of June bugs during his sermon. One emerges from the sprouts climbing over Momma's shoulder and down her back. Popping its wings it flies away Momma never seeing it.

If the preacher says we have to eat June Bugs is there a difference? Green and not trying to crawl off my plate like undercooked June Bugs there is no escape from Brussels sprouts. June Bugs, equally appetizing, may be preferable. Picking them up and giving them a flick with my finger, I would make them fly away. Momma, thinking that I ate them, would spare my stomach the duty of digesting them. I look at Momma, slyly thinking about it.

Loving, feeding and taking care of me, Momma makes me eat. Shaping me, always there, more than anyone else, she is creating the girl reflected in her eyes, pound by pound. Daddy, a fleeting influence, only there when not working in the plant, teaches me to count, has a way of getting in my head and being heard even when he isn't there, his remembered voice competing with Momma's real one. Will counting them help? One Brussels sprout, two Brussels sprouts, three, four--- that is a lot of Brussels sprouts, too many for a girl to eat!

Teaching me measuring too, Daddy carries me outside with him as he talks to my brother. His talk this Sunday is about systems of measurement.

"Here watch me," Daddy says.

He puts me down and puts his face in mine making sure my eyes are locked on his.

*What is he going to do this time?*

Daddy lies down on the porch with his feet against the wall leaving a pencil where his head ends. Getting up, he measures putting one foot after the other heel to toe until he measures out the distance between the wall and the pencil.

"One, two, three…six, seven, I am seven times the length of my feet tall. You lie down and let's see how tall you are, Sharon."

I do, Daddy putting the pencil down where my head stops.

Measuring it out with my feet Daddy counts, "One, two, three… six, seven. Amazing, Sharon, you and I are the same number of our feet long! Sammy, this is what they were thinking when they called the basic unit a foot. The originators wanted to have something that the people could use and have handy to measure by, the human foot. You do it," Daddy says.

Sammy stretches out on the porch. Daddy and I are the same tallness! He is seven feet high as am I, but I am a little girl and he my big Daddy. My brother is shorter than Daddy measured this way even though he really is taller than my father by more than three inches.

"Sammy's feet are like King John's. If God hadn't turned down so much for feet Sammy would be over six feet tall," Daddy says calling him King John the rest of that day to make his point.

Bigger feet than the rest of us, and bigger in proportion to his body, my brother's feet are long. His shoes have to be ordered from the company store rather than buying them off the shelf. Daddy's feet are size eight. He buys shoes at any shoe store. It is harder to get shoes for Sammy than Daddy. King John's feet are a problem too, being 12 inches long, the king, and the royal basis for the English measuring system, few citizens of his country can wear his shoes or approximate his foot in measuring.

That is what Daddy thinks. He can't be sure about the story, not being written down; it is legend.

Daddy says, "It is better to write things down. It gets too confusing otherwise."

The legend of the foot is clear enough, what isn't clear is whose foot. Is it King John's foot, or a third of the distance between King Edgar's nose and his outstretched thumb? None of the books Daddy reads makes it clear. A professor at the College in the Mathematics department tells him the story of King John. Liking that story best, Daddy shares it with us.

"Can you imagine, Sammy, how the planner of this measurement system felt when King John joined in? 'Here I am, the King, let's use my foot for the basis of measurement!' The originator of the idea must have been, well, flabbergasted. King John probably had the largest, if not near the largest feet in the whole kingdom. Average people like me, couldn't use their feet to measure; they had to approximate them to match the royal English foot!"

Sunday, usually Daddy's only full day off, this is Sammy's talk for the day. Does Daddy expect any of us to answer? Listening, if he pauses and waits for our opinion, we answer. Otherwise we know it is a one-sided discussion. Sammy, a high school graduate for two months now, Daddy is getting more and more advanced in his conversations with his eldest child. I am sure that he plans this lesson for days before giving it to Sammy. For most of it we younger kids watch and wonder.

"Sammy, what do you think of using King John's foot as a basis of measurement? Would you have done it different?"

"I don't know, Daddy. Maybe I would have used a more average foot allowing more people to use the measurement easily."

"That's good, Sammy, a better idea, but what about people without average size feet. Do I have average size feet?"

"No!" My brother looks down at my Daddy and his small feet adding, "You are our little Daddy." Sammy, a normal teen, is reveling in being taller, broader and bigger footed than his father.

"The idea of measuring is to use something that is easy, accessible to people, constant. Is our system of doing it best?"

"I don't know, Daddy. Maybe. The French and other countries use the metric system. Is it better?" Sammy's teacher at school has that opinion. Sammy wants Daddy's opinion.

"The metric system is better, more scientific! For measuring length maybe it is a little arbitrary. The metric system is more logical, based on things out of nature that can be more easily and accurately measured. King John has been dead a long time and digging him up to be sure how long a foot really is supposed to be isn't practical. For the average guy building a house measuring in meters may not be much differtent from measuring in feet, except metric units are more standardized to each other, easier to work with if you are a carpenter or a physicist. The metric system is based on 10s and is more mathematically friendly. It is easier to multiply by ten than twelve," Daddy says.

That is too big a number, 12. Being five years old I can count to ten, but 12? He won't teach me bigger numbers like that until I am in first grade. He and Sammy keep talking. I fall asleep on Daddy's lap. Listening to Daddy talk about measuring systems is not as interesting as listening to him tell bed time stories. I fall asleep faster when he talks about mathematics.

I listen, being interested because it is my Daddy talking, even if most of it is going over my head to my brother. Is Sammy going to college in the fall? Does Daddy think he should be thinking about things like this? Even though my father never has the chance to sit in a single college class as a student he loves knowledge. Is that why he takes us to walk on the grounds of the college some Sundays? Is it to him like church is to Momma?

He isn't a preacher, or teacher; he is a working man, but when he walks through the College with us there is awe. He feels and makes us feel as though the College is a gateway to heaven. One time a janitor, a friend of ours from church, lets us in one of the classroom buildings. Daddy handles the chalk like Momma handles her Bible and goes over each word left on the blackboard by a professor with that same kind of devotion Momma has for utterings of Pastor John. Being important to Daddy makes it important to me. I am his girl cuddling in his arms on the porch swing. Momma calls us to dinner.

Day dreaming about this, I wake up from Daddy's ivory tower looking at Momma's everyday china, the only kind we have when I am young. Rolling a sprout from one side of my plate to the other I wonder, "How wide is my plate in Brussels sprouts?" Rolling one endwise it keeps flipping to its round side. Pushing it with my finger I line it up. One Brussels sprout wide, two, three, then it turns, a five-year-old finger pushing it back in line.

Out of the corner of Momma's eye she sees me, "Eat what's on your plate--- all of it, young lady!"

Momma isn't interested in the width of her plates in Brussels sprouts!

"Yes, Momma," I say. If I count them will they taste better? I force myself to eat. *One Brussels sprout, two---* choking down one last mouthful I am done, can go play.

Learning, eating, a child absorbing Brussels sprouts, I fill my stomach. Do I need to learn to continue eating when I am full at age five? Do I do what Momma teaches me at five?

"Yes, Momma."

At 25?

"Yes, Momma."

At 65?

"Yes, Momma."

I grow up and out fleshing out her vision of me. I eat my Brussels sprouts and everything else that she puts on my plate. Looking in the mirror as a grown woman do I see a woman that cleans her plate?

"Yes, Momma."

"Clean your plate, Sharon. Then you can play." Did Momma say that?

The reflection in the mirror many decades later speaks scornfully, "You are fat?"

"Yes, Momma!"

Is it Momma's fault; always eating everything on my plate. Am I what I eat?

"Yes, Momma, and more."

I am who I was born to be, what Momma fed me, what others make me, who I chose to be, who I am.

## *Chapter 9*
# DADDY

A special day, first Sunday School, then chicken for dinner then I learn about King John's feet. That night, after Sammy's story, it is my turn to be the center of attention.

Looking up at Daddy as he gets out my pajamas, he is looking back at me with the opposite of a banker's smile. Bankers are supposed to practice warm grins covering their whole lower face with joy, while maintaining absolutely expressionless eyes. Straight faced, serious, without the least trace of a smile, Daddy has that stern, mean look. His cheeks sag and the corners of his mouth pull down. Given away by smiling eyes, do I know that look? He isn't mad at me! How is he such a good boxer? Telegraphing everything he is going to do, his eyes give him away, at least to me. Is he going to tell me a story or tickle me? He is going to do something!

I hold up my arms for him to get my dress off. Pulling the tops of my favorite pajamas over my head, the ones with the bouncy kangaroos, Daddy is putting me to bed. When Daddy puts those pajamas on me they come with tales, bed time stories. He is going to tell me a story! Excited I want him to tell me a story. I don't wait for his expression to change. I start jumping up and down like the kangaroos on my pjs.

"Please Daddy, Please Daddy, tell me a story! Please! Please! Please!"

His frown fades. His mouth puckering, words begin pouring out on me. This time it is the three pigs— his version! There are pigs running everywhere: the big bad wolf chasing them around. Picking me up and swirling me about, Daddy spins his love into my heart.

I giggle, "Stop Daddy! You're silly!"

I love my Daddy.

Not always getting a bedtime story from Daddy; they are special treats, words, touches, spins--- his loved stories.

Bouncing more, "Please Daddy! Tell me another story!"

This time it is the three bears, complete with sound effects, growls, super delicious porridge with oatmeal, raisins, bananas, wheat germ, honey, yeast, oat bran, cashews and flax seed oil— yummy, but hot! The front door goes cre----eeak and the bears go for a walk in the woods while it cools.

Goldie Locks comes along banging on the door, ka-pound, ka-pound, ka-pound. The house is as quiet as a church at midnight on Monday evening, except with that pounding the door goes cre---eeak and opens. Sneaking in Goldie locks smells the porridge, yum. She tries to take a bite of Momma bear's porridge except the spoon freezes stuck straight up in it. When she chips off a piece it almost freezes her tongue. Shivering she decides to try Daddy bear's porridge. The spoon sinks in nicely, it isn't too cold. But when she sticks it in her mouth steam starts coming out of her ears and the frozen part of her tongue from trying to eat Momma bear's porridge not only thaws, it sizzles.

"Hot, hot, hot!" Goldie locks sputters backing away from Daddy bear's porridge.

Then discovering Baby Bear's porridge she carefully takes a nip, then a bite, then begins shoveling it in her mouth like an armadillo digging a hole.

"Good, good, yum, good!" She says.

She finishes shoveling it in with the spoon and begins licking the bowl. As clean as if it had been washed except for a few slurp marks she puts it back on the table. Patting her belly, it being warm and way past the full mark, is she ready for more walking? Does she need a good sit down? Goldie Locks hurts her bottom sitting on Daddy Bear's chair. She does youches and ouches all over the living room! It is too hard! Then she almost suffocates in Momma Bear's chair. It is so soft she mires up to her eyeballs! Seeing Baby bear's chair she makes a dive for it. Baby Bear's chair goes crunch, crack, snap, pop, crash, etc. She breaks it to pieces!

Oh well. She really is too tired to sit down anyway. She needs a lay down. Going up stairs it is the same, bruises from Daddy bear's hard bed, eye balls sticking out from Momma bear's too soft bed and snoring in Baby bear's bed.

"ZZzequabble, Zzaquaghsnarf, ZZZZaghbuffquarkflubidid." Goldie Locks is asleep.

Meanwhile downstairs the door goes cre---eeak. Clomp, clomp, clomp Daddy bear comes in. Swish, swish, swish Momma bear comes in. Pat, pat, pat Baby bear comes in.

"Someone's been eating my porridge and ate a whole spoonful," Daddy bear says.

"Someone's been eating my porridge and chipped off a whole chunk with the ice pick," Momma bear says.

Baby bear is boo hooing everywhere. His mouth is open so wide the doctor driving by sees his tonsils and his uvula through the window. He is a health bear. The doctor doesn't see anything to worry about.

"Someone's been eating my porridge--- what porridge! Did Momma Bear give Babikins Bear any porridge? Momma Bear didn't give me any porridge. Does Momma bear love Baby Bear?" Baby bear squalls.

Momma bear thinks he is becoming a nut case and gives him a new bowl full of porridge, one unslobbered on. Baby bear wolfs it down and keeps eating until he is fat as a bear, but then being a bear, that is normal.

Daddy bear lumbers, Momma bear glides and Baby bear waddles into the living room. Daddy bear and Momma bear sit in their chairs. Baby bear looks for his chair. He finds one arm under Momma bear's chair, another in the corner and bits and pieces of his chair scattered around the room. He shows his tonsils and uvula to everybody one more time. Squall bellering round and round the living room he is a fright to behold! Thinking Baby Bear has real problems now Momma Bear is tempted to give him something to calm him down then put him to bed— and does! Poor little bear!

Discovering someone asleep in his bed, it's Goldie Locks! His pupils get as big as quarters. *A person, is a person supposed to be in our house, in my bed?*

Jumping up and down like a sort of round kangaroo he shouts, "Look! Look! Look!" until his Momma and Daddy come running.

"K-yawn, K-yawn, huff sub wulfult qwaugjwubbles," Goldie Locks wakes up.

Her eyes dilate like fifty-cent pieces. *Bears, am I in a bear house?* She checks her dress to make sure she is not bare too.

Baby bear grins at her with little white teeth. Momma bear grins at her with medium size white teeth. Daddy bear grins at her with the biggest, yellowst and meanest looking teeth she has ever seen.

"What are you doing in my Baby bear's bed, little girl?" Momma bear says.

Right then Goldie Locks promises herself never, never to go into the bear's house again, unless she smells porridge cooking, then she might slip in, or even knock on the door and see if Baby bear wants to play--- after they have porridge. Now she is more concerned with the look on Daddy bear's face and the way his tongue licks around those big teeth. Do bears eat little girls? She resolves not to find out.

Grinning back at them she says, "Oh, I think I hear my Mother calling!"

With that she jumps out of bed and runs over Baby Bear, under Momma bear and around Daddy bear. She runs like our cat, Underfoot, being chased by a stray dog! Zing! Savoom! Pitter pat, pitter pat! Running home so fast her shoes untie themselves and slide under the bed before her Momma folds her covers back. She is bed ward ho.

Being over Daddy's shoulder heading that way myself, I wiggle.

"Oh Daddy! I don't want to go to bed now! I want another story!"

Nevertheless, bed it is! Pulling the covers back Daddy souses me in. With the covers over my head, he can't figure out what happened to his girl.

I pop them off with my arms, "Here I am!" I giggle, "One more story Daddy--- Please!"

Not telling me a story, he tells me about the night I am born, and how pretty I am and how much Momma and he love me. It is then I meet my Daddy for the first time. He doesn't tell me The Three Bears story until the next week. He introduces himself and talks to me. His voice is deeper and more resonating than Momma's. Having become a girl the moment he gave me an X chromosome I know there is something special about voices like his. I listen to him as the first and most important man in my life. I am his little girl. He is my father, the man I see the first time I open my eyes.

The day I am born I look and look at him. Being happy to be in the world I give him a look of love that lets him know I am glad to be his baby girl. Once I am dry and wrapped up in a white blanket, he kisses me, calls me Sharon, and hands me to Momma for my first meal. Momma falls asleep with me in her arms. We are happy. I am happy he is my Daddy and Momma is my Momma! They are special parents, my parents, all I will ever have. Daddy gives me a hug and tells me to go to sleep!

Snuggling me in, he gets up and turns off the lights. But I'm not sleepy. I lay there thinking about the stories he told me. My Daddy, the master storyteller, no one ever tells stories like my Daddy! Thinking about me being a special baby to him and Momma almost dying to give me life, I love my Daddy and Momma.

Watching Momma work, wishing he could stay home and be with me always, I don't understand why he has to work. I want to go to work with him. I can't. They don't let little, or even big girls, in the plant then. I settle for stories and having him read to me on Sundays. Working hard, on call at the plant, often he comes home long after my bed time. Missing my Daddy, missing his stories, he has to work.

Time with him or Momma slices thin. Being the youngest of eight is not like being an only child. Needing attention are other kids. Dividing his time, Daddy plays ball with the boys, dances with the girls and reads to all of us.

Passing out of doors, short sleeve shirts, cotton dresses, Daddy in a baseball hat, my brothers carrying a ball, two bats and a glove each we take the whole side walk down Elm street to main, then four blocks to the high school. Being the smallest I go between Momma and

Daddy holding both their hands as we march onto the field leading our team.

Other fathers, families and boys at play my brothers join in. Being there for my brothers, Daddy lets the real players work with the older boys. They hit, catch and run. As the numbers grow men and older boys take over. A real game starts. Working on the sidelines with my younger brothers my father is called. Daddy a boxer, not a ball player, plays outfield a better player moves infield. Girls cheer. Momma shouts, cheers and argues with calls, always taking the side of her boys.

Taking the younger children home after a few innings when we get bored, the game goes on. A few hours later my older brothers and Daddy come home grinning and cackling about some great plays, or scowling about ones they should have made. This changes with the seasons. In fall, no bat, a football--- one foot ball is all we carry. In winter bundled in hats, coats and gloves, bouncing a basketball down the sidewalk, Sammy leads, passing and throwing to others. The high school principal, opens the gymnasium. Always a Sunday afternoon game of some sort, we always go.

My brothers enjoy it, but like Daddy they wear small to medium underclothes. Baseball is all right. Doing pretty well they are still playing when the lesser players are winnowed out. But in football or basketball, too small, they are never going to be super stars or even Sunday afternoon local stars. When the last of our family is eliminated from the competition it makes for an earlier day.

Does Daddy encourage any of his sons to follow him into boxing, a sport divided by size, giving smaller boxers the chance to compete?

"Brains are more important!" he says.

Seeing too many people hurt boxing he steps out of the ring before someone lands a punch making his thinking fuzzy and his reactions slow, and too late to stop before doing it to someone else.

It is during the week when he is home that he plays HIS game with us, *Chess!* Learning it from a teacher after school Daddy saves for three months to buy his board as a boy. When Grandpa finds him, a skinny 12 year old who hadn't eaten in three days, he had left everything behind, except that board and the box of pieces. A plain old board with simple wood carved pieces it sits on the mantle, waiting for my Daddy to take it down. His board, once shinny hardwood, scratched, is old.

Reflecting the image of a skinny young boy when it is new, the scratches now mirror gray streaks in the hair of the man who owns it.

Being chess players we are always ready for a game. Going through several cheap boards, cardboard, plastic pieces bought off the shelf we practice for THE board. Daddy home for lunch, the children's board beyond repair, I hold Daddy's hand as we walk into town to buy a new one.

Waiting for Daddy, our cheap pieces move on a school yard diamond. Home, he brings down Yankee Stadium from the mantle, the pro board, the World Series, Super bowl and NBA championships are played on that board. Oak pons in the front row, we watch in the bleachers when THE BOARD comes down.

Beating Daddy at basketball my brothers are proud. Daddy smiles. Beating him at chess is the mark, a hard mark, the mark for which you earn his respect more than anything else in sport. Only two of my brothers ever beat him. Only one takes him two out of three. When he tips his carved king, a chip of paint flakes off revealing the gray wood below, there is a look of respect for my brother, a new, permanent respect.

Decades later, after Daddy's funeral Momma packs the board, the pieces and gives it to that brother. When visiting them my daughter asks me why Uncle Sam has that old thing on their mantle below a framed letter from the President? I know. He knows. My brother carefully takes it down and starts a game with his grandnephew as we watch. It is Daddy's board, special to all of us. My brother's most prized possession, one he works harder to earn and relishes owning more than the presidential commendation. It deserves to be on the mantle, the place of highest honor.

Striving for that mark with passion each of my brothers trys, but the old man doesn't give much on the chess board. It's his game. He is a smart player, a smart man. Daddy works each boy with until he finds their game, something they are best at. One by one they each best him, earn the tip of his king, his nod of respect, self respect and become who they are, a garage owner, an engineer, a plant superintendent, a long haul truck driver and a chess player who after he retires from the Army still teaches at the war college.

With the girls we don't have to, or want to, compete with him as the boys do. Not driven by testosterone we are happy to be a part of the team playing or on his side cheering. With us it is Momma that sets our marks of the woman to be, and earn her respect. It is not beating her that counts, but pleasing her and being accepted as one of the women as we sit together stringing beans or sewing.

Knowledge, effort and sportsmanship are what Daddy values most in competition and instills as values in us. Both of them inspire us to the highest goals a man or woman can have--- being a husband and father for a man, or a wife and mother for a woman. Everything else is less important. Then as now it is success in the home, on the chess board which we live, that counts when the game is played and night falls on the field.

After the games my time comes curling up next to Daddy with my head on his chest, I hear his heart beat and words through lungs and bone pressing my ear to his body. He reads the funnies with all the other younger kids peering over his shoulder. The comics come to life. Pointing out then asking letters and simple words to me, then others at their levels of learning Daddy always teaches us.

Miss a word and he frowns, swats you with the newspaper or tickles you--- actually the tickling is all mine. Tickling me is something he does a lot. Tickling me till I get it right then we go back to reading. He doesn't tickle the older kids. Knowing he tickled them too when they were five, it is a little kid thing, something they watch, remember, and envy. Me squealing, the others waiting patiently, he always loses his place.

"Where were we?" he says.

Mary points it out to him. We begin again.

Loving it, I balance my desire for his tickling with my desire to be a good girl and get it right. Choices! choices!

I ask him, "Why don't you tickle me when I get it right, Daddy?"

Sometimes he does. I never know what to expect! Making it fun, learning, just for learning is something that Daddy thinks should be fun, makes fun.

After comics there is always a library book to read. It takes weeks to finish Tom Sawyer. But, his time is not sacred to the plant. One time they come to get him the moment he opens the book. He's gone!

Coming home without my father from a game my brothers tell Momma there is a problem at the plant. These times I go to sleep without funnies, stories or seeing Daddy again until the next day.

Taking his time, the plant is a part of his life none of us understand as children. Several of my brothers work with him after high school. Most do it as a summer job home from college. One, the engineer, comes home to work in the plant after graduation. Daddy's boss, my brother never gets used to that. Greasy overalls, long nights and a weekly paycheck it is our father's, our life, a necessary part, a part that feeds, clothes and keeps us alive.

Remembering them coming to get him to go fix something, I have a dread of the plant. It takes the man I love as a child from me disappearing behind its fence into a world of pipes, steam and tanks. Engines pound. I hear them on the street, an extension of him, his heart beat, his life.

Brilliant, he keeps the plant running. Living, it is a part of him more than a job. He loves that plant. With a formal education, and desire, everyone knows that my father would be more than a maintenance lead man.

He outlives his beloved plant. It sits quiet now, a rusting fence and old buildings. I can't pass by without seeing my father, hearing his engines, remembering my Daddy.

He is my Daddy, the man I live to please until I become a wife and mother having a man of my own. Play and reality, fathers are for play, husbands are for reality. I make real biscuits for my husband, imaginary ones for my father.

Oedipus rex, isn't that the syndrome? Playing, Daddy is my man. When he comes home I run, jump and grab him, leg locking, my groin pressing to his. He spins me around. Wanting him to kiss me, he does, on my cheek, blowing with slobber and buzzing. Then he puts me down. I want him, my father, in ways I don't understand as a child. He loves me, his daughter--- as a daughter, his little girl. Daddy never makes me ashamed or rebuffs my little girl advances, yet he never touches me as I play at touching him. He is my father.

Moving me on to other things, unlocking my pelvis from his, he asks, "Now what have you and Samantha been up to today?"

Samantha, my doll, lying on the porch where she falls when I see Daddy coming, has been fixing dinner.

"Samantha made biscuits, Daddy."

Climbing down I show him her rolling pin made from a stick in the yard. Picking up Samantha in one hand, holding his with the other, we go inside to Momma.

Does Momma like it when I do my leg locks on Daddy? She gives me a look. I smile. Holding Daddy's hand I'm protected. Being negative about anything that smacks of sex, and often assuming I am doing or thinking something wrong, Momma isn't Daddy. Sex is something I don't know she and Daddy are doing! As a five year old, I am learning, playing. I don't want real sex any more than I want to have to make real biscuits every night.

The biscuit part comes the next year: Momma lets me make them when I six. It is great fun, at first, then I have it to do every night. Being OK, it is work. Part of taking on the role of being a real Momma someday, scaled down to kid size, it is part of my education. I and my sisters have chores to do as do the boys. Amber does everything Momma does without asking if Momma is busy. Mary is an apprentice cook. Momma looks over her shoulder at critical steps.

I make biscuits under Momma's watchful eye. She makes sure I wash my hands first. Forgetting that often, my biscuits would be brown before cooking if she fails to check my hands. She lets me mix the flour and water with a sprinkle of yeast and a little butter. Mixing it is work. It takes me four times as long to do it as Momma takes. She checks that too. Before I stop kneading it has to be real smooth dough. Cutting is fun using the little tin biscuit cutter. Then I dip them in plain flour to coat them and put them on a tin sheet to put in the oven. Momma watches me most closely there, hovering over me every inch of putting them in the hot oven.

The girls' chores usually have something to do with cooking, cleaning, taking care of the house or the younger children. My sister Amber's has to do with taking care of me. Forgetting sometimes I ask her what to do instead of Momma. All right most of the time, Momma listens, only countermanding Amber's orders occasionally. Teaching me cooking, cleaning and house work, Momma prepares me to be a wife, mother and homemaker.

Daddy prepares me to be a lady, a woman loving and pleasing a man.

Frowning when I get too flirty with Daddy, my Mother doesn't want me playing at that part of being a Momma.

Daddy says, "Momma, You want her to grow up and be a wife and mother don't you?"

Momma not answering gives him a look.

"Who do you think she is going to learn from, the mail man," Daddy gives her a look. "She's growing up. She doesn't know what she is doing. The only way she is going to get the wrong idea is if you make a big deal out of it. Let it slide."

Momma looks at him, not saying anything. He is her husband she has to listen to him. The law by divine decree, Daddy is king in our home. Gone, working most of the time, his regent, the queen, rules. Who is queen? Who rules our home? We respect and obey Daddy, unless Momma has that look.

When Momma has that look we say, "Yes Daddy" knowing we will do it Momma's way when he is not there. Since what bothers her is my leg locks on him, I am safe. I can't do it unless he is there.

Does Daddy understood this part of me better? Maybe is it something between daddies and daughters.

Loving their children most is a Momma thing. It is rare that any child loves or is loved more by anyone than their mother. Mother's love is the most special. What is it about Daddies? It is that most daddies tend to see children from a distance and are more objective in what they see. Understanding, and knowing that someday I will need to do what I am playing at doing, he tries not to make a big deal about it. Daddy does not want me riddled with phobias and fears about sex. When the real time comes, as it does with my husband, it will be an even bigger treat than making biscuits.

Still, envying Momma, his touch on her bottom, the time I catch them in the kitchen, her dress up, him touching places, secret places, I want that! I am a girl too. Ignoring it, meeting my every advance with a diversion Daddy lets me play then moves me to other things.

Fleeting, unsupported by hormones, and unopposed by morays, I forget about it. Some years later when those hormones normally missing or at very low levels in a child hear an alarm clock go off in my brain, then I am even more confused. At that point I know I am not to do leg locks on my Daddy, and he will not play with me as he did, no birthday spankings, no wrestling and no cuddling in his arms. I miss my Daddy's affection, love. I miss being a little girl with him. I feel rejection. We love each other as a father and daughter. We play by the rules, the changing rules.

## *Chapter 10*
# SEX, BAD SEX

    I snuggle under the covers that night after Daddy carries me to bed and tells stories. Not sleepy, I finish thinking about good things, then a special part of me calls. I want something, crave it. What it is I want? As a little girl my anus is more sensitive and interesting than my clitoris. I like touching my anus.
    My clitoris gets very sensitive to being touched when I reach puberty. Before puberty that little spot, my clitoris, is there and I touch it. Is it more sensitive than my fingertips? Undeveloped, like my breast, it is dormant, will be interesting and become a large secret part of my life-- when the time comes, not now.
    Tonight it is my anus that is calling. Finding it a little finger slips in and is exploring up there. It feels good! Closing my eyes I play with myself.
    Do I hear or see Momma coming?
    Momma thinks I am doing something dirty. Being smelly in the mornings and leaving little brown streaks on my sheets she notices. Do

I think about such things as forensic evidence when I am five? Slipping in on bare feet, she makes no sound, is spying on me.

Before I know what is happening, she yanks me out of bed!

"Sharon, that is naughty! You bad girl!"

My pajamas down I land bottom up over her knee before I realize what is going on. Pow! Pow! Pow! Her hand comes down on my bare bottom. I rouse from that wonderful sensation of touching where it feels good to sharp pain. I cry.

"Please Mommy! I'm sorry!"

*What am I sorry about? Do I know why I am sorry? My bottom hurts, that is why I am sorry!*

"Sharon, do not play with yourself! That is being a bad girl!"

I was happy. Now I sit on my bed crying.

Stuffing me under my covers, lights off, a silhouette in the doorway, Momma says, "Sharon, stop being a bad girl!"

The door closing in the blackness, I sob. Am I a bad girl? Why am I a bad girl?

I hear them at the door talking, two feminine voices, Momma and Amber, my sister.

"Momma did you tell her what she did?" Amber says.

"The preacher says I explain too much. She knows what she did."

"Momma, she is a little girl, are you sure she knows what she did wrong? Why don't you make sure Sharon understands, like you always did with Sammy and I? I don't think she knows what she is doing wrong."

"The preacher says I've been doing it wrong, taking too much time explaining."

"Momma look at the preacher's kids, look at yours. Are they better than us? Do they do better in school? Do they get in more trouble in school or do we?"

"You are good children, but the preacher says---"

"Momma, you are a good mother. Sharon is a good girl. Your children are good. Love Sharon and treat her the same way you treat Sammy, Nathan, George, Thomas, David, Mary and I. She is a good girl. She will be a good like the rest of us."

"But the preacher says---"

"Trust yourself, Momma, you have raised us to be good children. If the preacher is so good at raising children his own would be better. The preacher is raising two, both of them, hellions, in trouble most of the time." She is crying and doesn't know why. "Please don't change, Momma. Be as good to her as you have been to me."

There is silence at my door. Amber's eyes beg Momma.

Momma gives Amber more latitude than any of her children. Her first girl, the one that as soon as she toddles, staying up on two feet, follows our mother trying to help she is Momma's girl. Now Momma's conscious Amber's serious look drifts Momma through the years and back to the present.

Saying without saying Amber asks, *Momma, you raised me in a different way, made me, me. Am I a good girl? Don't you want Sharon to be a good girl like me?*

"OK, you can stay with her this time, but she has to learn."

"Thank you, Momma," Amber turns the knob.

A figure, thinner, taller than my mother appears at the door comes to me.

"It is ok, Honey," Amber says sitting down on my bed.

"Amber, Momma spanked me really hard." I whimper climbing into her arms.

"Sharon, you can't touch yourself, Momma doesn't like it. The preacher doesn't like it." Amber rubs my back.

Whimpering taking a deep breath I lock my arms around her neck as I have been doing since infancy. "I'm sorry!"

Amber tells me another bed time story, not a story, something real.

I am a baby. Momma changes my diaper. Amber is there. The preacher is there. I like having my diaper changed. Stinging urine goes to a warm wet washcloth and talcum powder. It feels good. Momma always pays attention to me when I wet myself or go poo poo. Being my baby way of getting her attention I am squealing and giggling. Bouncing up and down my hands discover something, something interesting! Finding that part of me even more wrong to touch than my anus, I get quiet. Not knowing it is there my eyes get big with the joy of discovery. I find a new pleasure. My hand plays.

Momma notices, "That is naughty, Sharon!" she moves my hand and puts another diaper on cinching it down tight.

The preacher frowns.

"Sarah, this is more serious than it looks or seems, sexual play. Sex is ordained of God for a man, her husband to touch her there and make babies, not for play. You need to nip it in the bud. Swat her hand when she touches herself inappropriately now, and spank her when she is old enough," he says.

Momma looks at him and thinks, *What is he saying?*

Amber, having cared for me all my life, says, "Preacher, she's a baby. She doesn't understand what she's doing is wrong!"

Looking at Amber, Momma doesn't speak, thinking, *She's right*.

Is this Momma's oldest daughter, the one she worries about because she will never stand up for herself, say no when she needs too and never speaks to the preacher unless he asks her a question? Now she is becoming a fire ball. She speaks up, stands her ground, knows what is right. Momma wishes she would stop challenging the preacher. He doesn't handle teens standing up to him well.

The preacher, saying nothing, looks at her, *a girl headed for trouble*, he can sense it.

Amber, born two months before the preacher assigns Momma to teach her Sunday school class, grows up under the preacher's tutelage, has a feeling. She thinks there is something not likeable, not on the surface, not right with the preacher. What is it that Amber sees? Disciplining a baby, is that right? Disciplined herself over the years at the preacher's behest she knows he favors the paddle and cries each time he recommends it for her without speaking back.

I am Momma's baby. Amber is 12 when I am born, entering puberty. With the emerging woman hormones that surge through her Amber adopts me, thinks of me as her baby. Her love for me fires a backbone in my sister that defends me more than herself.

"Ladies, you know my thoughts. The interest, the soul, of this baby is my only concern." He leaves.

Why isn't this like playing with my toes or learning about the rest of my body? Learning to eating everything on my plate, and then having to work at it to stay pretty for my husband by not eating when I grow up, my mind is forming, warpable. Momma is to warp my thinking about sex too, only this time instead of teaching me to over do it, it is under doing it!

Anything that feels good between my waist and knees is something to not do. Confusing, when does it clear up? Not until my husband touches me as the preacher says a husband should touch a woman on our wedding night do I comprehend. Until that night there are desires, conflicts and guilt waiting for his touch.

The night Momma spanks me, Amber holds me and rocks me to sleep. What is it she wants to tell me? Is she going to tell me about pleasure, sex and touching myself? Holding me she kisses my forehead. She wants to tell me, make me feel good about myself, but what does she know? She is having desires, conflicts and guilt too. She is as innocent as I am about men and sex. What can she tell me?

"Sharon, don't touch your self down there, Momma doesn't like it," Amber says.

The last thing I remember of that night is my sister holding me. I wake up. The birds are singing. It is morning.

Momma is my final authority in this area. Are there other times? Does the preacher get his way? Am I spanked for touching myself as a baby? I don't know. I don't remember.

This gap in memory creates an enigma. Accounting for many illogical unbreakable taboos permeating every society, it explains: it doesn't help remove irrational institutionalized human behavior.

I feel guilty about my sexual feelings, who I am. I crave intimate sharing and care in personal, unmentionable ways my whole life. Why is that wrong? Why do we hide our passions, our needs? Why do we do most things in life robotically never questioning or understanding? It's simple! Most of what we are taught to do we learn when we are babies, under three years old. Built as strong as a granite mountain in our beings and as obscured from memory as the stone a mile deep under that mountain, what we learn as a baby is with us forever. The only windows into this formative world come when an adult or older child shares their memories of our younger years or there is a flash back from a parent or person practicing what is done at that age.

Our family reads! Every child of my parents is an avid reader. Like a window on my soul, I watch my Mother. She takes my less than a year old baby cousin in her arms and reads to her. My Mother cooing to her, reading to her, she falls asleep her eyes moving as the pages turn. Momma gives her a book in her crib, a card board one, a new chewy she tries to eat it, then looks at it. Little hands and eyes seeing colors, words, wonders, she is playing, learning.

Daddy passing by, I ask, "Daddy, did Momma read to us like that when we were babies?"

She did, incessantly. Then Daddy starts reading to us. I try to remember the first time I sit on his lap to read the Sunday comics. Can I remember the start of it? Daddy tells me, I was a baby in diapers! I wet on him more than once. Is that why I read incessantly, why all my siblings read incessantly? Momma and Daddy lock it into us. We can't stop reading if we want too.

How about other things? My sister, Mary, when I am a teen, tells me Momma punishes me for playing with myself when I am little. As she remembers it, Momma has trouble making me stop. She prays about it and asks our pastor for help. He reinforces how important it is to suppress these wrong acts as early as possible. Babies need to be taught not to do that! Everyone knows that back then, especially the preacher! Remembering events in flashes as the specific memory centers in my brain become active there are glimpses.

I am about three and half, maybe four. Daddy cleaning me up after a toilet accident, it feels strangely good, right to have him washing me, scrubbing my bottom and putting new undies on me. Usually Momma's job, having Daddy do it is special. I am afraid to touch myself down there, but I like doing it. It feels good. It feels good to have Momma clean me up, but seems to be something that someone like Daddy should be doing. I am a girl, like Momma. I need a male's touch.

Putting his hands on Momma's bottom Daddy touches her. He is supposed to touch her. Doing it when they don't think any of us kids see them, it is something naughty, secret that they do, like my playing with myself, only together. It seems more right at that age to have Daddy clean me up.

Soon I am formally trained to never let a male see or touch me there. Not locked in my brain like things learned before memories can be recalled and talked through, my husband helps me unlearn that negative when it is appropriate.

It is hard for parents to teach children it is wrong to do what they are doing and God designs to be pleasurable for everyone to do. Did I say it is confusing? It is bad! There is good and bad. Kids understand that. Icky is bad. Food is good, or at least so our parents teach us. Is sex bad, or is the sexual part of us bad? It feels good. They teach us it is bad. This is confusing. I am a bad girl from the beginning. Does God make me that way?

When I am born, I know God. I know God's love. God loves me. With him before I am created I float in a space filled with pure love. That loving of God gets lost in concepts beyond my understanding as a child, concepts swatted into me. As I cry I wonder, *Why is Momma hurting me? Doesn't she love me? Doesn't God love me anymore?*

Is it God's fault? I do not want to be a bad girl. Wanting to be a good girl I never understand why God makes me have these little areas that feel good to touch, if I am not supposed to touch them! If it feels good, doesn't God mean us to enjoy it, if he is a good God? Maybe everyone like the preacher has it wrong! Maybe the thinking of society about this is bad— bad society, not bad me or other boys and girls being ourselves as God makes us!

Is it a big question? Maybe Momma was spanked and taught sex is bad when she is a baby and not remembering why is passing this down the line.

Then I discover the reason for this--- Boys! My older siblings don't have any mystery about what girls and boys are like. They see me having my diaper changed and are bathed together. I am four years younger than my youngest sister, and two, than my youngest brother.

Not seeing many babies, I am one of the younger kids in the neighborhood too. Being born in the worst part of the depression there are fewer children my age. Trying not to have babies then, Timmy is the only boy my age in our neighborhood. Helga is one of the only girls my age!

We play together. One day Helga is either sick or gone somewhere, and Timmy and I are alone in his back yard. When Timmy offers to show me his, if I show him mine, it sounds interesting. His is little, like a little Vienna sausage. I don't have one! Fascinating! I show him where mine should be but there is just a hole! This is interesting! Seeing us, his mommy doesn't think so! Getting to see his bottom too, and how red it can get, she spanks him hard! Taking me, Timmy still crying, to my house, I sense this is not a good time to go home.

Giving me an even harder spanking Momma is angry. I cry like crazy.

Momma says, "Never! Never do that. You don't show yourself to boys! Do you understand?"

Do I understand? I don't understand why what we did is wrong. I am four years old. I don't know girls can get pregnant and have to be careful not to let boys put babies in there. I don't know why I have a hole and Timmy has a Vienna sausage in his pants. I don't know, but I am learning. Those feelings kids have, those good feeling sensitive areas under our panties, mean old God put there to get us in trouble. That is what Momma is teaching me! I am wrong to touch them, or for anyone else to see them. I am a bad girl because I love touching myself. I am a bad girl because I am interested in my body. I am a bad girl because I am interested in Timmy and why he is different. Learning, exploring, trying to know, I learn that God is a mean God, who makes me be something bad.

A few years earlier, as a baby, I know God and everybody loves me. Then I forget thanks to discipline via the preacher's teachings about God. I learn shame. I learn to be ashamed of my body and my feelings about it.  Momma teaches me what a good girl is. That is her job. Learning this is a painful lesson, one that makes me civilized.

Is being civilized good? Why, if we feel good about these things, are we forced into being neurotic sexual perverts viewing pleasant touching as bad and painful swats and hurting as good. Why not let us grow up like natives running about the jungles without clothes or shame smiling and being happy? Because we are civilized we need shame to make us feel bad about ourselves. With shame we produce and do what we are supposed to do, even if it hurts and is bad for us. Is this logical? As a foundation of society, is it perverted?

Timmy, Helga and I are in church. We sing "Jesus loves me." The preacher is watching, smiling. Crouching in front of us, our Sunday school teacher guiding us, the congregation watches us sing. With much coaxing and shy little kid wiggles we struggle to get out, "Jesus loves me this I know, for the Bible tells me so."

We breathe and try to remember what comes next.

Our Sunday school teacher whispers, "We are weak but he is strong!"

Awkwardly after her we repeat, "Jesus loves the little children, all the children of the world!"

Keeping going, our parents are smiling. The preacher is nodding approval. Our Sunday school teacher pats me on the back and herds me off to class.

I get the idea. Loving me when I dressed up in my Sunday dress, singing and being a good girl, Jesus and Momma are telling me how to be a good girl. A good girl is like a doll. We are always cute, always filled with smiles and always nice. We do not think of touching ourselves in "bad" places. We do not think. We sing repeating what someone else sings. We pray repeating what someone else prays. We do nothing original. Our minds and our sex organs are meant to remain virgin until we are married. Then we can use our sexual organs. When do we get to think? The preacher says not to think about it. When we girls get married, our husbands will do the thinking for us. He says what ever we do, not to think about, or touch things down there. Think of nice things, singing church songs, making little projects for Momma, or sitting on Daddy's lap and him reading us stories.

Things about down there aren't nice. Things down there feel good. It feels good to go poo poo or let my water tinkle in the toilet. These things are not nice, are done only when absolutely necessary and in private.

A good girl on Sundays, my Sunday school teacher always pays attention to me. I am eager to please her. It feels good to sing, and when I do that thing that feels good, singing in church, Momma, Daddy and the other adults say nice things about me. Being a kid is about learning to please adults, not what displeases them and learning to ignore pleasing ourselves.

I have a special place in my family. I am the baby. Having all those brothers and sisters, all of them good kids, can I get away with anything, and if I do something good, is it new and noticed? Whatever I do it has been done many times before and is a rerun. Even good reruns are boring, Daddy snores and Momma, one eye open, smiles before nodding off. Bad reruns get a response, or at least some motion. Momma or Daddy gets up to turn it off.

To Amber there are no reruns. Amber's first baby, a surrogate one, everything I do is new to her. She sees the good I do, feels the pain I feel and loves me as I am, but a sister, she is not my mother. She is there some of the time, at school with friends and in a world of her own most of my waking hours. It is Momma that counts. To her I am rerun number seven.

Finding out that there are two ways to Momma's attention, one, is being the pretty little girl singing in church, perfect, innocent, and pure. Momma smiles. Second, is do something bad, Momma spanks as quickly as she smiles, and puts many times more energy in the spanking as she does the smile.

One of these paradigms works in any situation. A few months ago my brother graduates from high school. Everyone notices my brother! Momma gets his gown ready ironing it with care. Running around like crazy, Momma is getting everything for him and not paying any attention to me. I start school in the fall, then she will pay attention to me for doing good things in school, but now. I am getting NO attention!

Being in his graduation gown my brother looks really--- good? Well, maybe not good, he looks strange. What sort of clothes are graduation gowns? Can you work in them? They get dirty. They are too black to be comfortable in the sun. The hat falls off really easily. Can you imagine trying to pick cotton in one of those? But he is in it, clean, a gold tassel, smiling and the center of everyone's attention. In my Sunday dress I am ready. I wait.

Deciding to play one more time in the sandbox in our back yard, while waiting, seems like a good idea. Who would think a nice clean sand box would have mud in it? It does. Brushing it, the more I brush the more it spreads. Will Momma like this? Will she notice me? She notices.

"Sharon, what have you done to yourself? You were pretty. Now you are a mud ball."

Taking me in the bathroom, striping off my dress and rubbing fiercely with a washcloth, she is not making me happy.

"That hurts Momma!" I beg, begging unheeded.

A new dress and we are off. Momma is peeved. The graduation goes well. Well— it goes as graduations go, lots of talking, the kids my brother's age marching in together and having to sit a long time. Then my brother makes a speech. I can listen to him talk at home, why do I have to listen to him here?

I ask Momma, "Why is Sammy talking?"

Momma smiles a proud smile. "He is valedictorian, now shush and listen to him!"

Sitting a long time is not always easy for a little girl! I squirm.

I tug at Momma's sleeve. "Is it over yet?"

After a few minutes of this, Momma is more peeved! FINALLY, the people in the funny black robes march across the stage one at a time. I think it is over! It is not! Talking and hugging, more talking and hugging and even less paying attention to me, am I a happy girl? I keep tugging at Momma's sleeve. I want to go home. I want Daddy to tell me a story. Looking at him, he is all smiles at my brother, he doesn't notice that I am alive!

My brother is going to go to college! He is the first person in our family to go to college. Everyone is proud of him. Right then do I care if he goes to hell? I want to go home. Maybe if I talk a lot more and begin to complain, Momma will listen to me!

Thinking for a minute is it working Momma has my hand taking me toward the door? Wrong door! Why doesn't she go out the front door of the school? Finding an open room, she drags me in. In one motion, she walks to the first chair, spins around, hoists me up, sits down, and lands me bottom up on her knee.

My panties are down before I can say, "No Momma!"

Her familiar hand on my bottom is popping out its message. "Sharon, be good!"

What she is really saying is that if I am naughty enough, no matter what is happening, I can get her attention! I cry! As I cry, I know she is paying attention to me. Being a bad girl is bad, not as bad as being a girl unnoticed! Working, method two becomes more and more important to me.

Wanting to be a good girl, I want Momma and Daddy to pay attention to me for being a good girl. That is always my conscious focus, but underneath runs another current. Bad girls get attention when good girls are ignored. By the time I start school I am a bad girl. That gets attention. It stays that way a long time. Inside I am a good girl, but outside, I am a bad girl.

Being hard enough at home to get attention with seven brothers and sisters, I go to school! More than thirty little kids crowd around one teacher! Trying being a good girl, I smile. I am cute. I do sweet little girl things. Of course, seventeen other little girls are doing the same things! One of them, Janet, does everything right and first. Being great at it, she and her best friend Annabelle are little darlings.

Not having a chance against them I am lost, and even these girls can't get the attention the boys are getting, aggressive little creatures that they are, even in first grade! Thirteen boys, two fighting, one picking his nose, another one going tinkle in the trash can--- they get attention!

Boys are always a problem, girls can be too. Doing something that makes me mad, even madder than her getting attention, Annabelle gets the bunny as I reach for him. She pets him. I want to pet him! Kicking her in the shin, you would think I had killed her the way she screams. Noticing me, my teacher has me over her knee.

I get to sit in a special chair at the front of the class sniffling with this funny pointed hat on my head. Everyone notices me! This is something! I am a bad girl. My teacher pays attention to me! Becoming one of the best fighters in first grade I hit, punch, gouge and kick better than most of the boys! I never try going tinkle in the trash but I can pick my nose well enough that I can get my finger up to the second knuckle.

My teacher is impressed when I go up to her desk and say, "Deacher. I can'd get my finger oud! Ids sduck!"

Squirming with my bottom burning on that special chair, I find my place at school!

At home I sing, "A, B, C, D, E… X,Y and Z, aren't you very proud of me! What note? Why would the teacher send you a note, Momma?"

After my bottom cools down and I quit sniffling, Momma feeds me.

At home bottom up over Momma's knee, at school bottom up over the teacher's knee at least they feed me. At church, bottom up over Momma's knee, Pastor John watches. At least at home and at school I get food. Whipped puppies and little girls always come back when fed.

Church doesn't feed me, why do I go back? Momma's hand holding mine, where Momma goes, I go, food or not.

Church is supposed to feed my soul. If Momma is supposed to feed my body and the church is supposed to feed my soul why are there Brussels' sprouts on the table at church again? How many of those things can the preacher grow in one garden? Is this his version of feeding me?

There should be a union with rules. At Daddy's plant he is a mechanic, he does mechanics. Electricians do electricity and other trades do what they are trained to do. Ok, teachers and mommas can both teach and give food or treats, unless my teacher learns how to make candied Brussels' sprouts.

Should preachers be allowed to mess with food? Ok, if the preacher retrains and learns how to grow something besides Brussels' sprouts we will keep an open shop and take tomatoes home from church. But if I see one more table piled high with those evil green things I am going to ask Daddy's steward for a picket sign and march in front of the church.

I think it. Do I do it? Before I get the sign made and out the door Momma will spank me with the sign handle. The only striking will be on my bottom, so much for having a little girl's union. I pray for a Brussels' sprouts eating bugs to move to the preacher's garden.

What a girl eats is important. If I am what I eat will I to grow up to be a bitter green thing?

## Chapter 11
# LOVING AMBER NOT BRUSSEL'S SPROUTS

*Summer 1936*

Am I what I eat or am I what I am fed? An innocent baby girl, born perfectly normal in 1931, perverted by the time I am five years old, Momma did it, didn't she, or did my teacher do it, or the preacher?

"Momma, I want to go play!" I say, listening to other children already in their yards.

"What is that on your plate?" Momma says.

"I ate my hopping john (peas mixed with rice) with fresh tomatoes on top, all of it. It was yummy, Momma." Not only that, I eat my salad and everything else… except!

Pointing out the except Momma lifts an eyebrow, "What are those, Sharon?"

"Brussels sprouts!" My nose wrinkles.

"Eat those then you can go play." Momma dries another dish putting it in the cupboard.

"But, Momma, Brussels sprouts are yucky! They taste awful. Why do I have to eat them?"

"The preacher grew those for us and says they are good for you. Eat them--- now!" Momma puts another dried plate back in the cupboard.

"Yes, Momma."

Nature or nurture, are you what you eat, or are you what your Momma feeds you? Why does she listen to that preacher? He thinks it. He preaches it. She does it. Forcing me to eat Brussels sprouts it is Momma's fault. I am what Momma feeds me!

A little girl, made by Momma, Daddy and God, I am growing, sometimes inside in Momma's kitchen with Brussels sprouts in a pot boiling. Sometimes it is in Daddy's arms, secure, listening to his heart beat between words as I snuggle close consuming a story. Once a week it is in God's house, behind closed doors.

We sing, "Amazing grace, how sweet the sound, that saved a wretch like me!" A little off key when the whole congregation sings. The choir sings loud to drown out Daddy and other off key singers.

Eventually no matter how pretty the singing and nice the Sunday school the preacher preaches. When he preaches, he can't help himself, the sound of his voice echoing off the rafters is the best music to his ears--- not mine!

"Sin, all are sinners, fall short of the glory of God. But, sin, less than perfection, less than the requirement of God--- the price! What price? Stealing, lying, adultery--- fornication!" With this reverberating condemnation he comes from behind the pulpit and approaches us. Not the congregation, but me, me in particular, why is he talking right at me? I schooch over by Momma as close as I can trying to get under her arm, but she pushes me upright right into the blast zone of what I know will come next.

"Sin!" he shouts. "Sin, the ticket to HELL! Adultry, the ticket to HELL!" Walking down to the first pew he stops. Looking over it to us on the second pew, he glares.

I feel Amber slide closer to me. Is it her he is yelling at? Or me?

"Fornication, lust, sexual evil, an abomination to God, an abomination to God, A TICKET TO HELL!" His shouting sprinkles Amber and I with spittle.

What did I do to make him yell at me? Afraid a chill creeps over me. Summer heat, over a hundred people packed in the sanctuary, two roof fans cool us. I feel my hands and feet go cold. In other parts of the church people are fanning themselves. I shiver, cold, shaking. Ice of fear flowing through my veins, the preacher leans closer to me, a big man with penetrating blue eyes, his face glows red. My face pales, I tremble.

Amber slinks down in her seat. The last soreness, blisters tingle as her bottom slides over the hardwood pew. Three days ago, Wednesday night at Bible study, I color a picture of baby Jesus and his mother, Mary. Momma cogitates a verse from St. Mathew. The rest of my brothers and sisters in various classes, it is a time of pious study for us.

Where is Amber? Where is Albert? Where is the preacher?

A nose for sin, an instinct for the evil that lurks in men's hearts and teen-age pelvises the preacher smells evil. Following his nose he heads for the basement. A door ajar. He pushes it open. A swath of light illuminates the darkness. In an unused classroom, her dress is up. Albert's hand is high on her thigh. Their mouths are glued together like Louisiana love bugs. The man of God's faith in sinful nature of adolescents is consummated, or about to be consummated.

"WHAT is going on here!"

In the shadow's edge a skirt tumbles down. A long leanness moves deeper in the darkness. The preacher moves toward him grabbing a hand full of air as the boy eludes him dodging toward the door. The preacher, broader and stronger than the youth, is no match for "Speed" in maneuvering. The big man falls twisting his ankle. The young Satan moving on feet as fast as cloven hooves escapes the man of God.

The best wide receiver in our school's history he is fast, earns his nickname, "Speed." He goes to college on a scholarship and does as well there in football. His speed on the field is legendary. His slowness in opening a book is legendary. He is home to stay at the end of his freshman year with a .7 grade point average and a blood alcohol level higher than that many school nights. The peacher sits on the floor holding his ankle.

"Are you all right, preacher?" Amber moves to him.

"Son of perdition! Filthy Gypsy! Worse than a Jew! Those people don't deserve to suck air. All they do is steal, use up space and seduce Christian girls. That boy is the filth of the earth, unworthy to live. What were you doing kissing that filthy Gypsy. You have grown up in my church. I thought you knew better! I should have said something about it the first time that piece of trash came though the church door." The preacher continues a tirade of accusations about Albert that would make a foul mouth sailor proud, yet never uses a curse word.

Casting a dark and accusing eye on the young angel from his own flock who almost fornicates with a Gypsy, one lover escapes, the other is his.

Amber helps him up.

"What are you doing with a boy like that?" He speaks to Amber. "Don't ever bring trash like that to our church again!"

Amber winces, is afraid. *Why is the preacher talking about Albert like that?* Pastor John never said anything like that before. Albert has been coming to church with her for two weeks. He's not a Gypsy. His father is a Gypsy. His mother was a local girl who inherited a farm. They don't steal! His father works hard. Albert works hard. Albert's hands are like leather from farm work. Albert never hurts anyone, steals anything or is anything but nice to the preacher. *Why does he say these things?*

Taking a deep breath, the anger fades, the man of God slips back into his preacher suit. "Amber, what were you doing?" There is a note of concern in his voice. His look of compassion is reattached.

The preacher has several faces. This one, the concerned one, is reserved for times like this. A young girl, a compromising situation, a rogue, the need for counseling, correction, he cares. On Sundays in another suit the preacher speaks loud, thunder in his voice. He thumps the Bible. His yelling, compels tears of repentance in wayward eyes. Does it always reach the heart, does it always work? Amber, inclined to cry, does not shed a tear as he speaks down to her in condescending tones. She hears him the first time. She loves Albert. She hears what the preacher says about him. She loves Albert.

Her first kiss, ecstasy filling her heart, if there are tears, they will be of joy not guilt. Did they do anything wrong? Amber's thoughts are not the preacher's.

She smiles and thinks, *Albert kissed me!*

The preacher thoughts do not match his compassionate look. *I have had enough of this girl's attitude!* Breathing deep he does not speak, he continues thinking, *I let niggers in my church, treat them like people, and she acts like this!* The demon flashes in his eyes. She sees it. He sees terror in the girl's expression. *Is she afraid of me? Does she see? Does this timid little nigger see what I'm thinking? Maybe she does, ever since her sister is born she has been reading my thoughts. It is the time to put a stop to this. I need her mother. Her mother is useful.*

Momma, a believer, trusts him, listens to him. When he speaks, she acts. Calling Momma out of her women's group, the preacher speaks to our mother.

"Sarah, does Amber know what fornication is? I'm sure she would had I been ten minutes later. I believe I saved her, a virgin angel in danger of Satan's seduction."

Momma listens, looks at Amber. "Thank you for telling me, Preacher. I will take care of it."

Momma speaks softly, lightening in her hand, her paddle does the thumping. Unlike the preacher's sometimes effective sermons, Momma's paddle brings tears of repentance to the eyes of all who bow across our kitchen table receiving its message.

Her paddle stays quiet and cool in the kitchen cabinet for months. The preacher shouts every Sunday. His words toothless to those disbelieving nor under the authority of those he influences, he lacks the power of an inquisitor's rack and lash, with one exception. The homes of believers, there may be no rack, there is the lash. Every child in his congregation knows the paddle, knows tears, knows the lash. There is no surer way of enticing Momma's paddle from the shadows than a few directly placed words from the preacher. This will bring the power of God down on Amber and bring her back into the fold.

Words, not heard over the pounding of love in Amber's heart, will sound again, become flesh, wood on flesh, the sound, the message, the pain heard well by my sister, the errant angel. What the preacher doesn't consider or understand is Amber's love. She wasn't trying to ferret him out when he wanted me punished as a baby. She was protecting me, her loved sister. She wasn't in the throws of lust in the church basement. She was in the arms of love. There's a difference.

In ecstasy, Amber knows what is coming, knows her love, her joy in that longed for moment in Albert's arms is greater than a paddling can extinguish. Looking at her daughter Momma recognizes there must be an adjustment in thinking, repentance, that the preacher is right and that Amber is in love. Two other girls from the church are pregnant, good girls like Amber, seduced in moments of passion. Amber will not be the third, not if our mother has any say in it. The preacher's warning words spoken thunder echo in Momma's ears. Becoming lightening striking her daughter a bit lower than her ears there will be regret, better behavior.

Is that all Momma sees, a girl headed for trouble? She sees the excitement of a girl, a first kissed girl. Momma, looking at her oldest daughter, the first one of her daughters romantically kissed. She sees the ecstasy of love, wants to smile, and remembers her own first kiss. A moment of joy, this should be a happy time. Why did she have to do it at church letting the preacher catch her and Albert?

"Amber, what were you thinking? Were you not thinking?" Momma says entering her court of justice, her kitchen. Around the table we eat three times a day, talk, play, can our winter food during long summers, and Momma holds court.

"I don't know, Momma. It just happened--- he kissed me!"

Amber, dreaming, happy despite knowing from a lifetime of sitting in the public gallery of Momma's court and a few times in the defendant's chair, is in love, the pleasure of the first male gentle touch on her lips.

She smiles. She knows Momma is district attorney, judge, jury and executioner. Does smiling affect executioners? King Henry VIII, ordered a special sword's man from Calais to behead Ann Bolen, the woman he loved with passion for years then tired of loving. Her smile won the king. Did the sword hurt less than the axe?

My sister smiles in defense, can woos a judge with a winning smile. It always influences the chief judge on the court of appeals. Daddy can overturn a conviction. Daddy staying out of courts and kitchens, that's rare. Worse yet Daddy isn't home. At work he is on a break grabbing a snack, sitting with other men talking, his bottom comfortably supported by a long 2 by 12 wooden bench.

Never having the time to sit in the defendant's chair, or file an appeal to Daddy, Amber does not sit, does not move. Her bottom supported by a much less-substantial piece of wood her trial will be over and her punishment complete before his break is done. Her seat will not sit comfortably anywhere for days.

Opening her interrogation Momma asks, "Leaving your class, ending up in the basement, Albert's hand on your thigh, just happened?"

Amber doesn't answer. How can she answer? Albert plans it, asks her to slip out to meet him. She follows, never resisting, never saying no.

"--- kissing, petting, improper touching. Amber, a girl doesn't do that sort of thing until they're married!"

"Albert," Amber says.

Watching Momma get out her paddle Amber she wants to plead innocent, is innocent, wants to avoid the paddling and knows nothing short of Momma dropping dead will prevent it. Without being asked she bends over the kitchen table lifting her dress. Tan young legs, a thin waist, clean white cotton panties hold broadening feminine buttocks, the kind she shares with Momma and the women of our family. She is ready.

Ready to scamper upstairs to my room, I turn as do my other brothers and sister. A paddling contagious to young buttocks always has spreading potential. We never stay unless told to stay, and then with trepidation.

"All of you--- stay!" Momma says.

Huddled near the door we line up, watching.

"Aren't the boys going to go?" Amber turns her head.

Knowing what Momma always wants, she doesn't want her brothers there. Amber stands up reaching for her panties. Embarrassed by the presence of the boys; she doesn't want them to see her naked. Momma paddles bare bottomed. Ready to pull her panties down her face reddens.

"No, Amber, leave them on!" Momma stops her. "The point of your paddling is to keep your panties on, not off." Then to all of us our mother says, "I am not mad at Amber, she is a good girl I know that. I know she wouldn't take her panties off and go all the way with a boy deliberately, but what if it just happened." Momma stares at Amber, "It does just happen!"

Seeing a chance, a reason to avoid the paddling Amber cuts in, "Momma, I wouldn't go all the way. I wouldn't. It wouldn't 'just happen.'"

"You are wrong, honey. It does just happen. God designed boys to always be ready. Any time a girl drops her panties they can be ready. Girls are different. Once you have your period, you have that once a month, then once a month, right in the middle, you have another sort of period. It doesn't hurt or make you uncomfortable like your menses, it makes you hungry, hungry for a man. Any girl, good or bad, when a boy kisses her, holds her, touches her just right will drop her panties during that part of the month. What did you feel like when Albert was touching your leg and kissing you?"

"I wouldn't have, Momma. I wouldn't have!"

"Honey, you are a woman now, a young inexperienced woman. A man that knows how and when to seduce you, can seduce you. It is the way God made you and every other woman. Maybe you do have the willpower to say 'NO' when your hormones are saying yes, but it isn't natural. Do you know why?"

Amber shakes her head staring back. She wants to know.

Momma teaches her.

"What do you think would have happened to you had you gone all the way with Albert tonight?"

"I wouldn't be a virgin anymore!" Amber looks down. She wants to keep protesting, but she knows her mother is right. Momma isn't talking about sin, evil and it being wrong like the preacher, she is talking facts.

"More than that, Amber, you probably would become a mother. That is what sex really about, making babies. You are two weeks past your period. You are putting out odors that attract boys, makes them want to love you, lets them know you want to love them. You are at that one time of the month that you can get pregnant. Didn't you feel that? Didn't you want to let him take you and do what ever he wanted with you? Didn't you want to pull your panties down for him?"

Amber blushes. Feeling the joy, the ecstasy, the love for Albert that she feels since 8th grade, that is exactly what she wants. She wants him. Amber looks down, doesn't answer. How can her mother understand feelings like this?

Momma knows. Momma remembers. She knows exactly how it feels to be young, to be in love, to kissing him for the first time. She puts the paddle down, and hugs her daughter.

How can Amber admit these feelings to her mother?

Better said through clean, pure, white panties untouched by a man, her flesh will answer the question. She bends over the table.

"No stay up a minute, honey. We need to talk. You need to understand. You are human, a woman. I want you to be a virgin when you marry. Don't you?

"Yes Momma, I want to be a virgin when I marry, with a pretty white dress, your dress."

A realization of how serious that moment of joy might have become trickles into Amber's mind. She doesn't want to get pregnant--- not until she is married. The choice is simple in the 1930s with no birth control, marry as a virgin, or, most likely, marry pregnant.

"Momma, I wouldn't have--- would I?"

"Amber?" Momma hugs her.

"I'm sorry, Momma!"

"It is OK, honey. Do you think it was wrong to kiss Albert?"

"Unhuh!"

"Really? I don't. It wasn't the kissing him that was wrong. It was the kissing him the basement, alone, where no one could protect you from him or your own feelings, Amber. Be glad that he kissed you. Beware where he kisses you."

"But Momma, the preacher said it was wrong to kiss him. He said---" Amber flashes back on the awful things he says about Albert and stops, not wanting Momma to know, and concentrates on her own actions.

"You are a girl. Didn't you feel like a girl when he kissed you?" Momma says.

"Yes, Momma."

"Do you want him to kiss you again?"

Amber nods.

"Do you want to marry him?"

"I have wanted to marry him always--- always!"

"Then don't be sorry you kissed him. Do it here in the living room when no one is with you, and I am close by in the kitchen. Do it quickly and discretely in the back of the movie theater, under the mistletoe at

Christmas, but don't do it in the places that seem most natural--- alone with him in dark private places--- until you are married. After you marry him, then every night in your bed kiss him and do what your body and he tells you to do. It is not wrong to kiss him, or make love to him, honey, just when and where you do it. You have to save the best until after you are married!"

Amber nods her head understanding then looks at the paddle. "I'll be a good girl. Do you have to paddle me? Please don't paddle me. Please!"

"Amber, You are a good girl, there is no question of that, there never was. You are a good girl that made a bad choice. You slipped out of class and you were doing things you should not have been doing, a mistake, one I know you won't do again. To make sure of that it is important that you have a good cry and a sore bottom for a few days to help you set it in your heart."

Does Momma need to paddle her till emotional lakes of regret unfilled by dry mental rain overflow with storms of physical pain? Does she need to paddle her till rivers of regret flow from those lakes and cascade from swollen eyes? Does she need to paddle her till a flood of emotion, knowledge and belief meet in her heart changing her? Will these tears make the commitment to being pure, a virgin on her wedding night, part of her soul as it can never be from a dry eyed, 'I'll be a good girl?'

Amber needs the emotional release of the tears, pain and the reminder of blisters to imprint a lesson. Before Amber cries in pain a tear drips down Momma's cheek. She remembers the first time Daddy kisses her, the passion and what could have happened if he had not been the man he is. As a giver of pain to one loved hurts, Momma hurts. Empathy and memories of youth, first kisses, the joy of the years in bed every night with my father, her husband, flowing through her heart Momma knows Amber must remain pure, a virgin, obey the against nature rules of society or risk never knowing years of joy, of marriage.

Amber is sorry to receive the paddle as all are sorry to have pain. Knowing, understanding, the emotional release needed to open the soul does not lesson the primal desire to retain cool buttocks beneath dresses or pants. Lessons brought to the depth of tearful emotion though a burning bottom rarely are sought by those that receive them. Amber not having the years and depth of Momma's having lived can not know the joy and fulfillment Momma seeks to protect by giving her this paddling. Bending over my sister doesn't want it.

Being a good girl, it has been years since her last round with the paddle. Momma not telling her to take down her panties, has not told her why she paddles bare bottomed. Momma has to help her feel what she needs to feel but Momma doesn't want to do it to the point of causing harm. With them down Momma knows when her bottom is well paddled, but not over paddled. With them on Momma may not give her the blisters she needs or hurt her by paddling too hard.

Amber expecting that "panties down!" order knows she wants her panties down for Albert? It is her first kiss, her first time held by a boy. It made her feel an arousal, a longing, that she feels alone at night thinking of him. In his experienced arms she wants her panties off. Is the preacher right, was she sinning, about to sin? Amber wants to repent.

Amber is to be paddled for holding and kissing the boy she loves, kissing him inappropriately. She would die for him. She will live for him, she will take her panties off for him--- after they marry. Will they marry? She knows he is going to ask. She is paddled and cries for him. No thought of the wrongness of their kisses or his touch is in her heart, only the thought that he will do it after they marry. Momma touches her bottom with the paddle, sets her stance and adjusts her grip on the wooden handle.

"Amber, do you understand that this is not for kissing Albert. It is for where you were, when you did it?"

"I'm sorry, Momma!" She thinks, *Why didn't I kiss him in the living room, sitting on the couch as Momma was in the kitchen pouring us some iced tea, not in the church basement?*

Amber feels the paddle touch her bottom, moving slightly as Momma sights it. That touch felt before on her bare buttocks, now though panties, the blood drains from her fingers and feet in anticipation. Her mind she feels something deeper. That touch, another reaffirmation of her Mother's love, tells her Momma loves her enough to share her joys, smiles and painful correction when needed.

Momma stops feeling similar thoughts. Momma, sorry to paddle her, is honored to do it. Tears welling in Momma's eyes, paddling, a duty, a painful duty, Momma empathizes, feels the pain with her heart, a place more tender than those feeling it on their buttocks usually appreciate.

Momma thinks, *Why did she have to kiss him in church and have Preacher John catch them?* The paddle rising over her shoulder she pivots.

The paddle popping with vigor, Momma's face turns red as the preacher's face in the climatic crescendo of a Sunday sermon. My sister's face white with apprehension darkens. Eyes flow silver tears. On Amber's upper legs and exposed buttock a red stripe with small white welts quivers. Fingers turn white as she grips the table lip. Rising off the table, her lower back tightens, arches.

Neither the preacher's or Momma's words enough to open regret for kisses craved, unwisely given, Momma's paddle does. The paddle sets the cadence pops out the rhythm as my sister chimes in singing a soprano lament. Serenading in strident, high-pitched, increasingly unintelligible words following each pop, Amber expresses regret as a girl untouched by the emotion of guilt best does when pain enhances conviction.

We, the congregation, silent, in awe, are in a tabernacle of pain. Thunderous popping, the wailing of the sinner, the repentance, the found respect for laws disrespected, these services in Momma's kitchen change lives. Momma preaches with her paddle. Amber sings. We fear the Lord, repent and believe. In less than a minute thunder stops, rain continues sprinkling the kitchen table. The preaching paddle having instilled repentance into Ambers bottom lays silent on the table having said more in one minute than the preacher can in an hour.

*Don't go where I have gone*! Amber sings the benediction in a melody understood in every language.

Amber sobbing, seeing Momma's point, understanding, crys and lets it out. The woman in her craving Albert's touches has no such feelings, blocks them from being part of her soul. Truly regretting once the pain overwhelms the pleasure she changes. Needing the paddle, the freedom of tears, the correction of thinking, Amber's sobs continue to echo off hallowed walls, pots and pans and bounce off the ice box door. The change last as long as she lives.

"Momma, I'm sorry. I am a good girl. I will be a virgin on my wedding day! I will, Momma!"

"I know you will!" Momma hugs her.

Her dress falling back below her knees Amber squeezes Momma, not letting our mother go, crying. Amber, tears dripping, faces us.

"Amber you are a good girl. Will be a virgin on your wedding night. You won't let yourself be placed in another situation that will endanger that, will you?"

Amber shakes her head.

"It was a hard paddling, one usually given for things far more serious in the eyes of a God that loves us than a misgiven kiss, but an important one, for Amber, for you all. Girls, if you put yourself in the situation Amber did, I will paddle you as hard. Boys, even though most people say that it is the girl's fault for letting a boy do what boys do, and let the boy go, I don't! If you put a girl in this position, I will paddle you as hard as I paddled Amber. Do you understand?" Momma looks each one of us in the eye.

My older brothers nod knowingly.

I nod not understanding what this is about. Maybe when I am six years old and in school I will understand better. It is closer to ten years later that the idea takes hold for me.

Albert from another world, alone with his father at their farm. His father's only friend his father knows him as he does every rock and tree on their farm.

"Albert, what wrong?" He says in his broken English.

"Amber. I kissed her."

The father smiles, pats him on the shoulder. "Good!"

Albert breathes deep looking at the heavy belt he has felt before, relaxes.

Is this the father that when he gets off the train from college says, "We have girl working. She good girl. You not touch. Understand. You touch. I beat you?"

"I--- we were in the basement of the church. The preacher caught us."

"Not good. What you say?"

"He tried to catch me. I ran."

"You OK. He no hurt you?"

"No Dad. He never touched me"

"Amber OK. He no hurt Amber?"

"Why would he hurt Amber?"

"I worry, Amber OK. You worry?"

"Dad why would he hurt Amber?"

"I no like preacher. Preacher not good man. Preacher no hurt you. Preacher loose something on farm long time back. He hurt you maybe I take back him. You tell. He hurt Amber. I take back him. Give back way he want give me. He understand. Preacher smart man. He understand good. You no go church there more, OK."

Albert sleeps light, restless, what about Amber. What about the preacher. What is between the preacher and his father? Is Amber OK?

Their kiss, he feels her lips on his. He kisses other girls, does a lot more than kiss with other girls. Being a football hero has its perks. Every big touchdown, every winning play, carried off the field by players, it feels good. Then there is the night. It is a rare night that some girl doesn't give him a little special cheer leading. Amber tries to kiss him like she knows what she is doing, but she doesn't. She doesn't help him. She is a statue frozen her hands going cold, trembling in his arms holding him. He feels it a moisture on his cheek. She cries.

"Are you all right?" He stops kissing her.

"I have wanted you to do that so long!" She says and puts her lips to his.

She doesn't notice what he was doing with his hands, lets him do it.

She says, "I've never kissed anyone before. I only want to kiss you."

The preacher breaks in. Does he get to say anything to her? What can he say? Kissing her isn't like kissing other girls. She is important. He likes being with her. He likes the way she smells, the way she works with he and his dad. He talks to her. She is more than a girl wanting to make love to the hero. She cares about him, the farm boy, who doesn't have a mother, doesn't know about women. He knows about making love, but never has a relationship with a girl like Amber. There are a few regulars in high school. Girls wanting to be on the arm of the star, does Sally Mae, Ruby or Mary Lou like him. If they talk at all it isn't a talking that interest him, and his talking doesn't interest them.

Amber talks to him. She listens to him. Within a few weeks she knows what he wants to talk about and opens ever conversation on a subject that interests him.

"How did you learn to cook, Amber? I've never had such good food," Albert says.

"You no like my cooking," his father scowls.

"I watch you, Albert. I know what you like. I fix what you like the way you like it," Amber says.

The old man smiles. Taking another bite Albert doesn't know what to say.

Wanting to stop work, go back to the house to talk to her and help her work Albert does women's work as soon as he leaves the fields. This surprises and pleases her. He and his father have done the canning before Amber. Shelling peas or stringing beans as fast as most women he likes doing it with Amber. They talk and can together. It is fun to do it in English. Albert speaks Romanian as well as English. Everything in the house is done in Romanian before Amber. She has to teach him some common English words for things, and she tries Romanian.

The smell of her one day is delectable. Shelling peas he moves his chair closer to hers and touches her hand several times as they get peas from the center bowl. His father comes in and in clear precise unbroken Romanian repeats the warning he gave when Albert gets off the train. Albert moves his chair back to its original position.

*What are they talking about?* Amber thinks.

He isn't sure he has ever kissed a virgin before. Is a virgin just a girl, another girl? Amber is more to him. He has known her all her life, but then she was a little girl, not a woman-girl, and not close enough to his age that they could have any interaction. Missing little he has eyes as sharp like his dad's. He noticed, she noticed. She would be on the play ground standing at the fence smiling at him. She was twelve and he was practicing for the coach. It was him she watched, no one else on the team. She would say "Hi!" to him as they came off the field, no one else. Did she mean it? She only wants to kiss me?

He can't sleep, waits for dawn, gets up. His father gets up.

"How did you hire Amber, Dad?"

"I no hire. She hire. I come house every day noon eat. She come house every day five time. Tell me I need help, house help. I say, no need help. No pay. She come. She say she take corn, cabbage, pig, what I have. She work house. Albert, woman difficult. Woman say. Woman do. Man no stop. Woman do. Amber do. Amber good woman. You kiss, OK. You marry OK. I like food! I like Amber. Kiss serious this time. Important. Not puff puff girl."

Albert doesn't sleep. Dawn, more hours, time for Amber to come to work, he starts walking to her house. Waiting for her on the road he will meet her part way.

Amber sleeps, her heart, her mind and the soreness of her bottom coming together. Dreaming of his kisses she is in the woods, her favorite place. Albert is holding her, kissing her, touching her farther and farther up her thigh as the whiteness of her panties moisten. They are on a blanket he folds and leaves near the meadow. Birds sing. Sunlight flickers through the leaves on her face. Lifting up she pulls down her love-wet panties tossing them over a small bush. He is on her, loving her, kissing her. Her legs wrap around him.

Momma is there, crying, saying, "You are a good girl!"

Blisters sting as she slides her bottom rhythmically over the bed sheets in the erotic dream. Her bottom wakens her. She rolls over. Kissing him softly she says, "Not now Albert, later, after we're married."

Her legs close. Drifting into deeper sleep he is nuzzling her cheek kissing her. Naked in his arms she opens her legs. Looking in his eyes she says, "I Love you!"

"I love you too, Mrs. Hensley," he says.

Blinking her eyes she sees the white wedding dress over a chair a black dress coat covering it. They are in a room, the door closed, alone, her buttocks sinking deep into a soft feather bed.

She hears Momma say, "You are a good girl. It is OK to kiss him." Momma is crying. It is daylight. The dress is hers, on Amber, a shimmering white veil over her face as Daddy gives her to Albert. Another preacher is smiling.

Amber wakes up Momma's hand on her shoulder.

"Oh, Momma. I had such a dream!"

"It is time for you to go to work, honey," Momma says.

Amber still half dozing tells Momma her dream then sits up. Hugging our mother she says, "Thank you for paddling me, Momma."

"I'm sorry I had to paddle you, Amber." Momma returns her hug.

"No Momma, if my bottom had not been sore, in my dream, I would have made love to Albert in the woods, not on our wedding night. Thank you for paddling me. I mean it. I do!"

Momma kisses her on the cheek, "I love you, Amber! Amber, there is something we need to talk about."

"Yes Momma."

"Your work. Your Daddy and I agreed when you told us you wanted to work for Mr. Hensley that it was something we would trust you with. Your Daddy knows Mr. Hensley. One of my friends worked for him when Albert was little. He was always a perfect gentleman. He told us he would not let Albert touch you. I have known how you feel about Albert a long time. And I understand what you did in going to work there. You want Albert. His father wants you to have Albert. We will be happy if it works out that way too, but--- Have you been kissing Albert at their farm?"

"No Momma, I wanted him too, but Albert never tried. I thought he didn't like me. I hoped but he didn't."

Momma holds both my sister's hands, "We have to have an arrangement, Amber. If you are to work there for the rest of summer, there can be no kissing on their farm, at your work. No touching. Will you agree to that? Will you promise? You can only kiss him or touch him if you and he are here at our house or some public place. If you and he marry you will probably live at his farm. You can't kiss him there until then. Is that agreed?

"Oh Momma! I have to be with him all day and not touch him, not kiss him. That is going to be so hard!"

"I know. Can you do it? Or do you want to tell Mr. Hensley this morning that you can't work there anymore?"

"Yes Momma, I mean No Momma, I won't kiss him on the farm until we are married, if we are married. He may not even want to see me this morning with what happened!"

Dressed, fed and on her way to work, what is Albert doing out here she wonders? It's a mile to his house. He sitting by a tree gets to his feet runs to meet her.

"Are you OK? I was worried about you. Dad is worried about you."

"Momma paddled me."

"What! Why did she paddle you? You told her I made you do it didn't you. It wasn't your idea to sneak out!"

"I did though. It was my fault Albert. I'm not sorry you kissed me and held me. It was the happiest moment of my life. It's worth a paddling. It's worth a thousand paddlings! In a few days it won't hurt to sit anymore. I will remember our kiss forever!" My sister looks up at him with new tears in her eyes.

"I love you, Amber!" They kiss, longer, slower, without stopping, not caring who sees. Not private on the road. A car passes by, blows.

The driver shouts, "A little early in the morning for that sort of thing isn't it?"

This is the kind of place Momma said it was safe to kiss him, isn't it? There is hugging and kissing after that and walks from the farm house to the public road, and honking a lot of honking. When Daddy finds out he expands the no kissing radius to one mile from the farm house and not on a public road. Albert starts walking her to our house and back every day, one point three miles, with our living room off the road.

Albert regrets Amber's paddling more than she does. If she had not been paddled, he was ready for another round of kissing in the woods, and knowing her special place he plans to slip an old blanket from the barn out there for such a meeting. The blanket stays in the barn.

Caring, he doesn't want her paddled again. Following the preacher's, Momma's and now Amber's rules and dreams he kisses her on the living room couch, in the movie theater and by our screen door every time he says good night. He steals one kiss behind the barn when Amber brings out the water bucket for he and his father, but she pulls away.

"I love you, want you too much to kiss you alone like this, Albert." My sister says reaching up to give him one more peck.

Two days later, Saturday, a half day of work, it is date day for Albert and My sister. Albert puts the mule in the barn having plowed enough and takes a bath while Amber and his father talk. Amber fixes his father's lunch before they leave. Momma has lunch for Albert and her at our house. Will Albert and Amber sit on the couch stealing kisses most of the afternoon, go out to eat then to a movie?

Walking her hand tight in his, my sister doesn't look where she is going, her feet following his. Her eyes and heart follow Albert.

"Amber, your dream, let's do it like in your dream. Will you do that with me?" Albert squeezes her hand tight.

"I love you!" My sister speaks from her heart.

She feels the grass against her legs. Where is the road? Looking her woods loom ahead, her favorite place in the woods, the place she retreats to as a child, her sanctuary--- the place where she dreams of making love to him. The place where she has come to twice since her dream sitting against the trunk of a tree dreaming in daylight of what by night she creates in her mind with Albert on that soft earth.

Albert is taking her to the place in her dream. On Pulpit Rock two blue birds sing. The buzzing of insects in the meadow is a love song. Sweeping toward the fulfillment of her joy her hand is in his. She is his. The sun in her eyes she looks up blinded by the light trusting Albert to guide her. A minute and they will be there! The wanting of a woman powers each step.

The lesson, the tenderness of her bottom, the change of heart, the repentance, her promise and honor sting her desires. Wanting him with all her heart, with ever urge, with every fiber of her body she wants him holding her loving her beneath that tree.

A voice speaks deep in side her, *Not now*! Hands turn cold with fear, of him, of herself.

Amber stammers, "Albert, I can't. I am a good girl, Albert, please! Please!"

Looking at her, questioning her panic, he stops by pulpit rock pulling the frightened girl into his arms. She shakes.

"Please, Albert. I can't. Please!"

"You can't marry me?" He gets down on his knees. The second part of her dream in his mind he sees his dress coat over her wedding gown them in bed, Mr. and Mrs. Albert Hensley.

Seeing THAT dream Amber never answers. Bending to him tumbling him back into the deep grass she tackles him. She kisses him. "Speed" wins the biggest game in his life by being tackled by a girl. She dreams a dream of what will be. Holding him she never lets him go, never leaves his side, makes love to him in bedrooms, woods every place where erotic fantasy can meet reality, any place where she can love her husband. He dreams a dream. They dream one dream.

Albert slips his mother's ring on her finger. Sized down two sizes it will fit perfectly. His mother would have liked Amber, loved her as a daughter-in-law. A kiss, a contract, pulpit rock becomes a place special to my sister and her husband-to-be.

"Meet me here after church tomorrow. Meet me here at Pulpit rock. I'll tell Momma you are coming to dinner." Amber gets in short sentences between long kisses.

Albert never stops kissing her.

## Chapter 12
# THE ENGAGEMENT

*Spring 1936*
*Back to Sunday's sermon*

The preacher in front of me shouts. I shake.

A little kangaroo I want to climb in my Momma's pouch and hide where it is safe. Being prey, my eyes wide, frozen in fear, I watch him. Unable to run or hide I shiver. Looking through his eyes I see into his brain. I feel his tension, his attack, his preparation to spring. Prey survives by melding into predator's brains predicting their attacks. Predators survive looking into the minds of prey predicting their escapes. He, not looking at me, is open, vulnerable to my entering the soul of the beast seeing him attach another. I enter his brain, see through his eyes, feel his rage.

He looks directly at Amber. "If you don't repent your sins and come to God through the blood of the lamb, you are doomed to hell!"

He waits glaring. *Why isn't it working?* Amber routinely yields to his bullying. He retreats to the pulpit. Repent or not he has some satisfaction. Knowing Momma what happens when we got home is certain, an angel with a sore bottom. The session with her mother, why isn't it enough to make her repent? She knows her stubbornness will result in his calling for using the paddle one more time. It doesn't make sense.

The preacher looking back once more there is to be a response from our pew. He thinks, *She IS going to repent. I'll make sure of that. I'll not let Hensley's get this girl and take her to hell too. With repentance, her faith restored, she will realize the error of yoking with an outsider, a non believer and cut it off. If only there were a few more nigger families like theirs and a boy for her. That would make it easier. They are valuable, pay a good tithe, good workers in the church--- and her mother. Never was there a better follower. She accepts everything I say and is a talented teacher. Her knowledge is impeccable as well. Is it the Aryan blood in them, too much of it? Brains like that don't belong in niggers, it makes them too hard to manage.*

There will be time for thinking later. He has been standing silent in the pulpit. It is time for his finale.

A thought, a memory opens in his mind. Twenty two years ago he holds her hand, kisses her. Her name is Helen. If the preacher loves anything it is Helen, and she has property a good dowry, good land, not a big place, a good preacher's farm.

Hensley gets her. He has some foreign name then, nobody can pronounce it. He takes Hensley. It is close and doesn't stand out. Handsome, black hair, small, only an inch taller than Helen, speaking with that heavy accent, he works on her farm as a laborer. Together all the time, one day they are married.

*She is mine!* The preacher thinks. *How can she love that little shrimp? He seduced her or raped her and got her pregnant.*

Her husband keeps her working on their farm through the pregnancy and nursing. Coughing, it is tuberculosis. She dies. The preacher blames her husband, goes there with his derringer to kill him. When the little man's back is turned getting a cup of tea for the preacher he reaches in his pocket.

*My gun, where is my gun!*

The gypsy sees him digging in his pocket.

"You look for this?" The little man pulls it of his pocket and points it at the preacher's head. Making him sit, talking about shooting him in the head the gypsy has the preacher crazy with fear. They wait. A twinkle in the little man's eyes he plays with the gun cocking one barrel then the other, pointing it at the preacher. Then thinking of something the little man leaves the room. Seeing his chance the preacher makes a run for it. Inaccurate at any distance if he can get fifty feet ahead of him he will never hit him with that little gun.

As Albert's father plans he runs as a group of Gypsy wagons move down the road. He chases the preacher, not with his gun, with a pitch fork. All the way to the road he shouts. The preacher runs. The whole wagon train laughs and points. Then the gypsy puts up that sign.

*That Gypsy isn't going to get this one.* The preacher swears under his breath, clears his throat and begins his oration of salvation.

Amber is motionless, dry eyed and not running to the alter entreating Jesus, begging for forgiveness.

The preacher spews venom at my sister. "Sin is not hidden. God knows you, sinner. God will punish you!"

Snuggling to Momma, her child, I feel her thoughts in my head. Momma looks at my sister, hopes that she will answer the preachers call, repent and reaffirm her salvation. Letting the preacher, in his one tract mindedness move on to other sinners, other crimes, is important. Amber's stubbornness troubles Momma.

The preacher's long memory and hunger to save her will not stop with one sermon. Public repentance and tears on the church alter are the only way to gain forgiveness of God in the teachings of the church. The preacher sees Amber in every meeting thinking, *Sin, You are a sinner! And wondering what she senses, what the Hensley's know and how they plan to use it against him.*

Repentance is the way to save this one from Hensley and his son. Pastor John forgives what God forgives, nothing more and less where it involves the Hensleys. To sit unrepentant in the congregation is no better in his eyes than to sit unrepentant in O'Leary's pub and more irritating. The sinners in O'Leary pub are not of Pastor John's herd, not a constant reminder of sin.

I look at Amber. What is she thinking? The preacher's words to Amber are loud, long and deep, the bellowing of a great bull. Today the preacher bellows are in a pasture far away. She is in Albert's pasture listening to him. Albert's heart beats in hers. She sees not the preacher, only a man, Albert's enemy.

She fears the preacher as a young girl, as I fear him as a young girl. Out of that fear comes respect. The good things now in her life are because of Pastor John's long nose in their business. Wednesday catching her and Albert, the correction, the paddling, and the pain have turned to joy. Momma wielding the paddle, corrects her, gives her pain. Does she blame Momma? She's grateful to Momma. The preacher's interference brings the boy she loves to propose. She is grateful for that too. It is the preacher's words, things Momma nor the rest of us know he says.

"Son of Satan, embodiment of evil" and a string of other oaths not using swear words, but more swearing in intent than any nonbeliever ever utters, the preacher hates the boy she loves. Amber sees it in his eyes. An evil glow burns inside him. She sees it. The preacher hides from his flock in a practiced posture of concern. Would Momma believe it is there if she tells her? If she does, what would it do, shatter her, take away the church, a huge part of Momma's life, of all their lives? She, a girl wise beyond her years, says nothing, keeps it in, looks down. She sees it all the time now. His mask of concern no longer works with Amber. The preacher hates Albert's father. He hates Albert.

Amber thinks back a few weeks to the farm, to Albert, to his father.

No woman in the Hensley home for years, they need a woman's help. It takes Amber a month to clean the house and put it in order, Momma comes to help the first few weeks but has too much to do at home. It becomes routine until canning season starts. Amber comes home every day with her hands burning and goes straight to bed. She needs help, but they are not rich people can't afford another woman. She looks at the father, *How could he do it all. When did he sleep?*

The father never remarries. He loves his wife, can never seem to love another. He raises Albert alone from a toddler.

"I little man with big heart. Work hard. It good. I no need much sleep when young," Albert's father says.

Amber smiles, is gaining respect for him.

"My grandfather tall like Albert. It in family. Me grow hard time. I hunger. I small. I what I am. When boy grow with food, he tall. My people, like yours, sometimes have hard. I make so he have food. Have farm good. Have food. Being on wagon hard. People not like us. Our children not eat. People no care. I keep farm. It good. It make food for Albert."

"You are a good man," Amber says.

She smiles at Albert's father. He is a good man. She respects him. He is not as she is taught. Are Gypsy's like him? Do they love their families as much as he does? Do they drink and play all the time?

"I like drink. I like play. I have Albert. I have farm. I drink, I no work. I no feed Albert. I no drink. I no play. I work. Albert eat. The farm much for man. With Albert easier. I get bottle from moon shiner sometimes now. Gypsies in town. We go camp. Is fun. I like. Not good enough for boy. I want better than me. He have the farm."

The father looks at Amber. "He have wife, have children. Farm take children. A farm good with many children. Hard when young. When old children help. You want children?"

Amber stops washing the dishes. Blushing she looks at the father.

"You want Albert? You young girl, too young. Think you not die like my Helen. Think you make Albert good wife."

Amber thinks, *Yes, I'll make Albert a good wife.*

"He go church if you want. I no stop him," Albert's father says.

"I not have liking for preacher. He say my Helen in hell. We not members your church. I run him off farm with pitch fork. He run fast with pitch fork behind. He not come back. It important Albert go church, join church?"

Amber tries to start washing dishes, can't. "I have been in my church all my life. It's important to me. I want to share that with my husband."

"I put sign on road, 'No Trespassing Pastor John, shoot if come here.' Maybe that the reason he not come back."

"No wonder he doesn't like you, Daddy," Albert says coming in from the barn.

"Not like him either. Sign wear out, fall down. I not make new one. It long time, 20 years. You keep him off farm. No invite him farm. We be OK."

Albert looks at Amber. *What have they been talking about?*

"Albert, you go church with Amber. She like that. I like that. You go. OK."

Albert looks at his father. His father never lets him go to another church. They go to the Catholic Church and there only on special holidays. Orthodox Christians their closest church is 40 miles away.

Now she understands why the preacher isn't more welcoming of Albert and some of his rage. Knowing the preacher, 20 years isn't enough time for him to forget a thing like that. His pride, being chased off a farm with others watching, the sign he will never forget.

There is a shooting contest in town a week after the incident with the pitch fork. The father enters it. Hitting every bull's eye he wins. Where did a Gypsy learn to shoot like that? After the match he walks up to the preacher.

"I in army. Marksman. I shoot men. Win medals." He opens his coat revealing a row of gold and silver medals with foreign inscriptions. "I keep rifle. I like shoot head. Men I shoot. I shoot head. I find small pistol. I keep by bed, in pants sometime. If I you, I not come farm anymore. You understand?"

The preacher understands, a Satan with a gun, a crack shot, a Gypsy, a thief, a bandit, a professional soldier, a killer. The Gypsy is not as the preacher's Gypsies should be. Racial stereotypes work best when the inferior ones are under the heel, bound or unarmed seen through a rifle scope. A Gypsy eye seen down the barrel of a gun his finger on the trigger conflicts with reality as the churchman believes it should be, changes things. The preacher never goes near his farm again.

Albert's father teaches him to shoot, to run, to dodge, to catch a ball, to be brave, to be the athlete he is, to be the man he is, to be the man Amber loves.

Amber kissing Albert, in the church enrages the man of God. In the meadow, her kiss of betrothal to Albert betrays the preacher. When the preacher knows about it he will think it as Judas's kiss in Gethsemane, and hate her too. Amber makes her choice. She loves and follows Albert. She will be of her husband's family, bare his children and follow the preacher no more. She repents to Momma, says she is sorry. If the preacher apologizes for his statements about Albert and Albert's mother, if he can erase the hate from his eyes and apologize to Albert's father, Amber will go forward, confess her sins publicly to the pastor. If not, she will not--- not to him.

She chooses the wrong place, the wrong time, the right thing to do; kiss Albert and keep kissing him. She, a virgin, will remain a virgin until their wedding. Why should she repent kissing the man she is to marry, a man she adores, respects, the man that less than 24 hours earlier proposes to her? She is paddled, punished and her sins and forgiven. She is sure of her innocence. Sitting tight in her seat she will come to the alter with the man of her dreams to wed him, not to repent of loving him.

Being a little girl, I am less sure of my innocence, and do not understanding the words, the paradigms, the theology. I understand a man yelling in my face. I am a little kangaroo, young and afraid. I fear the big man. I hear his voice in the cathedral tower of my head vibrating with each toll of the bell. Shaking, I believed he is looking at me. I shiver as the preacher shouts. He scares the devil out of bad people, good people and little people like me. I do not want to go to hell.

Not understanding, believing the preacher has the keys to heaven or hell, I do not want Amber to go to hell. If to avoid hell and the preacher yelling she is supposed to run to the alter screaming and crying. Why doesn't she? I pray for her. Momma prays for her.

I pray, *Please God, I don't want my sister to go to hell! Please God! Make her obey the preacher and be saved!*

A special person to me, she is my second Momma. When Momma is busy Amber takes care of me as a baby, changing my diapers, feeding me. Now she takes me places. Last week before the trouble she and Albert take me to the Saturday matinee. He has an extra nickel from selling rabbits he catches in his traps, and Momma says they have to take me. They hold hands, a first for Amber too. Her eyes twinkle, she is following him. He would have kissed her then if I hadn't sat between them, Momma's idea too.

Following him she is his. I follow her. I guess that makes him ours. If she loves him I love him too, another brother, a special brother.

Every day of the growing season Amber leads me on our daily trek foraging for food. Sunday a big meal, we have more to pick.

"Amber, Greens!" Momma orders as she prepares our dinner.

Ready for this I have off my Sunday dress and on my ordinary clothes. Amber is not changed. Day dreaming about Albert, not even hungry, she is filled with love. If she is filled with love how can she have forgotten him and their date in the meadow? Sitting on the couch with that dazed love look she has on her Sunday dress. Not a forgetting, she wants her prettiest dress on when she sees him today, and keeps it on.

Is it a picking dress? Her mind on him disconnecting from reality, she needs frequent jolting from Momma to rejoin the living.

"Yes, Momma!" She comes to life and bounces upstairs to change. Obeying Momma's order her love waits, not for Cinderella in an evening gown, but her in picking clothes.

I slip out the door with my basket.

"Wait!" The screen door swings open. Momma calls after me.

"Yes, Momma!" I say, freezing in my tracks under the Maple tree. Looking for my blue bird I want a song. Inside I hear them, my sister and Momma talking.

"Amber, hurry up! Your sister is half way to the woods already. You need to watch after her."

"Ok, Momma. There's no reason to worry. There's a whole world of bugs out there. She won't make it past the first one without stopping."

I think, *Bugs! I know there is a big one out here--- somewhere.* I begin looking while I am waiting. Do I find any in the yard? The grass is too short to be interesting to any big bugs. Looking across the road to bobbing heads of long grass and weeds, real bugs are there.

"Come on, Amber!" I say, as if she will listen to me. Impatient I want to cross the road. Knowing Momma will spank me if I do without Amber holding my hand I keep looking in our yard.

The screen door squeaks.

"I'm coming, Sharon."

She bounces down the steps out of her Sunday clothes. Albert won't care. He falls in love with her working on a farm, no Sunday clothes there.

I run to my sister grabbing her hand saying, "I love you, Amber!"

It makes her smile as if anything can stop her smiling. She looks down at me never breaking her stride except to scoop up a grunting Wuffie, who will cross the road with four feet splayed out and her stomach squished by my sister's arm.

Looking back and forth down the road then down at me, Amber smiles, "I love you, too!"

Crossing the road she grips my puppy, my hand, and her basket. Holding three things with two hands is something older sisters learn early in their teens. Squeezing my hand extra tight compressed between the basket handle and her bigger hand, it hurts. Pain preceding freedom I pull her forward like Albert's mule plowing the last furrow seeing the barn grow closer, anticipating the harnesses removal. Scampering, jumping, being five, my lengthening legs enabled me to go more and more where I want, to a world filled with wonders.

Too little to cross roads or go through the woods on my own this makes these trips special to me. Leaving the road behind it is safe for me to be free. My hand released I take off running, stopping, bouncing from wonder to wonder. I look at new flowers in Mrs. Johansen's yard, and every new flower and thing of interest along the way.

"Amber, did you see this flower!" or "Amber, what's that?" We talk, well I talk.

"Come on, Sharon!" Walking fast that is her standard answer to almost everything I say.

"Come on, Sharon!" She, sounding gruff and bossy, but really only a teenager saddled with a little sister she loves despite the saddle. I hear her grumbles as a puppy learns to hear its dinner bell and come running. Being slowed by little legs scampering to keep up is inconvenient. Being worshiped, adored and the center of my universe she returns my love, even if gruffness and feigned impatience are required by her teenage status.

Amber taking me with her through the woods to a field of greens we walk, baskets in our free hands. A blue bird an apple tree warbles as we pass, singing, looking at me with quick darting turns of its head. The bird, a greeter, is there most days to welcome us on our trip to another place of worship. God's cathedral never closing, its doors are always open. No shouting, no paddles, no dogma, no preachers it is the original place of worship, the place every religion starts. The unroofed, unmade place of worship where from darkness light comes.

In darkness our greeter and feathered singers sleep on branches in the choir loft waiting for dawn. At first light birds singing "Hallelujah!" call us to prayer. Worship services continue till the last rays of sunset. The choir never stops the medleys of worshipful song and sings in duets, quartets and tabernacle choirs for as long as there is light to read the music. At night they leave the owl to sing a solo, "Who?" Humankind, daylight dependant eyes, sits in the dark wondering, thinks, wonders, answers the owl. Who? Who but God, the source of religion.

The temple's lights vary, some dark shade, some glaring light. I watch Amber, ahead of me. She leaves a leaf covered vestibule entering the full sunlight of a sanctuary. There she prays; there she worships; there she stands in the long grass, looks for God, knows his love, his radiant sunlight, and bows to pick arugula. There she is close to God and there she takes me sharing a temple of love with me.

The temple free, for everyone, unownable, it cannot be bought, sold or ruled. People require homes, that piece of the earth they call their own. Some require palatial estates larger than towns, for her it is two trees bent down a few branches for a roof. Her private place as a child she shares with me. Big enough for two big people, and a little person. She and I call it our place in the woods. There she talks to me. I listen understanding sometimes. Wanting to be my big sister I look at her.

Before retiring to our cloister, there is the sanctuary. Wild arugula dots the communion table. Planted oregano covers a rocky area along a granite communion rail. Unplanned dandelions mix with rye grass spilling from earthen cracks in pulpit rock. Greens peppering the field among stone pews, are a divine blessing unearned, a living gift of God to us. Picking minutes we have baskets of fresh greens to go with our cooked dinner.

It is here that God feeds us filling our earthly needs. Giving without asking payment God's sun grows our food. Contrast this to church. There in the darkness of trees once in God's temple now cut and shaped into rafters, planks and roof of our church an offering plate is passed.

Every Sunday Daddy stops me and each of the younger children, before entering the church, "Here is your dime to put in the offering plate."

A payment in tenths to God for debts unpayable we learn to give to the church. Picking a mint leaf in God's natural temple I munch the tasty green, look to the sun and smile. The smile, my offering, God accepts sending more sun, rain and greens. The preacher at church accepts the offering, the dime and gives us Brussels sprouts and words to digest. I like the mint.

I ask Amber, "Are you sorry you kissed Albert?"

She smiles, sways a little and says, "No." Then leaning down to me she hugs me. "I love him."

I do not understand. How can anyone have the preacher yell at them, have Momma paddle them then say she loves him. It doesn't make sense. Looking in her eyes I can tell it is a mystery, one I will understand when my hips get wide, when my flat chest unflattens, when I am 16 and old like my sister. Not understanding, worshiping her, I know we have a new deity, a boy, an Albert deity. If she loves him and worships him, I do too, even if it doesn't make any sense.

Flowers make sense. Sniffing blossoms, watching bees and bugs, listening to birds and chewing leaves of sun warm arugula makes sense. Gods natural temple, made with his own hands, makes sense. Liking God's temple better than his house it is reverent, the birds and other members of the chorus sing in perfect pitch and volume. No one shouts.

There to work, there to gather, to take rather than give am I useful. A parasite on the earth, do I create, make protein, do I have chlorophyll? Only plants create life by taking water, sun and rock and turn it into life. It requires chlorophyll. People live by taking life from life. I take from other people. Momma and Daddy love me and feed me with only smiles for rewards like God. At five I don't work, or pull my weight. I eat. I do what little girls do. I smile, play a lot, pick a little and think unique thoughts.

"Do birds and other animals kiss and fornicate in the woods?" I ask Amber.

Amber laughs, "You will have to ask Momma that one little sister!" Then she smiles, "On second thought little sister, you had better not ask her that unless you want spanked!"

The world of the meadow fades to silence. The choir tunes their instruments for the next symphony. In the quiet my five-year-old mind darts to a new subject. The noisiest thing in God's temple is Wuffie, my puppy, and I.

"Wuffie, look! Amber, look! It is the biggest bug I have ever seen!" There in the woods, pointing, squealing in my best little girl voice I want my sister and puppy to come look. I find a bug, a big bug, a giant bug!

Amber knows it is a bug, one of millions, trillions, the first I have seen that day. Will this be the last bug I want her to see today? Ignoring looking at this one with an unenthusiastic, "Unhuh," she trudges on.

Kissed and grown up she is not interested in bugs. Bugs are little girl things, and not for every little girl.

Janet, another girl in my Sunday school class, says, "That's disgusting," seeing me playing with a cockroach!

The preacher pats her on the head and steps on my bug.

"Good girl," he is always saying that to her.

She is always a good girl, when the preacher is watching. She hates bugs.

Not answering Amber is lost in memories of kisses and anticipation of others. Continuing walking her basket swinging at her side, her hips swish, she ignores me! Why is she in such a hurry to get to the meadow and our dinner greens?

Perking her ears, Wuffie follows my lead, thinking I am her alpha dog. As I lean closer to the insect, closer than I if my legs and body were longer, Wuffie sticks a cold nose to it barking supportively in high pitched puppy yelps. It moves. It moves! More than moving it flutters, red tipped wings coming out from under its shell popping noises at us! Not ready for that, why is it scurrying toward Wuffie and I?

"Wuffie, it's moving!" I say.

Short, limber puppy legs glued to oversize puppy paws bound back. My dog folding up over her tail tumbles before regaining her footing. My protector, my dog, isn't she supposed to be defending me? Barking in rapid fire she raises an alarm as she bounces around the bug in a widening arc heading behind me. Looking up at me, her head cocked to the side she emits another less secure yelp, this yelp saying, "Help me, I'm a baby dog!"

Does she expect me to protect her? The bug skittering on six legs heads for us.

Me backing, Wuffie barking, my dog and I meet, "Wuffie!" I tumble over her, rolling on the ground.

The bug disappears. Where is it? I panic! Where is it? Little fingers searching my dress, then my hair down to my feet I can't find the bug! Where is it? Is it going to get me?

"Wuffie!" I yelp, this yelp saying, "Help me, I'm a baby girl!"

Saving us Amber calls, "Come on Sharon!"

Running as fast as I can to my sister it's the last time I out-run Wuffie, her legs growing more over the next week than mine will that year. Yelping and barking she plants big paws in front of her and tries to keep other big paws in as much of a line as possible behind her. My pigtails bounce a little, from the wind in my hair. Wuffie's ears wave like flags in a windstorm animated by the up and down motion of her head.

The bug gone, no other bugs, mammals or vaguely intelligent creatures appear for our inspection. Finding bigger game is always difficult for Wuffie and I. Being able to hear us long before we see them, Deer and other wildlife cut us a wide berth. Do other wild forms of intelligent life consider us worth a sniff or a bark? A small human child and baby dog are not worth the clamor of animal talk or calls reserved for their own species. They move into the forest shade or behind a bush without making a sound reappearing when we are gone.

Unlike church there is no yelling about hell that scares me in the woods. Woods are quiet places. Punctuations of attention grabbing noise are danger calls. Shouting being the preacher's danger call for humans, is that why the noise scares me? I like quiet. The only shouting I hear is at church. Momma and Daddy, being sane, don't shout unless there is danger. Danger I understand. The preacher shouts about dangers in his head, dangers that I can not see, dangers that I do not understand, like fornication. This scaring me, I want to slip away and hide in the woods when the preacher gets noisy.

Funny, the preacher does not see much big game either. Those he intends to scare into repentance slip by in the shadows on the far side of the street. His voice booming, reaching outside the building through the trees, warns them. Warned, sinners tip-toe by our church. His rafter shaking voice does not reach O'Leary's Pub, a place quiet and shady on the outside, but alive with music and laughter within. On dark nights our church disappears, along with God's temple into unlit darkness. Electric bulbs through small windows act as beacons to this temple of human vice. Less than perfect ones, afraid of the preacher's explosive voice coming from the church, scurry to their chosen hiding place, a meadow of their own--- with libation.

They are lucky to hear the preacher's shouts without being able to make out the words. Me, I am a little bug tethered to Momma, unable to escape the roar of his voice. I hear him, see him. Window panes rattle as his face grows red. I never want to be that forceful, that loud, that filled with the rage, or be in the same room with anyone who is.

Momma wants to be there, listening, punctuating his sermon with verbal exclamations timed with others in the congregation, "Amen!" "Praise the Lord!" "Amen preacher!" A cadence, it spreads through the room in ripples and waves. Reflecting back the wave focuses and peaks on the pulpit, the preacher adding shouts to the breaking wave sending it back crashing down on the congregation.

Choosing for me to be in that room, Momma makes sure I am there every time the doors open. Walking by the Seventh Day Adventist Church on Saturday mornings, cars in their parking lot, we hear singing, then not a sound. Why can't we go there one Saturday? I wonder what they do, why it is quiet? Is it like my nature temple inside, peaceful and quiet? I want to go there.

Not our church, not our way, we need music. We need emotion. My mother melds with the preacher mumbling under her breath in unison with others making the services a rolling, seething, fluid interaction between congregation and orator. Growing up becoming culturized to its rhythm, the flow of the services, should grow on me like Brussel's sprouts. Not happening yet I wonder if I will ever love and follow a vivacious strong-willed preacher as my mother does.

Little girl chatter and squeals is all I have the desire to emit or hear. Quiet, sedate worship, isn't that an option? In the natural cathedral I feel the reverence, the presence, yet I am to the animals as noisy as our preacher. Deer walk away when they hear me. They never run. They run when they hear our preacher. He is dangerous, a grown human.

Not limited to loud things coming out of his mouth, the preacher has a taste for things bitter too, Brussels sprouts. Going in or coming out, it seems we view the function of our mouths with a difference.

Listening close to the quiet of the woods I only speak to announce a new find to Wuffie or my sister. The taste of wild strawberries from a clearing--- sweet, and song birds singing, those are things that I love. Shouting and the flavor of Brussels sprouts are not to my taste or part of my nature. Have you ever seen a Brussels sprout growing in a natural setting, God's temple?

Food and sustenance from different sources, woods, gardens, other people, church and nature divide for me, each offering a different set of parameters. Every person, thing and experience has a different agenda. The preacher in his Sunday suit or politicians in their Sunday suits every day, each provide different cuisines.

The man running for Congress promises a chicken in every pot and hands my father a small bottle of peppermint schnapps. Not a drinker, my father smiles, takes it, thanks him, passes it on and votes for the other man, the man Mr. Roosevelt recommends.

From a table covered with stalks in front of the church, our preacher delivers Brussels sprouts to every plate. Putting the Brussels sprouts in one pot, buying a chicken, putting it with other vegetables in another pot Momma feeds us.

As we pick greens, my sister keeps watching the other side of the clearing. Where is he? Our baskets full she stops sitting on pulpit rock admiring the still crushed grass. Her body and his, two become one, their impression together in grass. Saying silently with more emotion than Momma can evoke with her paddle Amber says "YES!" Yesterday lying in grass she kisses him "YES!" It is yesterday, always yesterday for Amber in that field, in his arms. Soon she will hear--- "I love you, Mrs. Hensley."

Not telling me what she waits to see I wonder why we aren't walking home. Albert appears in a white shirt and Sunday pants coming out of a dark shadow his shirt radiating in the full sunlight. Amber runs to him kissing him right in front of me. From his pocket he pulls her ring. She puts it on.

"Amber, what is that?" I ask looking at it.

Amber takes it off giving it back to Albert.

"Sharon it is a secret. We are going to tell everyone after dinner. You keep quiet till then, little sister!"

I giggle, loving secrets, I can keep quiet. I can keep quiet at least an hour, or two, till dinner is over. Is Albert forgetting something important? Amber kisses him yes. Hers isn't the final word, he has to ask Daddy. Daddy won't kiss him yes. Will he say yes? Albert worries, doesn't worry. If Daddy says no they will elope.

Amber kisses him taking my hand, and his. No spare hands my sister bubbles and giggles. The center of a world she is a young girl engaged holding us both. I carry my basket. Albert carries hers. Together we walk home skipping in places smooth; walking in rough spots.

Amber letting me go we reach the edge of the clearing, a cool dark spot under two large leafy trees.

Amber says, "Albert as soon as I am old enough to go to the woods on my own, about eight or nine, I came here, to this spot. When I was ten I built a little shelter. It was my house. I brought you once, to ask your help in bending down the trees. Do you remember?"

"Yes." He says gripping her hand, kissing her cheek.

"It's my special place, my special place as a child. It's the place I dreamed about with you. Will you bring me here after we are married?" Amber turns kissing him full on the mouth.

Albert doesn't answer. They are kissing a lot. Making love to her alone in the woods will be special. I don't understand this. I like a good night kiss from Momma and Daddy, even Amber's kisses, but why are they so lovey dovey? Why teenagers get that way; I have no clue. They kiss. I walk around in circles looking for something to do. Looking back at them, their spot, it will be my special spot too when I am old enough to come here alone, and they are too old, and have a real home. Till then I will leave them there kissing while I look for wood bugs in the forest.

I find an interesting one. Amber is in a rush to leave. Impatient, a teenager, she wants Albert to have a chance to talk to Daddy before dinner, not after dinner. An understanding sister, not that many years away from my point of view, she keeps me moving, and lets me explore. Today is not a day for exploring, it is a Daddy asking day.

We walk fast. Not fast enough, Amber tires of waiting for Wuffie and I. Scooped up wuffie bobs along grunting in my sister's arms. I am going through the woods at new heights sitting on Albert's shoulders. They speed walk us home.

Daddy, reading the newspaper, waits, hungry, and curious when we burst through the door. Not waiting Albert approaches him.

"Sir, can I talk to you," he asks?

Daddy, never having had a boy approach him this way, looks serious, "What is this about, boy?"

He looks at Albert. He looks at Amber. Momma tells him everything after Amber's paddling.

"Do I need to get out my boxing gloves?"

"No sir!" Albert says, "Can I marry your daughter?"

"Most of them are too young for that, boy," Daddy says looking at me and Mary Rose.

"Can I marry Amber, sir?"

"What do you think, Amber."

"Yes, Daddy, he can marry me! Please, Daddy!"

Momma runs out of the kitchen ignoring four pots of food boiling on the stove. Tackling Albert and landing onto the couch, he is toppled by my sister's pounce. Eighty pounds heavier Momma flattens him. She is hugs him. She shakes his breathless frame as his eyes bug in surprise.

"You can marry her," Momma says.

"Do I get any say in this," Daddy asks?

"Sure you do. You can say yes," Momma says.

This is the other thing they talk about after Amber's incident. When will Albert ask is their only question. Passionate as they are, sooner is better than later.

"Yes, then. Unless my dinner is burned and I get in a bad mood," Daddy says.

Momma hugs Albert, then Amber, then kisses Daddy. Eventually she hurries back in the kitchen. Daddy can't get in a bad mood today.

"Sit down, we need talk--- When?" Daddy says.

"We haven't talked about that, Daddy," Amber says.

When are they going to get Married? All they think about is they are, not when.

"Albert, I said most of my daughters are too young to get Married. I should have said all of them!"

What is Daddy doing? He said yes!

"Albert you finished high school and tried college."

"Yes sir."

"Amber graduates in nine months, Albert." Daddy wants my sister to finish high school.

They look at each other, almost a year! Their faces drop.

Nine months to a sixteen year old girl with love on her mind is a twenty year sentence.

"We haven't talked about it, Mr. Forest," Albert starts. "I, we, need to talk about it," Albert looks at Amber. "Does she need to graduate from high school? Nobody in my family ever graduated from high school, sir. I did, but I don't need a high school diploma to get a job in the plant or for most other jobs. Amber doesn't need one to raise our family."

They hadn't talked about that either.

Amber smiles. She wants to be a mother, the mother of Albert's children.

"True enough, Albert," Daddy answers, "And I know it is hard to wait that long, but I believe finishing at least high school is important and will open doors for both of you during the rest of your lives. I want you to think about it."

My sister looks at the love of her life. I am going to be a flower girl. Momma looks over our flower garden, what sort of flowers do we have for Amber and Albert's nuptials. Can Daddy get them to wait until Amber finishes high school? True enough, Amber doesn't need a high school diploma to be a wife, have babies and take care of a family. Do most girls drop out of high school to get married in the 1930s? Albert, having a diploma, will benefit from it. Even to be a foreman in a plant, high school diplomas are required some places. There are choices.

Amber wants jonquils. How is he going to get Jonquils in August?

*Women!* Rubbing his head Daddy thinks, *Why do these women love Jonquils so much? Haven't they heard of roses?*

## Chapter 13
# ALBERT'S ARMY

Amber and Albert's engagement is announced: a month passes. The happiness, the smiles, the joy, my sister is going to be Mrs. Albert Hensley. It doesn't fade. Looking at her I sigh. She remains on a cloud, a cloud of snow white innocence, an angel on earth. I love her.

We play. We sing. We are oblivious to the world. Amber bounces, still a girl, a woman, is she ready for marriage? Daddy holds her back.

"Get your education!" He wants her to be the second high school graduate of his children.

She listens, says, "Yes Daddy." Never being able to tell anyone no.

Marching to two sets of drums, is it hard to stay in step? Two men pulling, a man and boy, Daddy holds her ear, a life time of obedience to his words. Albert holds her.

Not ruling her as hard as in the past Momma frets. Why won't she repent in church. Pastor John is adamant about that, no repentance, no salvation. Knowing her daughter, a girl in love, she slacks the reigns, lets her run freer, there will be time, there are years yet to come. Amber, raised in church every time the doors open, is committed. She will come back.

"Momma, I need to see Albert."

The afternoon sun, not yet setting, leaves time to walk to his house and back before dark.

"Will you be home for supper?"

An opening, a chance for more time with her beloved than she expects, "I think I'll fix supper for them. Albert can walk me home after that."

"OK, Honey."

Amber doesn't say a word to me. My mood changes. Do I love her? Does she love me? I don't say a word to her either, not even "Good by" as she bounces down the stairs. Being mad at her, all she thinks about is Albert, never me. I look at her dead mother-in-law-to-be's ring always around her neck now and remember what she says to him in the forest.

"Albert, I will always love you, always," she fiddles with his mother's ring, now hers. A tear rolls down her cheek. "I will never take this off. I will always be yours. I will always love you."

Being five, being left out, I want love too.

"Amber, what about me? Do you love me too," I worry thinking, knowing that another love in her life will intrude on us.

"Of course, silly, I'll always love you. This ring symbolizes Albert's and my love. Wearing it means I am his, always his. There is a ring in my heart for you little sister. I will always love you too. Ok, this ring, seeing it, when you see it know that I love you too, OK?"

Soothed I accept her blending of loving Albert and me. Over the weeks since that there is less time for me, less time for my dolls, less of everything from Amber. Every time she can run off to Albert, she does.

Mad that day I want to go with her, "Please let me go with you Amber. It is lonely without you!"

She doesn't listen. She wants to be alone with Albert.

"I hate you. I hate you. I wish you were dead!" Anger spills out of me as I run to my room slamming the door. I need her too.

"I LOVE YOU, SHARON!" ringing out from my sister I hear the screen door slam.

Gone. I wonder, will she be home to tell me a bedtime story? Daddy will if he is home. Momma will if they are not, but bed time stories are best from Daddy. If he is not there Amber is second choice. She jumps, makes funny faces and makes them almost as exciting as Daddy does.

I watch her round the corner, never looking back.

I play with Samantha, my doll. The afternoon is longer without Amber. I miss her sitting in her chair, eating beside me. Will I need to get used to that? When she marries, she won't be eating with us anymore. After supper Momma washes the dishes. My new chore to pick them up one by one and bring them to the sink, I have responsibilities now.

No Daddy, he is working late. I look through the screen into the darkness. Amber will be home soon, Albert will bring her.

Momma joins me, "Amber is not home yet?" Momma calls my brother, "Nathan, your sister is not home and it is getting late. Can you take Sammy's truck and drive over to get her?" A request, not a request, Momma wants her home then thinks to her self, *I wish the Hensley's had a phone.*

It is after nine, she has been gone over six hours and engaged, or not, a girl does not stay into the evening with a boy.

The hum of Sammy's Ford pickup springs to life on the second crank. Lights disappear around the corner. Momma puts me to bed, one of her stories, a little dry, induces sleep. I am nodding off when the front door opens.

"Momma!" Nathan calls out, "Momma!"

Momma noting the tone in his voice is up leaving me. Not yet asleep I tumble out of bed following her.

Albert is with him. Where is Amber?

"Momma, Amber never got to Albert's house!" Nathan and Albert look worried.

Momma sends the boys to the plant, "Go get your father!"

Nathan goes, Albert walks home alone checking along the way.

"Have you seen Amber?" he asks everyone along the road.

With a lantern he walks through the woods. Out of the way, why would she go that way? Knowing her, sometimes she does, she likes the woods, the meadow.

Nathan, Daddy, Albert and two men walk the road to the Hensley farm twice before midnight beginning to knock on doors repeating

Albert's question. Men with lanterns scan the trail through the woods. No Amber. She didn't stop at any friend's house.

"We had better call Officer Clancy and the sheriff!" Daddy says coming back at near midnight.

Nathan takes Daddy to the sheriff's office. Officer Clancy joins them.

Finally noticing me, Momma puts me to bed. I am so tired I can't stay awake. I feel it. Momma is shaking, afraid. I wake up, it's morning, no Amber!

In the afternoon Officer Clancy comes to get my father. He goes away sitting in the front seat of the squad car. Hours pass, the last slivers of sun sliding below the horizon, officer Clancy brings him home. Daddy is shaking, his face is wet with tears and he is bleeding. Both his fists are cut, his knuckles as raw as if they were whipped with a board. Officer Clancy shakes too.

Momma starts screaming. She never screams. Her voice, the wail, the anguish, scares me with a deeper and more profound fear than any sermon I ever hear. Momma puddles in Daddy's arms: they are both crying. Women from the church come. What is happening? Where is my sister? Where is Amber?

Two ladies from church gather some of my clothes and take me with them. The next day Uncle Jim and Aunt Mindy are there. I see Grandma and Grandpa, other relatives but not Amber. My mother is not my mother. She sits hollow eyed, unresponsive in the living room. When I see her and go to her why doesn't she hug me? She sits.

Grandma takes me home on the long bus ride to our family farm. Playing in the fields by where the Jonquils bloom is fun. No one talks to me, will tell me what is wrong. Why didn't my sister come home?

I ask grandma, "Where is Amber?"

No answer.

Being five, I don't question long, I adapt. Grandma is fun to be with. No children in her home I get all the attentionS. I get read too and she lets me play everywhere on the farm, so long as their dog, Kimo, stays with me. He is twice my size and follows me everywhere. When I get near the creek or any place he doesn't want me he gets between me and where I am going. A herd dog, I am his little sheep. He always brings me back to grandma's porch no mater where my course is planned.

A month is a long time to a five-year-old. The first few days I cry, I want Momma. I want Amber. I want Daddy. Then I am used to the farm, accepting it.

As I play in the yard I hear an engine. There are no engines on the farm. Grandpa uses horses, neighing and whinnying horses. They don't make sounds like that. It is an engine. Looking to where the road appears for about 100 feet between the trees across the creek I see a car, DADDY'S CAR, his Knox!

Running I head for the road. Kimo, excited too, thinks that is a bad idea. He blocks my way. Ducking under him crawling I keep going. The confused dog has never had a little sheep crawl under him. I am not a good herdee. Bleating for my Momma I run. He follows me barking. Kimo needs help herding his little human; I have a goal no overgrown dog can block. I will get to my parents! It requires Grandma or Grandpa, hands, to stop me. Running the fast I am unstoppable.

The car comes up the road straight at me. It skids on the gravel stopping crossways in the middle of the road as I run right to the door.

"Daddy! Daddy!" I cry reaching up to him.

Scooping me up, squeezing the breath out of me he spins around with me.

"I've missed my girl." Daddy plants a kiss on my neck.

"I knew you wouldn't leave me! I knew you wouldn't leave me," I cry.

Momma grabs me dragging me into the car, my old Momma, the one that loves me. I see it in her eyes, the sparkle is back, that loving sparkle. I am mad at them for sending me away, but in that moment, I can't be mad, I am crying in happiness, my Momma, my Daddy!

"Please, don't leave me, Please! Please, not ever!" I break down in more tears of joy. On Momma's lap, my arms clamped around her neck, my head over her shoulder we pass bushes as high as the car. "Momma the black berries were in, millions of them. Grandma picked them. But she isn't fast like Amber. She needed Amber to help!" Loaded bushes line the road with black dots, still green leaves, thorns and long straight runners reaching out to us.

Momma cries holding me tight as we drive the last few hundred yards to the house. Glad to see me she cries, more she sobs that blankness is in her eyes. What is the matter with Momma?

We stay a few days. During those days I hear things. Little ears can be big, and ignored.

"I think she is going to be OK now," Daddy tells Grandpa. "It was pretty rough for a while, but Sarah has stopped crying all the time, is becoming herself."

Grandpa nods. "What did you tell the children?" Grandpa asks looking at me playing in the yard as if I am deaf and can't hear.

"There is not much to tell. The older ones know. The smaller ones, well what can we tell them?" Daddy no longer cries, but there is sadness in his eyes as he talks to my Grandfather.

"I guess that Amber is in heaven. That should be enough for those not old enough to understand," Grandpa says, having lost two children, one to the flu and one to pneumonia. He has bitter experience and has had to tell his living children before, but nothing like this.

"Yea, that is what we did. The only problem is the preacher. He says Amber never repented her sins, sins he knows she committed, that she died in sin. He never mentioned her being in heaven. That's what is wrong with Sarah. She believes Amber is in hell because she failed to make her repent! Do you have any ideas?"

"It is a matter of opinion. Amber was of the age of accountability, but I know she accepted the Lord Jesus in her heart. Our preacher says that's a one time thing. You accept Jesus, then you are a Christian always, go to heaven when you die. Other preachers say you have to repent every time you sin, and that only one sin can keep you out of God's kingdom. Your preacher one of those?" Grandpa looks at Daddy.

"Yeah! Sarah believes it too, that's the problem," Daddy puts his head down.

They head in the house for a cup of coffee. I keep playing. Is my sister in hell? Why didn't she go up when the preacher asked her to go up? Is she dead? What is dead? Seeing a dead cat in the road, is Amber like that? What is pneumonia, the flu, and why do they kill children? I have questions, a lot I don't understand and no answers. Why doesn't anyone talk to me? If they do can I understand?

After we go home our preacher preaches a sermon about hell, as if he ever preaches about anything else. It's a place where bad men, women, boys and girls go and live forever. He talks about it a lot and emphasizes repenting as soon as possible and not putting it off like a sweet young girl in hell because she delays repenting. Momma cries every time he says that. There is this other place, heaven, where good men, women, boys and girls go!

If good people go to heaven, and Amber is dead, then Amber is in heaven. She believes in Jesus. She is in heaven. That is what Grandpa's preacher believes. Why does our preacher think she is in hell? It doesn't make sense. Why do you have to follow different rules in different churches to go to heaven? Churchmen talk about one God, then believe that their God is different from other churches' God.

I know that if Amber is dead, Amber is in heaven where God lives, and waits for me.

When I get there she will be at the gate saying, "Come on, Sharon!"

I think that and will think that unless our preacher scares me into thinking something else. Besides, no one has told me Amber is in heaven, I over heard it. She will come home. I believe that. It is time to pick apples at farmer Miller's place. Amber will take me. After we go home I sit by Amber's door or on the front porch watching around the corner. I do this for days, whenever I think of her, but no Amber. Keeping up my prayers, I pray at every meal for her to come home.

Holding Momma's hand walking down the street I see Albert. Breaking away I run to him.

"Albert, Albert!"

Reaching down he scoops me up hugging me like an old friend.

"Albert, where is Amber, please bring her home! Please bring her home!"

Time and distance heal some things, some things never heal, some men, some women never heal. Albert loves my sister. Does he ever stop? Tears rain down his face. He falls to his knees still gripping me in his arms. What is the matter with Albert? Standing, he hands me back to Momma never saying a word. He walks away.

Months later, winter, Sunday, Sunday school over, preaching services are starting. I am looking forward when he appears beside me, slipping in late walking to our pew. It's Albert! I smile at him. Momma smiles at him. Daddy smiles, with a question in his eyes, *Why is Albert here?*

The preacher starts, softly speaking, loud then soft. Setting a rhythm delivering one of his best hell fire and damnation sermons he plays for Albert. At the end he comes down to the front and gives the invitation looking directly at Albert, sitting in Amber's place.

Without wasting a second Albert rises and walks to the alter kneeling before the preacher tears in his eyes. Albert is repenting? Momma smiles, glad Amber's passing has a silver lining. The preacher ecstatic over a new convert glows, turns to the congregation and starts to extol the power of God to reach the most heathern sinners and bring them to the light.

Albert stands sheepish, uncomfortable in a long winter coat before our congregation. Turning to the other side of the congregation the preacher takes his eyes off Albert, a mistake. Albert's expression changing, he slips his hand in his coat pocket. Daddy's mouth opens. He knows Albert. He knows the boy is not there to repent.

A short plain clothes officer's billy club in his hand Albert frees it from his coat pocket.

The preacher thinks, *Is something wrong?*

Expressions of the congregation say, *something is wrong*!

The preacher turning toward Albert, his mouth open, wonders.

The boy, with a strength festering since Amber's loss, swings the club meeting the preacher's mouth. Teeth and blood splatter. The preacher, the same height as Albert and twice the weight, freezes blood pouring from broken teeth and cut lips. In the presence of a boy now a man the preacher is not towering over a pintsize girl. Not verbal, real violence this is not the preacher's kind of war, but a war he starts nonetheless.

"I'll go to hell with Amber!"

Turning to walk out Albert has repented enough. Three men move into the isle to stop him.

Daddy steps out, "Let him go!"

A path clears. Albert walks toward the door steadily with the anger and the fire of hatred in his eyes.

Turning as he opens the door he yells back, "You ever say Amber is in hell again and I WILL kill you!"

The preacher never again mentions Amber or uses my sister as an example in a sermon, fearing Albert. Passing the offering plate for dental work it takes three months and jonquils blooming again before he speaks clearly. Gold in his smile he has shinny new bridges, old thoughts.

Seeing my mother's pain the preacher consoles her, in ways my father does not see or hear. Heart broken I hear my mother crying after his visits. Is it her fault? Was Amber a bad girl? Is my mother too lax, to permissive?

The preacher says she is. "Sarah, I know you love your children: everyone does. How often do you spank them? How often do you with righteous rage blister their bottoms? God says, 'Spare the rod, spoil the child.' There is an innate evil in the hearts of people, Sarah. Let it slip out, let it fester in the night or during the day and it grows. Hell waits. Strike against evil when it is young, growing and it dies."

"Amber was a good girl, preacher. She loved the Lord," Momma says.

"I know she did, Sarah, but she died in sin. Your life is not over. You have six children in your home. Six more chances to bring souls to God. I know you will do what is right," the preacher pats my Momma's arm, says a prayer and leaves.

Momma spanks me for having a bad thought an hour later.

"I am a good girl, Momma. I wasn't thinking anything bad!"

"We are bad, bad inside," Momma says leaving me crying on the porch.

Filing a complaint against Albert Monday morning after the incident the preacher has no sympathy for the young man, a willful sinner, who removes seven of his front teeth and a piece of jaw bone.

The judge, not a fan of the preacher or a man who can let an assault on a high ranking citizen slide, sits impassively on the bench. No jury necessary, Albert denies nothing, is ready to take his punishment.

"Son, we can't allow you to be detoothing one of the most toothy leaders of our community. Do you understand that?" The judge says.

"Yes sir," Albert says.

"If I let you loose will you do it again?"

Albert doesn't answer.

"I understand you said you would kill him if he does it again. Is that right?" the judge says.

"Yes sir," Albert says.

"Son, I understand how you feel, but---" the judge speaks directly to the preacher. "Preacher, if I were you, I would shut up about the girl this boy loves!" then to Albert, "I can't have it son. Do you want to go to prison? I can send you there for two years if that is what you want."

The preacher smiles, the hole in the front of his mouth exposing his tongue.

"No sir, but he IS going to stop talking about Amber!" Albert says.

"I can't make him stop talking, but I can put you away," the judge puts his hands down on the table.

"Sending you to jail is a waste. OK, two years in the state prison, or enlist in the Army for four. Which is it?" the judge raises his gavel.

"The army, sir!"

Satisfied, would the judge have been any less angry than Albert at the Bible thumper saying his dead wife is in hell? Being older and more callous, would he have done anything about it? His sympathy is with the boy. The night before, peace time, a stagnant army, no recruits needed, it cost the judge five drinks, and a get-out-of-jail-free for a brawler of the recruiter's choice to make a place for Albert.

Waiting, watching as Albert signs the enlistment papers the judge knows the boy, a Gypsy's son, smart, a high school graduate, settled and descent, the judge wants him away from his past in a better place with a future. The recruiter has the papers filled out before the hearing starts and nods to the judge.

"Case dismissed pending completion of four years military service." Then looking more closely at Albert, "Son, look at me!"

"As a further condition, except for a family emergency, if you enter this county any time in those four years you are to be arrested on sight and the charges reinstated. Do you understand, Mr. Hensley?" The judge has to protect one loud mouthed preacher.

"Yes sir."

In the court room, quiet, sitting in the back, Daddy watches. Albert leaves tomorrow on the night bus for basic training. Daddy invites him for Sunday dinner on Tuesday night.

I am glad to see him sitting by Amber's chair at supper that night.

Albert insist on leaving her chair empty for the meal saying, "She is always with me. I will never forget her. I will never stop loving Amber!" he starts to cry. Then the anger comes, "It doesn't end here. Nobody is going to ever do to any other girl what was done to Amber, I swear it!"

Daddy says, "Son, Albert, you were going to be my first son-in-law. I think of you like a son. You are my son. Let me talk to you." He motions for Albert to come with him. Putting his arm around Albert's shoulder, it is time for one of Daddy's porch talks. The Knox hums. Daddy drives him home.

## Chapter 14
# THE PREACHER'S GOD

Bette Davis and Joan Crawford, actresses, are not friends, even in old age. When Joan Crawford dies Bette Davis reportedly says, "You should only say good of the dead. Joan Crawford is dead. Good!"

Cute and witty for a Hollywood feud, not so for a man talking about a loved young woman, the preacher's example makes an impression. Working hard to learn political correctness, to say the right things at the right times, I learn that a person with power and authority, must remember the rules.

Shouting, rattling windows, people remember Pastor John's sermons. That day silent, spitting teeth, the preacher's visual image is louder than words. Are his words remembered? The sound of teeth clinking as they hit the sanctuary floor is remembered. Everyone remembers that sermon. Talking openly about Amber through his own front teeth, does he talk about her being in hell once he is toothless? Fearing the preacher, not liking what he says about Amber and how it affects Momma. It is better after Albert stops him.

His talk changes, not his mind. The churchman adjusts little when corrected. Steadfast in the faith he calls it. He is the preacher, a bull, a man. Does he look to the cause of his injury, or is he satisfied with punishing the messenger? He mentions Amber no more, even in our living room on his visitations.

He starts to once.

Before he gets it out my brother Nathan asks, "Preacher, Albert wrote me a letter. He is doing OK in the Army. He won a marksmanship medal. Is there anything you want me to tell him when I write him back?"

The preacher blinks, moves to another subject.

The day of my sister's loss is an oak tree falling on my Mother's heart. She screams. Daddy holds her. She changes. She goes silent, unresponsive. Over the next month others care for my brothers, sister and I. Helping with daily visits Pastor John works with her. She comes back.

Intent, meek, entreating, he comes doing his job, caring for a parishioner injured of soul. A dead child, a wonderful young woman gone, is that what it takes to make a change? Pastor John sees. An illegitimate son of a Jew, born to a gentile mother, can be white, Aryan, can put his ancestry behind him, can become a chancellor, the leader of a nation, or a pastor, the leader of a church.

African ancestry, how do you hide that? We are different. Among Africans is the widest variety of genetic adaptations among humans. Features that help to breathe and dissipate heat, melanin that protects against sun and skin cancers, blood that is immune to malaria and other tropical diseases, height that makes reaching high, seeing far and moving fast easier, height that makes running under low bushes and hiding in small places easier, how many useful traits among us are missing in other races? Africans are the tallest people on earth, and the shortest. We have broad deep noses in central Africa, long straight ones in the northern African deserts. We, from the land of the original humans, have adapted to the Dark Continent's varied and severe climates. Tropical heat, diarrhea, and ideal conditions breed parasites and diseases originating in Africa and brought to us from every point on earth. We adapt.

Swine flu and other European diseases destroy the Native Americans leaving vast unpopulated expanses of good land for white settlers. Disease resistant whites live and prosper in the New World, especially the temperate New World. American Indians lacking the resistance to white man's diseases are overwhelmed by European invasions. A small percentage dies in battle. Most die in their homes racked with the fever of infection.

Africa? White invasions? For how many thousands of years have Caucasian hordes rode into Africa and disappeared? Are the conquests successful? Are the occupations? African diseases, jungles and climate affect Africans, are deadly to other races. Whites come, they conquer, they settle, they die, the Africans come back. Africa remains unoccupable to white masses until modern climate control, technology and disease abatement.

African conquests outside the highlands and southern tip remain colonies with a few white overseers, colonial rulers and African workers. In the non tropical Americas European whites do well replacing Indian populations killed by disease. There is a sustained immigration from Europe. From the Southern United States through tropical South America there is a problem. Indians dying from European diseases leave no labor force.

Tolerating tropical diseases and climate blacks are needed to work these hotter climate zones after the mass death of American Indians. Black slaves work and survive from Tidewater swamps to Brazilian plantations. In heat and sun that gives cancer to pale skin and heat stroke to brains cooled by small nasal passages, black people produce. Africans, hard to kill, hard hide in populations of less genetic diversity, the unwilling immigrants to America, are they ever appreciated, ever accepted?

My sister, visibly black, amber, and a Gypsy boy, visibly white, betrothed, preparing to wed, didn't we see trouble coming? Pastor John did. He sees more ahead. The illusion and foundation of racial superiority depends on preventing intermarriage. Where intermarriage occurs racial lines blur. Where blacks are part of the blend their increased resistance to challenges of disease and climate results in numerical domination. Maintaining racial purity prevents European rulers being overwhelmed by brown masses who become more and more difficult to tell from masters.

This happened with the Jews. The Jews, a Middle Eastern people, were dispersed throughout Europe two thousand years ago. Originally identifiable by darker skin and other Middle Eastern traits, after two thousand years of inter breeding only yellow arm bands make them identifiable. Eastern European Jews, the classic look used to depict Israelites, is also the look of Eastern European Christians. Anti-Semitic discrimination depends on registration. Some modern European countries put religion on passports and identification papers, most don't.

In America custom and law prevented Africans, brought in as slaves, from genetically absorbing the ruling population. Other groups intermarry (with the exception of a more limited and shorter lived legal discrimination against Orientals). American Indians, looked down on, but legal to marry remain somewhat identifiable on reservations, with a good number of chiefs and tribal elders passing more easily as natives on the streets of Dublin than Muskogee. They are being absorbed.

After 300 years in America African Americans are excluded from a fundamental human right, two people in love marrying. Remaining illegal and unacceptable for a black and white to marry in most states until the 1960s only our minority is uniquely excluded from the American melting pot. Jews, Greeks and others having distinct cultures on entering the United States and tend to live in their own communities and marry within their own groups for a generation. Two or three generations later the majority of their grandchildren marry outside their culture resulting in blending and acceptance in the main stream. Until discrimination ends in marriage it continues. In the Caribbean interracial mixing and marriage is usual, and racial discrimination is going.

Recently on a trip to Puerto Rico I heard a conversation. A person of obvious racial prejudice makes a comment, "Them niggers sure do move slow!"

The person to whom the comments are made, a Caucasian Puerto Rican man, says, "I know what you mean. My sister is exactly like that."

The conversation ends. One man retreats red faced and necked. The other spits as he walks away.

Intermarriage on the island is common and accepted. It is impossible to tell if the person you are talking to is or is related by marriage to someone of African descent. This is ending racial prejudice. Prejudice against sisters, wives and brothers is rare.

Throughout the history of the United States it is acceptable for white men to spread their genetic material through out the black population. It is not acceptable to marry them. Had Albert taken my sister to his house and had ten children with her, without marrying her, racists would not have raised an eyebrow. Giving her potential children legitimate status violates white Southern racial law. White women, unlike white men, are not permitted black lovers, marriage or not.

Missing, presumed dead, what happened to my sister? The only Black family in town, in a community never inoculated with racial hate. We are accepted. We are free to be ourselves, except in times such as these, the depression. Poor white Southerners coming north, hobos on trains spreading throughout the nation, people move. Hate moves. People dispossessed, angry, blaming something they blame another people, another tribe. In Germany it is the Jews. In America it is the blacks. In Germany, the hatred of one man, elected, can extinguish Jews, Gypsys, Homosexuals and other minorities where the people acquiesce. Stopped by the people it publicly ends. Harbored in the hearts of thousands wandering the roads, hungry, seeing a man in a clean pressed suit, a nigger, looking on their own white skin in dirt old clothes, hatred flairs, violence happens. Harbored in the heart of one person, an assassin, it waits, strikes without warning, can take a girl walking to see her love on a sunny summer day.

Prejudice relating to sex knows no depressions, no prosperity. There is always a man, or woman longing, wanting, not having. The rule, the anger against interracial marriage flairs in the best of times. "Why could she (or he) love that nigger, when they could love me!" It starts. In silent disgust or violence it ends. Being a child, does it matter, does sex and marriage come into it? When sex does and we want marriage, to be with the one we love, the problems start. Hate appears. Jealous eyes stop seeing a man or woman, but a nigger, a Jew, someone else less than human fondling a member of their tribe, one they should be fondling.

Defined as a race noted for broad smiles, happy ways, idleness and lack of intelligence we are made so by laws prohibiting our learning to read, or allowing us to pursue occupations requiring literacy in an era when 75% or whites cannot read or write. During slavery Black men, like my Daddy, are the overwhelming majority of mechanics. Black men use and repair the equipment and tools of the South. Without their technical skill, many of the machines of the plantations would never have been invented.

The second generation beyond this legal repression, Daddy teaches us chess, science, mathematics, the value of work, thinking and self respect. Momma reads to us and gives us a better education than others get at school. In a town of whites, we are accepted. They, my parents and the people of our town, let us think we are human, like everyone else, as good as everyone else.

Pastor John sees the error. Intelligence, hard work, values and acceptance in one small community do not make white. The preacher allowing us in his church we should be grateful, and are. Other churches overseen from a distance cannot accept us, have rules against us in their congregations. Some churches have it in their dogma that Blacks do not have souls are not fit for worshiping God. Four score years and seven ago Abraham Lincoln believes we do not have souls. In 80 years since Lincoln the times they are a'changing, they have not changed.

A victim of discrimination, the preacher never reveals his history and passes. Thomas Jefferson has Middle Eastern blood. Was he of Jewish descent? Most Middle Eastern DNA in Europe is Jewish in origin. Who knows until modern genetic scientists check his DNA? The preacher knows his past. Making the Aryan jump he goes through a special transition of self hate. No one hates Jews, like a Jew, that is not a Jew, that doesn't want to be a Jew. This is our preacher.

He understands and doesn't hate us as he hates his own, but sees us as others hating us see us. He empathizes with both. Did Jefferson know? Did he compensate by opposing slavery, by living with and loving a black woman most of his life and by creating the free nation we love? Sinning, hiding, compensating and changing can be good. Hiding his confusion well does the preacher hide it from himself? Does he like Jefferson seek to create a better world? Or does he seek to destroy the evil within himself by destroying those who are what he is.

On the one hand he accepts us. He gives us the chance to pass and become part of the church. On the other he loathes us. Nonwhite, not being what we are supposed to be, openly sinning as he secretly sins he watches us. From one who knows because he is, he knows a nigger when he sees one. He smiles hides the anger not revealing himself. He helps consciously and hates with hell's fire when the demon slips out walking in air.

Through the years the local people never suffer prejudice because of their race or religion. They see us as different and have no emotion about it. We are people, neighbors to them. Are we stupid, slow, lazy? Having seen no others of our kind, they know the truth about us from us. They know my daddy is smart, hard working and a friend worth having. They know my Momma knows the Bible inside out, as well as the commentaries and reads better than most school teachers. She teaches the women's Sunday school class for five decades.

A homogenous society with no racial, ethnic discrimination or experience, problems of the South don't follow us until the mobility that brings us to a place we can be as we are, brings old demons behind us on wheels. Other Southerners come, real white Southerns. With them come old thoughts. With them come old prejudices.

We owe Pastor John. Momma and Daddy know that. He welcomes us into his church in an era when few American pastors would. Now devastated, eaten alive by the greatest sorrow a mother can have, she is open to change more than at anytime since her youth. She needs her pastor, the support of the church.

Momma, following the preacher, listens to what he says. This time he goes to the core of parenthood.

"Sarah, I have watched you and your family a long time. It is too late for Sammy or Amber. The older ones are set in their ways, but the young ones. You can make their lives better, more in tune with reality. Sharon is smart. David is too. They all are. What is missing is the recognition that all have sinned and come short of the glory of God, their inadequacy, their place in the scheme of life.

"You have failed to instill in them their place. Sarah, you are what you are, what you were born to be. We are all sinners, and need to focus on that. From the time I have known you, you have given them logical explanations, made everything a learning experience, expected them to be learners, logical and knowledgeable. What place in the world is there for them with that education? Can they go to a good university? Can they be officers or leaders? Can they marry whomever they please? You know they can't. You need to put the focus on what they can be, not what they can't. Humble them. Teach them they are sinners, unworthy of the glory of God. Make them ready to take a lower station in life. Humble them, Sarah. Humble them before they are lost!"

Saying this in our living room, Pastor John asks Momma, "Let's pray together."

Kneeling by the couch they pray.

"Lord, Lord Jesus, we pray you visit your rod of chastisement on this family. Protect them, correct them. Make them as they are--- sinners, having fallen short of your law, needing your staff and your rod. Break the arrogance of uppityness, bow them down before you. Bow them down. Visit your Holy Spirit on them, help them, protect them from themselves and others as they learn thy ways," he says.

"Amen!" Momma begins to open up, "Help us Lord. Help us Lord Jesus. Help me take the uppityness out of my babies. Help me take it out before sin kills them. Help me. Help me God. Please help me!" Momma cries.

"That's it, Sarah, that's it. Let it out. It has been in you a long time. You have wanted to be what you are not, and let the children see that in you, grow into it. Now you've got to whip it out of them, whip it out of them," he looks on our mother.

She sees, "I am going to do better with my babies, preacher! The young ones aren't going to sin like the old ones. I am going to do my best to see to that."

For the next month, every afternoon, while my father is at work, Pastor John comes, bringing ladies from the church, praying with my mother, praying for change, telling her what that change must be, repeating it daily for a month as Momma cries, mourns and makes Pastor John's reality, her reality. The racial system born of relegating diversity to inferiority, every person born to their place, Momma accepts as most minorities accept creating inferiority where none is.

The preacher comes, comforting, talking, forming her thoughts until she is ready, then he asks Daddy to gather the family. We come home, to a different home, a different Momma.

The preacher has ideas, a complex web of theology and beliefs that is supported by the congregation and congregations over America. At age five or even eight or ten, do I understand theoretical Christian theology, do I understand the caste system, a system that makes me be less than I am, that tells me I am stupid, when I, and most of my brothers and sisters rise to the top of our classes in every subject? The preacher has power over our mother. That power makes his opinions facts that as children we must accept.

Nathan, the oldest still at home, is almost 16.

Daddy kids him, "That Clark girl, have you been making eyes at her?"

Nathan blushes, "She doesn't know I am alive, Daddy. She likes the big boys, the football players."

"Unhuh," Daddy gives him a sideways look.

Momma hears, waits.

Two days later she sees Nathan talking to the girl on the street. Two hours later he comes in the door hungry for supper.

"I saw you! I saw you with that girl! Get over the table--- now!" Momma has her paddle out.

Giving him the worst paddling he has ever had Nathan sobs, "I didn't do anything! I didn't do anything wrong!"

Momma says nothing getting dinner ready.

It is the same for George, Thomas and Mary. Almost every day at least one of them is bent over Momma's table wailing as she blisters their bottoms.

Most often they repeat Nathan's response, "Momma, I didn't do anything wrong!"

Being right or wrong changes nothing. Momma paddles them for sin and evil of another standard.

David and I, seven and five, at the beginning of the years of hell in our home, are we too young for paddling over the table? The smooth piece of polished cherry wood we take it in shorter strokes over her knee.

Wood in our stove cooks our food. Wood in our furnace heats our home. Wood in our fireplace blazes yellow-red sprinkling light and radiating heat in our living room. One small piece of wood in Momma's kitchen never burns; it stays warm heated by our bottoms.

I drop a cup. It breaks. Momma spanks. I leave Samantha on the porch, forgetting to bring her in. Momma spanks. I run hard hearing the thud. Wulfie yelping a horrible yelping my dog begs for help. She lies dying in a puddle of blood.

I scream, "Wulfie! Wulfie! Help Wulfie, Momma!"

Momma, not heading for my dog, she cuts me off before I reach the street.

Momma spanks, "You can not go in the street without me holding your hand, no matter what!"

"Wulfie!" I cry.

My dog closes her eyes, dead like Amber.

That time after Momma finishes spanking me, for a second there is a change.

My old Momma holds me saying, "I'm sorry, Baby!"

Then the preacher talks to her. "Sarah, you must be strong. Resist the urge to show compassion. Punish without letting emotions weaken you. What if it had been Sharon in the street? Teach them to obey the rules before it's too late!"

We enter a darkness, a hell, a place inhabited by sin, evil and danger. Momma sees it everywhere, the preacher helps her spot it and whip it out. Some days she is my old Momma, then in a minute she changes, is the new Momma. There is a cold fire in her eyes, the new Momma, the Momma I fear. Where is my old Momma, the Momma that loves me?

Daddy doesn't change, but away at work, the fireplace of light he puts in our lives is small compared with Momma's every-day presence. Momma, the furnace in the center of our home, takes on a red glow, as the preacher stokes log after log of hell fire and brimstone into her fire box. Hell's conflagration and bottoms burning, the fire in Momma's eyes rekindles every Sunday morning. Smoldering puffs of smoke in her stares she watches as Daddy plays with us and takes his day. Monday after Daddy is gone her paddle burns.

We once wait for Church with anticipation. We go willingly. Now we are forced to go. The older children see the preacher differently. Once looking at him with respect and fear, the fear is there. Is that what I see in their eyes, fear? Is that what I see in Nathan's eyes?

The preacher asks him, "Nathan how it this old truck doing? Is it getting you to work OK?"

The preacher runs his hands over the Model A's fender. It was Sammy's pickup.

"Yes sir, it's doing fine," Nathan says.

After the preacher leaves he carefully wipes the man of God's hand prints off the fender and looks toward the street with a cold stare. There is fear. There is something else in my brother's eyes--- hate!

Nathan goes to church the next two years, never wincing at the preacher's tirades, never responding to a call to repent and never attending church after he leaves home.

George, when grown, goes to church, occasionally, sits and listens. He follows his wife's faith. A dull stare as the priest talks, does he pay attention? At school, an honor student, sharp and alert, he hears. Church is a place he goes, listens and hears nothing, blocks its influence and leaves. There as he was in the days of his youth listening, does he absorb anything after Momma's change? Does he feel the spirit or love of God in church?

Thomas the youngest of my older brothers is eleven when this starts. At thirteen puberty hits as does Momma.

"I didn't do anything, Momma," he cries.

Having witnessed Sammy and Amber's fates, having witnessed Nathan and George's punishment for acts never done, he changes. Girls, white girls, the only kind there are in our world, is that the problem? If there were a black girl, would Momma approve? There is no black girl. He learns and changes. What ever heterosexual energy he has, what ever desires to kiss, hold hands or be with a girl pass. He never dates. He never marries.

Mary, unlike Amber, more aggressive, stronger, sees a way out.

Almost four years after Amber leaves, Mary leaves. A day after she has a terrible whipping from Momma she asks, "Daddy, can I spend the summer with Grandma and Grandpa. They don't have help anymore. I can help to them."

Crying Daddy puts her in the back of a bus heading South the day after school is out.

She and Grandma grow close. Grandma travels North with her for a visit when summer is over. Going to church with us I notice the same cold stare at the preacher in my Grandmother's eyes that I see in Nathan's. Has my sister talked to her? Does Grandma know what is happening in our home?

As summer wanes Mary asks, "Daddy, can I go to school at Grandma's? I'll be dating soon. There are boys I can date, and Grandma and Grandpa could use the help."

"We sure could use the help," Grandma says.

"It is important that she have boys she can date. I understand that," Daddy says

My sister never returns home to stay.

Five years later Mary marries a boy of our race, a boy that becomes a preacher, one who loves God and teaches love. She loves Grandma's church and her husband's church. Mary never attends our church again.

Younger do David and I fare better or worse? Our personalities and main paradigms of thinking already formed we can change our outer responses better than our older siblings. Used to the paddlings we change the outer layers of our inner selves. To an older child home turned to hell, is hell. To a younger child a home that is hell, is home, what we know. We adapt. We go inside. Outside we do what we need to do.

"Why is Sharon always in trouble?" Momma asks grandma. "Not a day goes by that there isn't a note from her teacher, or she is into something."

"Sarah, don't you know---," Grandma breaks down, cannot finish.

Sunday comes.

Daddy, avoiding Grandma, has to start the car. Before he reaches the crank Grandma corners him in the garage. Daddy can't look her in the eye. He knows she knows.

"Sam, can Sharon come live with us too, and David, the other boys?"

"She is not a bad mother. She is a good mother. Maybe a little to strict, that is all, a little too strict. I can't let you have my children. I need them. Sarah needs them."

Then on another part of reality, Daddy looks Grandma straight in the eyes, "You know it is different for boys. A girl like Mary needs to be with our people, can adapt. If she makes a mistake, smiles at a white boy, nothing will happen. We know that. If she makes a big mistake and goes to bed with him, nothing will happen, except he won't marry her. We know that.

"The boys, it's different, Grandma. They have been raised with white children. They don't feel they are any different. If they smile at a white girl, you know what will happen. It might happen here. It will happen there. I can't let the boys go South, Grandma. It is too dangerous. David, I could, he is young enough to learn the ways and not get killed while he is learning, but not the older boys," Daddy says.

David doesn't want to go.

Asking me, Daddy says, "Do you want to go live with Grandma?"

I say, "Grandma's nice. I like Grandma. But Daddy, I love you. I love Momma. You promised you wouldn't ever leave me again when you picked me up from Grandma's last time. Don't you remember? Please don't leave me again!"

Why is Daddy hugging me so tight? Why is he crying? He tells me his best story that night, then after I am supposed to be asleep I hear him talking to Momma.

Daddy quiet, I never hear him talk loud. He is talking loud.

He shouts, "Sarah, if the children need paddling clear it with me first from now on. Do you understand?"

"But the preacher says---" Momma says.

"I don't give a damn what the preacher says. I am the head of this house. You will obey me. You will listen to me, NOT HIM! DO YOU UNDERSTAND?"

I never heard my father swear before that evening or after it.

"You don't understand, Sam!" Momma talks back.

"If you ever paddle any of the children without my permission, I will use it on you when I get home. DO YOU UNDERSTAND?"

"But Sam, you know you can't do that. You can't. Don't you remember? Please Sam. You can't!"

A trimble in our Mother's voice she has heard the preacher now she hears her husband.

I don't hear anything else. They talk in quieter tones.

In the morning Grandma is all smiles. Momma is quiet, confused. She wants to do what the preacher says, will do what my father says.

Daddy has a cold set to his jaw. Kissing Momma, he looks deep in her eyes then goes to work.

"What did you say to him, Momma?" Momma says.

Grandma never answers her, smiles. They get up to do the dishes together. Momma helps, Grandma washes. A role reversal, a role as it was. Did Momma follow Grandma? Why is she following her now, acting as if she were in Grandma's home rather than her own?

The authority of the preacher's does not vanish. The teachings of the church remain the same after Grandma's visit and Daddy's changing the rules. A God of wrath, a God of vengeance and a God of punishment remains the God of our church. Mary hides a crucifix in the space over the front door to protect our home from the God of our church.

A month passes. Then Momma paddles Thomas without asking Daddy. Having let this slide because Momma is cutting down on the paddlings Daddy doesn't want to be involved in punishment. He wants her to use it reasonably without his presence or participation. This time she goes too far.

"Did I tell you to ask me before paddling the kids?"

"Please Sam, I'm sorry. I won't do it again! Please don't do it!"

Momma standing before Daddy he has the paddle out.

She starts to cry, "I'm sorry!"

Momma bends over the table.

"Don't let it happen again!"

Putting it back under the cabinet unused Daddy walks in the living room. In my entire life at home Daddy never paddles anyone. Momma asks if there is any question of my father's approval after that.

Four years after Amber leaves Grandma comes to visit. Normalization occurs. The preacher returns to a church authority. Daddy becomes the home authority. Momma drifts between them. The previous four years never vanish from my brothers', sister's or my memory. Stopping the unwarranted paddlings life is better. The new Momma still lurks after Sunday sermons.

## Chapter 15
# MY AUNT MINDY

*And I am nine*
    I watch a new side walk grow down Main Street. Piles of gray mud in wheelbarrows dump into frame squares. A man leans on a long handle with a flat board attached to the end, waits. Then as Momma lifts her paddle he lifts the board part way up and sends it smacking into the pile of cement. Pushing and pulling the man works the cement. He shapes it. Filling the square flat he jiggles the board vibrating the surface liquid smooth then moves on to the next square. He is efficient. He doe not waste a motion. A practiced worker, he makes concrete, has been making it a long time. Momma using her paddle, her trowel, is as efficient, and practiced in working our bottoms with her board. Am I fresh poured cement, concrete, smoothing into the shape I will be with the application of Momma's wooden trowel?
    Floaters level sections of gray mud into flat connecting squares extending down both sides of the road. Wooden sidewalks

downtown when I am born; concrete strips extend into residential neighborhoods.

Standing in front of the new chiropractor's office, on the corner of Elm and Main, his son gazes at the smooth gray surface. Pausing, then scratching something into the wet surface with a stick, once part of an oak tree in their yard, what is he writing?

*Are you supposed to be doing that?* I wonder then say, "What does it mean, E=MC2? Who is E, and who is MC2?"

"Energy equals mass times the speed of light squared. It's the equation whereby we know the amount of energy stored in matter, or the amount of matter that can be made by a certain number of joules of energy," he says.

*Is he going to keep going?*

He would, but I interrupt, "Are you supposed to be doing that?"

Good, that stops him.

He answers in English, "Why not? It's a blank slate for writing on, and will be here a long time, as long as the cement."

He looks at me like I should have known that. Isn't it obvious?

Taking the stick from him I say, "Sharon, my name is Sharon."

I scratch out the Sharon part in the corner of the gray square.

"What is your name?" I ask.

"Noble."

He scratches his name below mine. Now it's our piece of concrete with his E=MC2 and our names on it. That makes sense! In the morning when I pass by on my way to school it's already too hard to write on with a stick. With a chalk someone has put a plus between our names!

*Who did that?*

Being nine, in my last few years of basic formation before the girl thing hits, I talk to Noble. I don't want any pluses connecting us!

*Who did that?* I wonder all the way to school.

Mist gray eyes, black pupils staring right through you, a bigger girl can have plusses in her eyes for a boy like that, not a nine-year-old. I am still fresh concrete, not mature enough for boys to be writing plusses on my surface. I wonder all day, *Who did that?* I have trouble concentrating on my teacher's lessons.

Did Aunt Mindy put that plus on our piece of sidewalk? It can't be her. Her bus arrives while I am having lunch in the cafeteria. I see it

*When The Jonquils Bloom Again: Book One*

in the morning on the way to school. Never finding out who did, my name, his name and his equation are still there thirty years later without the plus. An spring downpour fixes the plus.

Aunt Mindy waits for me at home. A special person, Aunt Mindy puts plusses on my life. She loves me. Seeing that writing on the side walk every day as I walk to school, it reminds me: both she and my square of sidewalk appearing in my life on the same day, is that a coincidence?

She helps me. Is that why Grandma sends her? Five years passing, do I still miss Amber? Does anything fill the hole in my life Amber leaves? Momma changing, I change. Grandma sees it, a little girl hungry for love. Starving for the love I once had, I need love. What is this lack of affection doing to me? Of all her grandchildren, Grandma worries about me most.

Momma spanks me more lately.

The preacher's approach, "If the old paddling is not working, try a new paddle."

The preacher gives Momma a new paddle. He has a pile of them on his table outside the church door instead of Brussels' sprouts. Preaching a sermon on discipline his voice smacks the rafters and his eyes dance. Anticipating years of children dancing holding burning bottoms gives him joy. Every child, even Janet, is wide eyed and quiet as parents walk away carrying paddles home for later use.

Grandma hears about his sermon, and sends Aunt Mindy. Grandma thinks Aunt Mindy will help me and says, "The preacher's new paddle will make good kindling."

Can I help her? Am I what she needs? She is what I need, a grown woman that loves me as I am. Does she need a child's love? Does living quietly with grandma and grandpa work for her? Needing more excitement than being with people, living with us will be exciting, pregnant with hope! That is what grandma thinks.

Aunt Mindy's favorite niece, the one she loves from the first moment she sees me, she needs my laugh, my high pitched incessant chatter, my childish adoring love. If anything will save my Aunt Mindy, it will be me.

Before she comes to us, she goes alone to visit the Jonquils. Aunt Mindy picks her way down the hill. Crying, remembering the joy of that day long past, she, I, my mother, my grand aunt and most of all Uncle Jim admire the flowers in the field. She sees us in her mind, hearing our voices, feeling him holding her, smiling at her, happy two days before their wedding.

It's a dream, a fairy tale romance lasting seven years. She walks alone. Yellow blossoms, flowers sway in a light breeze as they did with all of us there, talking, smiling and drinking in their beauty. Holding me on her hip walking among the flowers those years ago, she is certain she'll be the mother of a little girl like me, Jim's baby girl! Every one of her sisters has at least two babies when she marries. She'll have a dozen. She wants a dozen! How many does she have? How many babies has she given her beloved husband?

Sitting among the flowers, yellow, they bob around her without making a sound. Quiet, like their nursery, with never a baby's cry, the field is empty. Aunt Mindy cries alone without a child to say, "What's the matter, Momma?"

"I want Jim's baby. I want Jim!" she sobs.

Her eyes flood dripping in rising water.

Water gurgling almost to the jonquils it is a spring flood. Waters of sadness surround her. Thinking, crying, looking back she wades out up to her knees in the creek. Up this year more than in the last nine years, it swirls, is deep in the middle. Aunt Mindy sees the girl, a child, waiting for her in the ripples across the water. A little girl in a blue old fashion dress, she too is a daughter lost, childless.

Seeing the girl, about my age, waving franticly to him, Grandpa stops plowing, looks. *What the heck is she doing in the creek?* Past her he sees Aunt Mindy already up to her waist in the muddy water. Grandpa running down the hill splashes after my pretty aunt.

"What the hell are you doing?" He says.

"I was--- I was---" Aunt Mindy says.

Going back to look for the girl after he saves Aunt Mindy, there isn't a trace, not a foot print on the soft ground across the creek. After that they watch my youngest aunt closely.

Grandma thinks being with me now will give Aunt Mindy a reason to live. She needs someone who needs her. Old, my grandparents, have nothing for her to do or be on their farm, yet aren't old enough to need her as she needs to be needed. Not a mother, not a wife, not needed by anyone, she drowns in uselessness.

"Nobody needs me!" she says over and over as Grandma holds her.

Memories overwhelming her, walking by the soda shop where she and her husband sipped vanilla malts, seeing the old tree where he first kisses her, the field of Jonquils, and the run down front of what had been his car sales. Being home is not good for her.

She loves him. A woman discarded, she needs a new place with people that love her, without reminders of Jim, without an empty four bedroom home with a fully equipped nursery.

Playing with me the night before their wedding my soft baby pudginess increases the hunger in her, a baby hunger. Jim knows she loves me, a baby, not hers. Looking back and forth between me and her husband-to-be she begs him to quench the hunger with pleading eyes.

"Isn't she cute," she says.

Two nights later they make love for the first time knowing their love will grow into a baby like me. She whispers in his ear, "Give me a baby like Sharon!"

On coming home, he builds the nursery. A room with a crib, baby toys and furniture await their first child. Finding her huddling in a corner in that room crying when grandma comes for her, Aunt Mindy loses more than her husband. She loses her life. My pretty aunt's doctor asks grandma to come get her.

Giving her husband and his new wife the house Aunt Mindy leaves her dreams and hopes. She never has a baby. Her husband and his new wife do! Their house will have children, the children he and Aunt Mindy dream of having, but don't.

All she wants from her husband is love and babies. Not wanting his money and all it buys them, she doesn't ask for money. She wants him. Children are important to him. What would she give to get pregnant? Rather dying in childbirth than being childless, now every month as regular as her periods there is a check, a cold, dead, paper check. Meaning most to her it is his hand that writes it. Folding the expensive piece of paper she keeps it by her heart before cashing it.

If he knows when she is sad, he comes to her. His gold Cadillac makes the trip from the city to see her every time my grandmother calls him. His visits are the only things that make her smile.

Both of them crying, holding each other when he has to go, does he love her too? A man, why does he cry when he has to leave? He loves Aunt Mindy. Another new model is in his garage, one that is able to do what he marries Aunt Mindy to do, she waits for him at home, pregnant.

Withering, having no place to go Aunt Mindy goes home with her mother. Staying in her old room crying, Grandma says she needs to be with a family, with children. We get her.

Having her to myself for that first afternoon she stays with us, I think momma plans it that way. My forth grade class lets out early for a teacher's meeting. Momma is busy. Bringing her home, showing Aunt Mindy her room and telling her to take care of me, momma leaves.

Does Aunt Mindy bring me a teddy bear? Teddy, brown with big eyes and one ear flopped over, has that look, that hug me look. Loving him from that first day, as I do her, starts it. Being excited to meet my other stuffed animals Teddy bounces up and down on my lap. Then sitting still on the couch flopping over by Aunt Mindy he waits to meet his new brothers and sisters. Running upstairs bear hunting, there are bears hiding in the toy chest at the end of my bed. They jump out of the toy box into my arms. I look around them going down the stairs to avoid doing a flop, flop, crash into the living room. Now with Teddy there are more bears than a girl can carry in a single trip! Old bears dive onto the couch by Teddy, waiting their turn, each one of them hugs him and introduces themselves as Aunt Mindy watches smiling. Piling them on her lap I race upstairs to get my dolls.

Aunt Mindy sits silent on the couch, up to her collar bones in bears. When I come back she is as still as Teddy without me to animate her. Bringing out my dolls, Samantha, Alice and Belinda and introducing each of them to her I put them on her lap replacing the bears. Teddy and his new family are next to her in a bear pile getting acquainted as bears do. Snuggling together they are in a make believe couch cave hibernating. It is my dolls' time to be alive, animated.

"This is Belinda! You can see by her uniform, she's a cheerleader!"

Belinda flies up in the air and lands on Aunt Mindy's lap doing a split.

"This is Alice! Alice is really, really smart. She makes all A's and her Momma is really, really proud of her!"

Alice settles on Aunt Mindy's other knee, very lady like.

Showing her my favorite doll, being smaller, not as pretty, nor as good as the other dolls, I never know why she is my favorite. She is.

"This is Samantha! Samantha is a--- well--- Samantha wants to be a good girl, but she is a bad girl! She needs this to be a good girl."

I wave a used paint stirrer I find in the garage for Samantha. It is mostly white with a little light blue on it. It makes a good toy paddle.

Wanting to sit by Aunt Mindy I push bears to the side. With three bears on my lap, three dolls on hers and two more bigger bears next to me it is getting crowded.

Is this going as I expect? Sitting peering over Teddy's head I listen to the living room as quiet as a cemetery at midnight. Is this how I plan this? Not in a million years! I love being surrounded by my babies, bears and Aunt Mindy, but sitting? We sit! Why are we sitting? We should be playing! Doesn't she remember how to play with dolls?

"Aunt Mindy, did you play with dolls?"

She nods, not making a sound.

I grab Alice and Belinda. They are up in Aunt Mindy's face telling her about school, cheerleading and stuff.

"You are suppose to be talking to them Aunt Mindy!"

Aunt Mindy tries. Starting to ask them questions, she is out of practice!

She being stiff I put both dolls in her hands and grab Samantha. Samantha begins running around the room chattering like the sparrow does when I pick up it's baby last spring, then she comes back to Aunt Mindy and dives on Alice pecking her head like the sparrow dives on my head, pecking me. Alice begins boo hooing and saying how much it hurts like I did. Does Momma love me enough to spank that mean sparrow? Momma loves me, but can't do anything about the bird pecking me. It is difficult to catch a sparrow for a spanking. The momma sparrow flies away leading the baby bird and is gone.

It is different with Samantha. Being my doll, I do something about it! Samantha's dress pulled up, I start looking for my make believe paddle, the paint stirrer. Does it make enough noise?

I have to make noise for it, "WHACK! Whack! Whack."

Aunt Mindy stops me! "Sharon, I think Samantha needs some loving to be a good girl, not a spanking!" Taking her away from me, she smooths her dress down then hugs her close to her chest stroking her hair.

Not looking at Samantha or the other dolls, Aunt Mindy freezes, looking at me!

*Why is Aunt Mindy looking at me?*

I am not doing anything, just standing there sucking my thumb.

*Sucking my thumb! Why am I sucking my thumb?*

Being a big girl, nine, I don't suck my thumb! My ears burning and my face turning red it's hiding time! As fast as I can I sit down close to Aunt Mindy, covering myself with bears. My thumb remaining in my mouth I am sucking as hard as I can. Why doesn't it come loose? I try to quit nonchalantly taking it out and making believe my thumb has never been in my mouth! Sneaking a glance I see. She is looking at me!

*Why does Aunt Mindy have this soft look in her eyes?*

Reaching over to run her fingers through my hair Aunt Mindy has a hint of a smile. Samantha falls off her lap and lands head first on the floor! Aunt Mindy drops Samantha! Bears explode into motion sailing to find a place on the couch. I dive to save Samantha. Retrieving my doll, I almost smile at my aunt as I put Samantha back in her arms.

"Aunt Mindy, I think Samantha needs you to hold her some more!"

She hugs me!

*Why does she hug me? It's Samantha she drops!*

Sitting with her holding me for a long time, maybe a minute, I move around. First I hug Aunt Mindy then I hold Samantha and give her a hug.

I wiggle around, Aunt Mindy comes to life too! I want her to hold me. Holding me for stories Daddy holds me sometimes, and even Momma holds me sometimes, but neither of them as much as they do when I am little. Getting too big for being held, I am growing up. Does

Aunt Mindy know that? Hoping no one tells her I want her to hold me like she holds Samantha.

*Why didn't I think of that, holding my doll instead of paddling her?*

Always paddling Samantha for being bad that is her role, the bratty little sister that needs paddling, not the little girl, the doll, that needs loving.

This is swirling in my mind when the look in Aunt Mindy's eyes changes from soft sadness to a sparkle.

*What is she thinking?*

Aunt Mindy wants to share something with me. Liking Jonquils she brings a sack full of bulbs from my Grandparent's farm.

"Sharon, let's you and I get on some old clothes, and plant some Jonquils around the house for your mother. Do you have any old clothes?"

"Un huh!"

After making two trips to take the bears and dolls to my room, then arranging them really neatly on my bed, we are ready to change. She going to the guest room to rummage through her steamer trunk; I change in my room. Ten minutes later we are digging in momma's flower bed. We dig holes with two hand spades. Sliding in, little cloves point up before disappearing beneath the earth. We plant a hundred of them.

Fall, everything else in the flowerbed is gone from frost it's the time to plant bulbs. Summer to me, summer is in my heart filled with flowers. Planting the flowers with her makes me feel a love warmer than a hot August day, a good heat. My heart melts.

"Sharon, I have an idea! Let's let this be our secret! Our bulbs are in the ground. Next spring they will pop up and the flowers will bloom. Let's not tell anyone else we planted them. Your momma will be so surprised when she has new flowers next spring! It will be our secret, our surprise for your mother! What do you think?"

She smiling a secret smile at me, how can I say no?

"Oh, Aunt Mindy, that is— Yes, Yes— Momma will love that. I won't tell her, if you don't."

I love surprises, getting or giving them! As we plant them she tells me the story of the jonquils in Grandpa's field, and their history, about the girl in the blue dress. It seems I have heard it before. It almost seems

I have heard it before from Aunt Mindy. Being there smiling at my aunt, thinking it is a pretty story, sad, but pretty, I hug her. My dirty hands stain her blouse. Hugging me back she tells me she is glad to see me. She cries, not long, just a little.

It is time for me to share. I have a secret! Being dirty and in our old clothes it is a good time to show her my secret place. Taking her hand I get her up. Off to the woods we go. I want her to be part of that secret too. Taking me there with her every summer when I am little, Amber creates the special place. I take my best friend Helga when we are old enough to go alone.

This place, natural, public, part of woods owned by the plant, Amber builds the first lean-to, I remake it yearly. Taking branches, I make a shelter big enough for me and a friend. Going there when I need to be alone or am in trouble, it is my special place, a little girl's special place. Aunt Mindy fits, her head rubbing against the branches.

We sit and talk. Well, I talk. Listening, mostly she is quiet. Some of it is that she is a good listener. Some of it is from her pain. Feeling she is a failure after her husband leaves her she can't talk about it, bottling everything inside her. She makes me feel special despite her pain. Being a grown up, a registered nurse even, she listens to me.

Aunt Mindy treats me like a baby at times holding me like one, but other times she listens as if I am grown. A nine year old, it's special to be noticed. Now we share secrets! A few hours on a warm fall afternoon and years pass, a friendship, a love born long ago on my Grandmother's sofa fills in time passed. Smiling, I am happy.

Knowing she and I have things in common I know she is going to be a special friend in those first few hours. She is the baby of the family, like me. Knowing what another baby of the family needs she reads me. Aunt Mindy, my favorite aunt, becomes something more to me. We understand each other. At least she understands me.

Making her happy is my plan. That is what I am going to do, make her happy!

Nothing can go wrong, then does!

What is Officer Clancy doing here? He is at the door talking to Momma. Maybe it is something about church. He and Daddy are always doing something for the church.

"Sharon, my girl, how are you?" He speaks directly to me, "And this must be your Aunt Mindy?"

"Un huh!" I smile at him.

"Can we go inside, Sarah? It would be better to talk there."

*Why is he talking to Momma?*

He never talks to Momma. Daddy is his friend. Bringing them something to drink as the men talk, does Momma ever speak to Officer Clancy?

"Sharon, would you be putting your name on the sidewalk down on Main Street?"

Other kids do it. I am doing what they are doing. Noble, the chiropractor's son, says it is all right. It is a blank slate for writing permanent things.

"It's OK isn't it, Officer Clancy?" I say.

"No, Sharon, it isn't. It is defacing public property and carries a fine of fifty dollars," he says.

Momma sits down hard on the couch repeating, "Fifty dollars!"

*Isn't that more than Daddy makes in al days work?*

"I didn't know! Other kids are doing it!"

"That we know, Sharon. Lots of kids are doing it! The sidewalks are new, and the Mayor notices. He is not liking it, Sharon. He is really not liking it! When his honor is not liking something, it makes my life difficult."

The last part he says looking at Momma.

"Sharon, there is another bit there, three bits actually. '$E=MC2$,' someone scratched 'Sharon;' someone scratched 'Noble.' Then it looks as if someone added in chalk a plus, Sharon + Noble. What would you be knowing about this, Sharon?" Now he is questioning, the officer, not the deacon I know from church. "Who would be this Noble fellow, Sharon?"

With this he smiles, trying to make me stop shaking.

*How can I stop shaking with Momma looking at me that way? How?*

"I don't know who wrote that (at least the plus part) I don't. I want to know. Who did write it?"

"Well, someone that loves you, Sharon. A boy, maybe, someone that thinks you are afternoon sunshine after a cloudy morning. You know!" The big officer smiles at me, "And how about the $E=MC2$?"

"I don't know!"

Knowing enough not to tattle on Noble, tattling is wrong, and if I am in trouble, why should he be in trouble too?

Finishing though, I remember what he said, "I think it means he is a Catholic. E=MC2. I think it means something about going to mass as fast as lightning, and something about being a square. I don't remember what E is supposed to be."

And Momma thinks I am not a good listener!

"That is interesting, Sharon," Officer Clancy does not try to get me to tattle anymore.

He talks to Momma.

"Sarah, I know $50 is a lot of money, and I have no intention of giving you a citation for this. It must stop. I talked to the mayor. He is agreeing too, it is too much for working families. Discipline her, and let the other kids in the neighborhood know about it. Make it stop. Is that copasetic with you?"

"Yes, of course, Officer Clancy!" Momma agrees instantly.

It is settled.

He leaves.

Momma glares at me!

I am in trouble!

Paying attention to me Momma stands up. Reaching in the kitchen cabinet without any discussion she gets out her paddle.

*Please, NO,* I try to say it, but can't!

I can't say anything in front of Aunt Mindy! A new friend she is being nice to me. This can't happen in front of her! She can't see this happen to me! I choke up.

I start crying, "Please Momma! Please Momma!"

I look up at Aunt Mindy. It isn't the paddling I am crying about, it is Aunt Mindy seeing me paddled!

"Please Momma, not in front of Aunt Mindy! Please, not in front of Aunt Mindy!"

Momma doesn't listen! She has me over her knee in a flash, with my dress pulled up and my panties, down.

I try to say I am sorry, but before I can, momma starts. Spanking me as hard and fast as she can, it feels as if my bottom is on fire. Sobbing out I am sorry so many times that I lose count, the spanking continues. I am crying completely I can't say anything, just cry. It hurts awfully! More than that, I have made a friend, and she sees me spanked! Hurting most is Aunt Mindy's watching! I smile and talk to her seconds before, I am being a good girl! Now my face is drenched with tears. I sob! Hurting more than the spanking is the embarrassment, the shame.

"Sharon, I want you to start being a good girl," Momma says as she finishes the spanking. "Writing on a sidewalk! What were you thinking?"

Looking up at Aunt Mindy's face a tear rolls down her cheek!
*Why?*
I don't understand. No one cries because I have a spanking before. She is sad, cries because I cry!

Pulling up my panties, I stammer back at momma, "I am a good girl, Momma. I am not a bad girl!"

I am a good girl. I didn't know it was wrong! Not wanting Aunt Mindy to think I am a bad girl, I look to her.

She cries.

Looking at her through my blurred vision I beg, "I am not a bad girl, Aunt Mindy! Am I?"

I don't want to be a bad girl.
*Does Aunt Mindy believe I am a bad girl?*
She cries! Is she crying because I am a bad girl?

Not saying anything she shakes her head.

Crying harder how can I stand it, if Aunt Mindy thinks I am a bad girl? Running to my room I throw myself on my bed, tears flowing. She is being nice to me, and I have to be a bad girl and be punished in front of her. Being the girl she loves and wants, I know she cares about me, I am her girl, a girl she holds rather than paddles! She cares! I am not a bad girl for Aunt Mindy! I would be good for Aunt Mindy if I were her little girl.

Time drips by a tear at a time. Then there is a knock at my door.

"Can I come in, Sharon?"

"Aunt Mindy? Just a minute!"

I dry my eyes the best I can then let her in. She hugs me. I dry my eyes. A wasted effort I start crying again.

"I am not a bad girl am I, Aunt Mindy?" Through my tears I am looking straight from my soul begging without saying, *Please tell me I am a good girl, Please!*

Talking to momma, momma tells her I am always in trouble. Watching me with Samantha, she understands.

"One, you are not a bad girl! Two, you are not a bad girl! And three, you are not a bad girl! Repeat this after me--- I am not a bad girl!"

Stammering it out, "I am not a bad girl." I do as she asks.

"Again," she orders!

"I am not a bad girl."

"Again, and this time say it like you mean it!"

"I am not a bad girl!" I don't stammer this time.

"I didn't hear you! AGAIN!"

"I AM NOT A BAD GIRL!"

I shout this one loud enough to make my bottom sting. Does Momma hear that one in the kitchen?

"You are not a bad girl, Sharon. You are the baby in a big family. It is hard to get attention when you have a big family, I know. I know your sister's death made things especially hard for you. I was lucky, before I started school we moved in with my Aunt Constance. She took extra time with me when no one else had time. I am here now for you. You are my special girl. Every day we are going to be together, be friends, and you are going to start getting all the attention you can handle from me, for being yourself, a good girl. Is that OK with you? Is that something I can do for you?"

For the first time since Uncle Jim sits her down for that talk about leaving her, there is confidence in her voice. She is being the Aunt Mindy I remember from our visits to their house in the city.

"Aunt Mindy, I want that more than anything!"

New to me, I believe her, but am less sure of myself. A good girl, can I be a good girl?

She is going to work with me and help. Not thinking I want to be a bad girl and in trouble, Aunt Mindy is going to help!

"I know you are not a bad girl, Sharon! I know you are a good girl!" She punctuates this with a strong hug. "Together we will find a way for you not get in trouble!"

"I don't want to be in trouble!" I hug her back, "I don't want to be a bad girl, Aunt Mindy. I don't!"

"I think you need love. Aunt Constance made the difference for me. I know I can make a difference for you. What do you think?"

"Un huh!"

Hugging her tighter with tear streaks drying on my cheeks, I love her. After school and in the evenings, Aunt Mindy and I spend time together, a special time that Aunt Mindy gives to me and I give to her. We help each other. Do I get in trouble as much? Does Aunt Mindy begin to smile again?

## Chapter 16
# GOOD GIRLS DON'T GET PREGNANT

Does my mother know her sister? My mother is more of a second momma to her than a sister when she is a little girl. Now they are both women, grown women. Accorded the status of a visitor the first week sitting and talking, my Mother and Aunt get to know each other. Being real sisters is new to them. Momma, being the second oldest child, she and her three brothers are closer, and share one life. Mindy has another with her brother and sister that are two and four years older than she. Living somewhere in between are Aunt Karin and Uncle John.

Are they from different families? Siblings wide spread in age often are from different families. Baby-sitting her along with another little sister and brother Momma's memories of her are as a little girl from Grandpa's old farm in the Piedmont. To have her baby sister, a nurse and visiting, is different. Momma marries Daddy when Mindy is four. A week less than nine months later my brother Sammy is born. Three months later after he helps Grandpa and Grandma with the move to the ancestral farm, Daddy moves Momma and Sammy Jr. north to another state. Before that Mindy is her baby, a baby taken back by her real mother when Momma goes away.

I have a life like that too. My sister Amber, the second child in our family, adopts me at birth lugging me everywhere on her hip. I don't remember her as a sister either. Other than the fact that she does not breast feed me, she is an alternative Mother.

During my preschool years I sit on the couch watching the door as I hear the high school girls chattering, passing by, coming home from school. A few seconds later my sister swings open the door and says, "Hi," picks me up and swings me around giving me a kiss. After I start first grade I come home, a few hours later the high school girls make the same chatter, pass by the same way. I stop and watch the door. Amber never opens it.

Momma does this too. She stops her work when she hears the girls. She sits with me and watches. She prays for it to open, sometimes she cries, then she goes back to her work. Amber won't come home from school again. Five years after she leaves hope is alive.

Missing my sister as Aunt Mindy must have missed my mother I appreciate that part of her life. There the parallel ends. Her Momma does not go crazy nor is there a preacher giving out paddles in her past. Her home stays the same after Momma leaves, not ours with Amber's passing. Growing up bathed in love Aunt Mindy did not have the pain I have as a child.

Will I have the pain Aunt Mindy has losing Uncle Jim? These are things I can not know, understand or feel as a little girl. Can my mother? Having never experienced the pain Aunt Mindy feels, my mother and father have never spent a night apart since their wedding day. Momma feels a twinge every time Daddy walks out the door going to work without her. Like all good wives she fears the loss of her husband and is drawn to her sister's suffering.

All my aunt thinks about is Jim.

"Jim wanted children," tears roll down her cheeks. "We were happy!"

"Sarah, do you remember my wedding," Aunt Mindy asks?

Momma nods, "It was a beautiful wedding!"

"You came. The house was running over. There must have been 40 kids, with all of you. Do you remember Momma had to make arrangements with two or three neighbors to put everybody up? You, Sharon and the two other younger children stayed with us and the rest of your family stayed at the Crawford's place didn't they?"

Momma nods listening to her sister replay a life wrenching love story from happiest memory to present through the movie theater of her mind. Over and over, every morning, every matinee, every seven o'clock performance, she sits in a front center seat watching in her mind, crying without popcorn. She keeps their wedding pictures on the dresser. Putting them up the first night she stays with us it is her shrine, her temple with pictures of her god. Every new person she tells about her Jim getting out the picture of he and her together on their wedding day.

"That was the way momma worked it out, so that my brothers and sisters could stay at our house. I don't think I said "boo" to any of the rest of my nieces and nephews. I played with Sharon all night. Wasn't she a good baby?" Aunt Mindy doesn't wait for Momma to answer, she keeps going. "I remember how she dozed off in my arms as I sang Amazing Grace to her."

Aunt Mindy sighs. They are good memories. "I told Jim the next night, before we made love, 'I want you to give me a baby like her!' He sure did try! Making love that first time I loved it. It didn't hurt. I wanted to be making love to him my whole life. Nibbling his ear, kissing it, I told him, 'Give me a baby like Sharon!'"

"Kissing me back, he nibbled mine, 'How about a boy to work on cars with me like her brother Sammy? How about two?'"

"'What do I have to do to get two girls like Sharon?' My most intent look beaming at him, I pleaded."

"He rolled me on my back, kissing, opening me, beginning to make love to me, breathing in my ear, answering, 'Just what you are doing, Honey, just what you are doing!'"

"I told him, 'We'll have to have a dozen--- at least one like Sharon, and one like Sammy!'

"Forgetting why we are doing it, I disappeared into his loving. We only got out of bed for a quick race to the bathroom or food for three days. I knew I would get pregnant right away--- like the rest of my sisters!" Aunt Mindy sobs out the last few words, she added. "When we went home the first thing he did, after our honeymoon, was to build a nursery for a girl with pink wallpaper! It was perfect. All I had to do was start having babies!"

Months passing since Uncle Jim leaves, Aunt Mindy cries every time she thinks about him!

Eight years since that beautiful wedding with its promise and hope, one day her husband sits Aunt Mindy down to talk. He has an affair with another woman. She is pregnant. Leaving my aunt to marry her Uncle Jim breaks her like a porcelain doll. She never stops crying.

"Sarah, I want a baby," she says.

Aunt Mindy never expects to be childless.

Momma holds her, nestles her like a hurt child, and tells her, "It's going to be all right!"

Is it?

Over and over she cries, "I love Jim. I want Jim!"

Every time she thinks of Jim she cries like I do immediately after my spankings. Momma holds her tries to comfort a pain, a whipping that burns without ever cooling without ever easing.

How can a man leave a woman who loves him this much? How can he live knowing how much pain she is suffering?

Uncle Jim calls Daddy at work. Coming to town to meet Daddy he doesn't want Aunt Mindy to see him. Does he come to discuss the car business? Daddy has rebuilt more than three dozen used cars for him over the years. Daddy, sending word he has to work late from the plant, doesn't come home from work at quitting time.

Walking into the restaurant, Daddy sees Jim in the third booth.

"It is good to see you Sam."

"You too, Jim." Daddy slides into the booth facing him.

"How is she?"

"Upset, she cries a lot. Sarah is trying to get her out, but all she talks about is you," Daddy's eyes meet Jim's.

Putting his head down Jim breaks eye contact. His eyelids fill.

Can a woman sense the presence of her god, her man, the source of her life? Aunt Mindy walks, first up and down our street, then into town. She sees it, the gold Cadillac, Jim's gold Cadillac, parked.

Running she reaches the bumper touches it, goes back reaches the driver's seat. It is warm. He is here! No longer walking she runs looking in every window, every shop. She finds them in the restaurant.

"Jim, oh Jim," out of breath she touches his back, kneels beside him.

He pulls her onto the seat beside him with a quivering in his hand, a joy in his eyes.

At first things go well. Aunt Mindy has happiness sparkling in her eyes, he is here! Asking about how he is doing, the people they know, his new baby is the hardest. Making conversation, doing better than in previous meetings she is the old Aunt Mindy. The crying starts.

"Please, Jim, let me rent a room in the city. See me, talk to me. I won't do anything to upset your marriage, please!"

Holding back, holding her, Uncle Jim starts sobbing too. Crying they hold each other. Everyone in the restaurant is looking at them.

*What do I do*, Daddy thinks, having disappeared from their world he is not there, nor anyone else.

Jim sees is the woman he loves, as she sees him. Not knowing what to do, Daddy brings them home. We kids pile on him until Momma makes us leave them alone. The crying stops, they hold each other as lovers.

Their wedding long past, his wedding, his new bride waits for him in the city.

Leaving, Uncle Jim talks to Momma, Daddy and Aunt Mindy. "Mindy, I love you. I will always love you. If there is anything you ever need, ask me, call me!" Then to Momma, "If she, you, ever need anything ask me!" To Daddy, Jim doesn't speak at first, he stuffs a roll of hundred dollar bills into Daddy's hand, and says, "Everything she needs, wants, get it!" Holding her he doesn't want to go; he wants to stay; he says,… "I love you. Oh, how I love you! Mindy, Mindy, Mindy!... I can't see you anymore, good-by!"

Shaking, his shoulders bent, he turns to the door not looking back, is gone.

None of us see Uncle Jim for a long time. Aunt Mindy cries softly in her room long after everyone is asleep.

Momma and Daddy help her. Staying in her room forbidden Mindy goes everywhere with Momma. Allowed to be alone barely long enough to go to the bathroom or take a bath Aunt Mindy is hovered over. Kept in motion, Momma makes her sing in the church choir. Two single men, both potential boyfriends for my Aunt Mindy, sing in the choir. Liking Aunt Mindy one of them comes calling. Aunt Mindy looks at him, bald, broad shouldered, built like a bull, a shy bull, he looks at her, peeping from under bushy eyebrows.

"Hello, Mindy," Ed gets out.

"Hello, Ed," Mindy says.

Nothing more happens. He looks. She looks. They sit. He goes.

What does Aunt Mindy think?

"He's not Jim," my aunt tells Momma her voice becoming shrill and adamant!

"Date him," Momma makes it short, an order!

Aunt Mindy must date him. Needing the practice, turning down dates is not one of Aunt Mindy's options!

Coming to the door Ed knocks.

"Hello Ed," Momma says.

There is a fuss in Aunt Mindy's bedroom after Momma goes in after her.

"Hello Ed," Aunt Mindy says.

Can we children stay and enjoy the show? Momma makes us kids go play leaving Aunt Mindy and Ed alone in the living room.

Not hearing what they are saying, I eaves drop. I giggle at them. Slapping me on the bottom Momma shoos me somewhere else. Are they saying anything? Sitting on the couch and looking at each other, the walls or something, is that all they ever do? Is Aunt Mindy better at talking to Ed than she is to my dolls? Why doesn't she hug him? Working for Samantha, it would work with Ed too. After he leaves, Aunt Mindy and Momma talk.

All I hear of their conversation is Aunt Mindy whining, "This isn't going to work!"

Then momma, playing her alternative Mother role, says, "You have to try, Mindy!"

When Momma talks in that tone to me, it precedes a spanking. When she talks to Aunt Mindy this way does it end with sharp popping noises? Does Aunt Mindy do as she is told, as if her obedience is inspired by the threat of a paddling?

Not liking Ed or knowing him is the problem.

"Sarah, he won't talk to me! I get more conversation out of Sharon's dolls than him," Aunt Mindy says.

She needs more time with my dolls, talking to them, hugging them, and then hugging Ed. Everything will be all right if she hugs Ed. But--- I remember Uncle Jim. How many times have I seen him at a loss for words?

Outgoing Uncle Jim spins magic with sound, charms the heart of my aunt with words not brawn, not looks, not youth. He talks. Talking constantly, Uncle Jim deals with people, charms them with the soft flow of words.

Ed, being Ed, doesn't. Never talking, with the arms of a bear, he moves steel not people. Being bald, gray and short, Ed has a body. Rippling with power is he some women's fantasy? Is he Aunt Mindy's dream man? Is he Jim?

Does Aunt Mindy prefer being home and listening to the radio on Saturday nights? Prefer and do are two different things. Momma gives orders. Aunt Mindy goes out. Does Momma need to use her paddle on Aunt Mindy? Swatting her with a broom once Momma makes my Aunt wait on the porch for Ed. Does it hurt? Does it scare her? Both Aunt Mindy and our cat, Underfoot, stay clear of Momma when she has her broom in hand. Going out with Ed she gets used to him and hides Momma's broom the night she has diarrhea.

I Like Ed. I smile at him and say 'Hi Mr. Ed' every time I see him.

He smiles back most of the time, will say 'hi' but if talking to grown ups is hard for him, talking to kids is impossible. A lady at church handing him her baby I see his hands quiver holding it, big arms shaking, he is afraid to hold the little girl. Her momma takes her back. Does he like kids? Liking it because he thinks Aunt Mindy can't have babies he has no desire for children. He sees potential for her and is smiling more intently at her date after date.

Tolerating my brothers and sisters, and most of all, me, a bouncy little girl, we are her family. He has no idea what I might do next. He watches me warily. Having never married, he is special in other ways. When he goes swimming the kids notice. A middle age man with his Sunday suit on, he looks much younger without a shirt. I hug him once, being touched his muscles tighten up. It is like hugging one of those Greek statues, as hard as marble with the same shape.

Momma says, "Leave Ed alone. You are bothering him!"

Aunt Mindy's eyes wander down his body too. Does she miss having a man? Ed is certainly a man. Ok his body is better than Jim's body. What would it be like to make love to someone with a body like that? Would those hard muscles hurt lying on soft flesh: would his weight crush her? Would--- I see it in her eyes, a hunger, a lust, then a shake of her head--- naughty thoughts, she can not be thinking them. Does she want anything more of him than his body?

Not feeling that way Ed truly cares for her. The longer she stays the more he cares. A few nights in the Sleep Inn Motel and he thinks she loves him. She says 'I love you' when they are making love. She does love his body, his quiet, hard, rippling, body. If the statue could talk, tells jokes, maybe things would be different.

He never tells her he loves her even in the heat of passion. Those nights, the passion, the sex, being held, does he help her? Drawing her out he makes her feel like a woman, a desired woman. Closing her eyes she moans. She works with a fantasy, a body magnificent, dreams it is Jim's body. Being with Ed, using him, is part of her therapy.

I am another part. Listening to me, I talk to her. Unlike Ed I know how to talk, can talk faster than most radio salesmen, and don't stop for station breaks. She seems happier with fewer times staring into space. Glad she is there even when she is sad, I keep working on her.

Momma tells me, "Stop being a pest," with every other grown up in the world. Does Momma let me treat anyone else like Aunt Mindy? Momma sits me down and talks to me.

"Honey, Aunt Mindy is really sad. When you see her sad, go to her, talk to her, sit on her lap, play with her--- anything to get her back, OK?" Momma actually says that to me! I can pest Aunt Mindy! Well, maybe not pester, I will love her without ceasing.

I nod, understanding, enthusiastic, ready to help. Knowing I cheer her up it happens from the start. Her wanting to touch me and hold me is wonderful, something I want too.

Whenever she is sad, I run, jump in her lap and hug her, "I love you, Aunt Mindy!"

She comes back into her eyes, sparkles ignite. She hugs me and plays with me. I make her happy. She makes me happy. Momma smiles at both of us, puts a small flower in my hair.

# *Chapter 17*
# A TALE OF TWO FARMS

Did Aunt Mindy and my Momma grow up the same? My grandfather moving the family to a new farm, the heritage farm that remains our family's, my mother and the older brother are grown and gone before the move. My grandmother immigrates from two counties over, an outsider accepted as a local in time, a green card holder, not a native. My Grandfather, a local boy coming home, old friends await a native son returning. Aunt Mindy, growing up there, is a local, of the new world. My mother, never living in the hollow, is an outsider, a flat lander, of the old world, grows up differtent from Aunt Mindy. Aunt Mindy is of the mountains.

Aunt Mindy's life is as different from my mother's life as now exists between neighboring nations. The mountains and piedmont are different worlds, different cultures, different peoples bound together in the same state and nation. One rolling hills; one rugged mountains; one easy to walk, plow; one a climb from valley to valley, plowing happening in valleys on flat pieces between boulders and cliffs. One becomes a carpet of continuous farms, tobacco, cotton, corn, sweet potatoes and vegetable gardens, spots of trees and forest, tamed. One becomes footprints of tilled land in wilderness untamed. The mountain forest as it was, as it will remain is natural, wild.

Ordinary farming villages, both communities, on the surface are similar, brown eyed mules, men in overalls and taverns named the Dew Drop Inn. The differences are subtle, behind closed doors. Saturday morning a mountain farm girl watches her Aunt buy a new enema bag through a drug store door. Sunday morning looking from the third pew back double doors close: different voices rattle the rafters with new and unfamiliar hymns sung in minor keys. On the porch the last of chicken and black berry pie swallowed: the Crawford's welcome new old neighbors to the hollow.

No television, no program news, no entertainment fed into the living room from a studio in New York City, neighbors visit, become friends. People sitting on porches and in living rooms, talk, think, form cultures and dialects distinct hollow to hollow. A good linguist can spot a person's origin, down to the valley, by listening.

Differences like differences everywhere disappear in moon light, are mostly the missing at noon day. It is a 90% world. 90% of the people, farmers, have the same physical world. They squint into noon day sun under straw hats. Plowing the world in rows men see the horizon over the back side of a mule and hear the past in bugs buzzing in weeds. Whether the field is bounded by a neighbor's fence or a wall of stone extending to the sky life is the same.

Have you followed a mule's behind up close, your hands on a plow? One looks like another. Basic farming, the same the world over, people plow to eat. The differences are not in the calluses on the hands but calluses in the brain. In the years before headsets, country music and news, sanitized and the same from coast to coast, real differences exist under straw hats of farmers plowing. Holding down the plow watching that brown backside swaying in front of them day after day the plowman's thoughts come from within. Shades of thought under straw hats left alone to think vary, come from words not on the radio, but said in person.

The input ideas come from local talk, listening to wives, children, a preacher they see once a week and a lawman they only see if they are in trouble. Another voice they listen to, when they have too, comes with pain, sickness and the birth of babies--- the doctor. From these different starting points distilled through millions of ploughman minds there is more diversity of corn whiskey flavors and thought than exist in the modern world.

The starting points are individual. Each person differs. Doctors and preachers differ. Preachers look back. Religious thought is old, basic before the pyramids are built. It fulfils the same needs for modern man as ancient. Personal interactions, love, anger, power and politics, men and women change little. Cavemen wander and eat, then plow and eat. Ancient men learn horses and breed mules. They live life and wonder what happens after they leave the body and breathing stops, death. Domesticated animals then plants then people, are they different than modern man?

Tools change. Doctors like preachers look back. Unlike preachers it takes more than words to heal. Life, the preservation of it, the healing of it, is the work of doctors. Their references are in continued breathing and "That feels better doc!" Their world ends at death. Science, observations, what is, shapes doctoring. Their role in society and tools change with time and skill. A physician's thinking runs on the same hormones and looks through the same eyes as the first modern humans. Like others they wonder what happens after breathing stops. When they know they are preaching, not doctoring. Politics, science and technology change doctoring, not the essence of man. As man was he is and ever will be.

### *Before the pyramids are built*

A big cave man grunts. Others move. He grunts louder, starts shaking and falls over his eyes remaining open. Others move further.

One comes back, kicks him, "You OK?"

A doctor is born.

Another comes back, kicks him, "You in there?"

A priest is born.

His seizure ends. He kicks the two who kicked him out of the cave.

A king is born.

Orders given by a big cave man are listened to as long as he is in sight or in body. Orders given by God are listened to while he is in sight. Since you can not see him, when is he out of sight? People pay attention to him when they don't see him.

What did the priest say? The king calls him back. He may be useful. The cave man has an idea. He is not epileptic, he leaves his body and wanders around, invisible. The priest tells others this. They leave the king's place open when he is not seen, and leave him unharmed when he has a seizure. The king is a god.

His kingdom grows. A favorite child sickens. He calls the doctor back.

"Where does it hurt?" the doctor asks.

"My stomach!" the little boy grimaces.

The doctor does the first brain surgery looking for the cause.

The boy dies.

The king does the second brain surgery on the doctor, the first using a club.

The doctor dies.

New rule for doctors: If the patient dies, you die. Medical schools close. Longevity in the kingdom increases.

The king codifies rules. Rule one: God is always watching. Rule two: God's priests say what King wants said. If rule two is broken expect new priests or a new king soon. Rule three: You are going to die, if God likes you, you go to heaven. If he does not like you, you go to hell. The king mourns his son, who is in heaven, and kicks the doctor's body, who he knows is in hell.

The priest says, "That doctor was a bad man, a very bad man!"

The king puts the priest on salary, gives him a nice cave. He lives long and prospers doing little.

Then there are other rules. Rules, theology and a government are necessary to the running of any kingdom. Doctors are optional until the discovery of prescription pain killers. Mead is sold over the counter. The prescription concept makes doctors necessary. A joint booze making and doctoring lobby group gets the prescription act passed through the house of wives with a promise of painless childbirth.

They also get rule 4 for doctors modified. Rule 4: If an important or influential patient dies, you die. This readily passes the house of lords, the lords having forgotten how to trim their own toenails, about plowing and the people who do such things. Rule 4 is abolished altogether after the king gets and infected toe from a careless toe nail trimmer and needs pain killers. The pain killers work. The infection spreads. The king dies of gangrene. In medical schools of the day curing illnesses like infection comes after pain killers which are number one, down through estate planning and wealth building, which is number four, to fixing what is wrong, number five.

The new king pardons the doctor and appoints him special physician on call and company doctor to vassals. He may be useful. He did not like his father or older brother anyway. He hires a new personal physician. When ever the old physician is called do patients die? Absenteeism from illness drops radically among royal employees. Assisted suicide is born.

The priest objects. The king comes up with a new rule: Objecting to the kings ideas is a sign of illness and requires treatment. He calls for the special physician. Rushing to his royal presence the priest now sees the rightness of the king's point of view. No treatment being necessary the doctor and priest go together doing charitable work. At the cave of wayward girls the doctor does research and tries to remember in which room he leaves his doctor's bag and pants. The priest gives blessings and looks for the girl wearing his collar as a garter.

The power of religion, unlike that of kings, is followed in dark as well as light and people will do anything for pain killers. The priest and doctor are useful to the king. He eats, drinks and is merry.

"Am I fat?" The king asks the doctor.

"Of course not, your majesty, a pleasing girth is good for the health," the doctor answers.

"Have I been a good king?" He asks the priest.

"Of course, your majesty, the people love to give and you and been most blessing to them in expanding their largess to church and state."

The king dies and goes to hell.

Remember rule three. You only have to put up with the king for a short time, or if you take enough pain killers, it does not matter. Rules four, five, six and seven for kings: Four: have priests and doctors wear electric dog collars and keep the controls handy. Five: Give free pain killers, also known as health care, to anyone who looks like trouble.

Six: Do not get between the people and their rice bowl. Remember the movie, *Feed them and they will come*. Seven: Ask someone who will give you and honest answer and a farmer for their opinion at least once in a while. Mess up on these and your royal backside will end up in the heaven or hell earlier than expected.

Were these guys Romans? Roman emperors decide they are gods. People listen to them when they can see them or as long as they are in power, whichever lasts longer. Human gods is that a good idea? The priests hold a convention. God is ethereal. Kings are not ethereal. Scratch what ever rule number it was that the emperor/god is using.

Rules vary, some are constant. Every society needs hard working farmers. Every society needs religion when problems occur that can not be reasoned away logically. Society needs doctors when problems occur that can not be buried quickly, but can be explained away with scientific sounding jargon. Farmers remain the key to royal success the rest is fluff. No farmers, no crops; no crops, no food; no food, no kingdom; no kingdom, no religion, no free pain killers. Religions grow from successful kingdoms, not unsuccessful ones.

Rule 8: God loves farmers. God loves everybody. There are more good farmers than good kings. There are good kings? If God has to pick between farmers and kings, do you think he is going to pick, kings? As farms and kingdoms succeed in numbers complacency comes. With complacency over kingdoms comes an empire. Some, like Islamic empires, spread to spread their religion, most spread to feed the ambition of a king on testosterone.

A successful empire can impose its religion on vassal kingdoms unless emperors marry pious vanquished queens or their relatives. Testosterone meets estrogen. If they do the empire incorporates the queen's religion as soon as she teaches it to their children and one of them becomes emperor or sooner. Religions can, and rarely do, change. Nor do new emperors usually want them too. Intelligent emperors conquer armies, reason with religious leaders.

A great priest of the ancient past once says, "The king is dead! Long live king (whatever the new ruler's name happens to be)!"

Lasting religions have flexible leaders in political matters. On theological matters religious leaders tend to be inflexible. They thrive or are abolished having central tenets that are divine and cannot change.

Kings and political leaders can live with that. Long ruling leaders are inflexible on their own political fates and flexible on their central values.

Both kings and priests flexibility and survival has been tested as science and industry change the world. Religion and politics based on farmers now face a world in which most people work for wages and farmers are a small percentage of the population. The change began in the industrial revolution and is accelerating.

America's entire existence has been in this period of revolution and change. Our founding fathers saw parts of this. They set up a political system with no kings. We have a changing pluralistic government capable of changing paradigms with changing times. Governed by a vote of the people with a constitution nothing is immutable.

Religion being inflexible is barred it from official participation in the government. Our nation uniquely gives the people the right to choose any or no religion. A consequence of this America is one of the most religious countries in history, and a birth place of new religious thought. Limiting enforcement of religious edicts to persuasion only more than a thousand sects vie for public support. A nation sold on God follows God more ardently than nations forced to follow a faith.

The founding fathers see this, and some see more. Preserving religious and political freedom for the people, Thomas Jefferson and others seek to make medicine and the choice of medical care a right of the people too. This fails to pass. Medicine is not an important issue then. To have or not have medical care makes little difference in most people's lives. About as many people survived from not having medical care as died from having it in the 1700s. Our first President, George Washington, is bled with leaches when he is sick and dies. Would he have lived longer without the leaches, without the doctors? It is debatable.

Medicine without the help or interference of government grows and improves. No consequences seemed to occur from this lack of freedom of choice in medical care until after 1900. A great diversity of medical thought, science and practice spreads and improves lives with the same flourish that grows religion in a nation where religious diversity is protected by law.

The new doctor is the product of that era of great diversity in Medical education and thought. Medicine is an art with little science in prerenaissance Europe. The art of medicine incorporates science gradually over the centuries, is an art with a growing base of facts, experimental truths. Subject to theories, some valid, some wild and quackerous, medicine, like no other science, is too personal for pure objectivity. In science we believe what we see. In medicine we know what we feel. Science gives explanations of things seen and unexplained. Medicine must treat pain, emotions, thoughts, fears and phobias, things not scientific in nature and things scientific.

Science, truth, is more unlimited than fantasy and explodes with new thought and ideas. Science gives facts. These facts weave within the fabric of medicine. From a single fact or theory can grow trees of knowledge, different approaches and schools of thought. In the rise of science in medicine many doctor/scientists use science to explain clinical observations and start a host of different approaches: osteopathy, chiropractic and homeopathy are three among many. It is a time that changes the world, changes health care, brings the foundations of great schools of thought into the minds of physicians and patients.

Freedom of thought and diversity, the soul of science, is that what people want? It is what Thomas Jefferson wants and why he supports freedom of choice in health care. Thomas Jefferson, more than a statesman, is a scientist. He sees opportunity in diversity. Is this what the people want, diversity? People are overwhelmed by dozens of healers hawking different healing approaches in 1900, they are no less confused than a customer, without a computer science degree, buying a computer today. In 1913 in America there is a demand for the known, the comfortable, the uniform. They get it. Thomas Jefferson's dream of a Republic with freedom of choice in health care ends that year.

After the Flexner report and its adoption by political medicine doctors are required to conform to practicing what is commonly practiced in their region, consensus medicine. Can they follow the multifaceted experimental approaches of science? Some approaches blossom, other successful approaches disappear. Thought becomes limited to broad highways of consensus practice. Exploration of mountain tops of knowledge via untraveled wilderness trails is prohibited.

The Flexner report and demands for uniformity in medicine do for medicine what McDonalds does for food. In the eons before 1913 medical doctors are as different as Cajun food from Fish and chips. Now if you go to a doctor you know what you will get, a big mac with fries. When my grandparents move there is only one Doctor McDonald. They have no idea what to expect when the new doctor is called.

With the old doctor it is, "Take two of these and call me in the morning."

With the new doctor it is, "Take two of these and I'll be back in a couple of hours to see how you are doing."

The difference is that the first doctor hands you some pills, the second hands you an enema bag.

Most doctors train as apprentices of practicing doctors rather than in institutions subject to accreditation and standards of practice. Few doctors have the same basic ideas or ways of practicing.

Their old doctor, a flat land doctor, educated in Charleston, on the coast, exposed to sea traffic and the latest fads, is a pill pusher, something uncommon in that era. Using primarily pills and elixirs in his practice he is an alleopath, a pill doctor, a pill for every ill doctor, a forerunner of the overwhelming majority of modern Medical physicians.

The new doctor, a free thinker in religion and medicine, is a natural hygienist, into natural things, foods, herbs, exercise and physical medicine. 70% of all medical doctors practicing in 1900 have similar beliefs and practices. These physicians are now considered naturopaths. Defeated by the advertising budget of alleopathic physicians, funded by drug company money, commercial manufactured pills win. Naturopaths now represent 2-3% of physicians and are only licensed to practice in 13 states. Politics older, leaders appear before abstract thought. Doctors and the role of medicine changes

His father practices before him in the mountains, is his teacher. Learning the medical trade as a bare-foot teen, he is delivering babies and setting bones before he is twenty.

His father says, "Boy, you have got the knack. You need the schooling. I've given you what I can, but it's been a long time for me in these hills. There's new knowin', new ways, you should know. I got a friend in the city. He teaches at my Medical School. Wrote him. Here's his letter back."

Looking at the letter it is formal written. At the end it says, "John McDonald is accepted as a first year student. He must be here September 2nd. Classes start the forth. Yours faithfully, J. Weinstein, MD."

The boy looks at the letter, then up to his father.

"You have to leave next month," his father says.

In a rough fitting suit, uncomfortable boots and a hat twenty years out of style he rides a mule into town and from there takes the train to the city.

With a letter from his father in his hand John knocks on the tallest house door he has ever seen.

A black skinned maid answers, takes the letter and looks him up and down.

"Wait here," she leaves him on the stoop.

A minute later the doctor himself is at the door, "John McDonald, come in! Come in!"

A warm welcome with two motives, Dr Weinstein is please to have the boy arrive. Country boys often will not come to or stay in The City. The second reason, a simple one, Dr Weinstein does not want his upper class patients to see an apparent vagabond standing in front of his door. It is bad for business.

Looking at the boy Doctor Weinstein sees the father, an old friend. A friend who makes his life among the poor mountain people helping, rather than become rich in the city. Doctor Weinstein respects his friend's nobility not his sense of fashion. Obvious is the influence of the father. His son knows neither wealth nor good clothes. There is work to do.

"You have to have the right apparel, John. These will never do. A doctor is respected for what he knows. People here won't ever know you, or what you know. It is a big city. They look at you. If you drive a fine carriage, and dress well, they listen. If not, you will not be respected, not given the chance to show your knowledge, or in your case the knowledge you acquire. In two days you join your classmates. You are a doctor's son and must appear to be one. Time is of essence. It will take my tailor those two days to get you presentable. For that time we need to keep you hidden," Doctor Weinstein says.

His gray suit, expensive, a perfect fit and an imported felt hat he can pass for a young Scottish Lord in Edinburgh. New shoes highly polished, uncomfortable on his feet, John hobbles into the University. He needs the support of the gold handled cane his benefactor gives him. Elegant, yet partly crippled by footwear, he meets his class mates, the best dressed of their number. Does anyone realize he is a country boy? Not saying enough to give himself away, he remains an enigma. The next week he strides in with his usual fast sure step and lets slip a string of hillbilly verbage.

Blushing he says, "I ain't nothin' but John McDonald. I been practicing medicine with my Daddy for three years now. He's a doctor. A good un', the best. He went to school here. He sent me. I come to learn."

Another student, one who would be a life long friend as Doctor Weinstein is to his father, puts his arm around John's shoulders and says, "John McDonald, this is the city. I have no doubt you will be the best doctor among us, but you must speak as a city doctor speaks."

"How's that," John asks.

"Like this, let's rephrase what you said… Pardon me, I am John McDonald. My father, a distinguished practitioner has employed me for the past three years as his assistant. An alumnus of this institution, my father, Doctor McDonald, insists that I complete my education here prior to rejoining him as an associate. Repeat that after me," the young man smiles.

Repeating it flawlessly on the second try a city boy grows where a country bumpkin stood.

Three years after entering the University he graduates at top of his class and is offered a position with a successful practice in The City.

"Doctor, you honor me with this offer. I would be most pleased to work with you, learn from you, but I came to the College to prepare to assist my father in his practice, and have given my word to do so," Doctor McDonald says.

To Dr. Weinstein he says, "Sir, Doctor, without you, your help and your tutelage, my skills would be dismal. You have my eternal gratitude, my respect. Thank you."

New travel bags he gets down from the train and hires a buckboard. Wearing a new hat and fine clothes he has an ornate diploma and a box of new surgical instruments. There is a new doctor in town with an old name, Doctor McDonald is home.

His father says, "What did you say to me, Boy, 'Antediluvian.' I know what antediluvian means. It means old fashioned. Now you know medicine. I think you have forgot English. Most folks around here, that can read, know what antediluvian means. They are Bible readers, know it means from Biblical times, but common folk, don't read, don't know antediluvian from antelope. They would as soon shoot a fella that talks like that as an antelope's cousin, a deer. If you talk like that they won't have a clue what you are saying and it won't be safe for me to let you out of my sight when we are in the hollows. Now show me what you mean. What is the best way to handle this thang. I didn't send you to college to be uppity. I sent you so you can come home and teach me what's new."

Three years later the young Doctor McDonald's grasp of spoken English is as good as it was the day he left the hills. Their practice thrives, chicken, hog and even a few dollars wise. Most people pay in moon shine. This limits their opportunities. Both father and son are teetotaler temperance men, who turn a blind eye to the stills as a necessity of practicing in the mountains. Wholesaling moon shine is not one of their options. A long term compromise is reached with real wholesalers. Patients give their doctor bills to the wholesalers. Returning from the city the whiskey sold, their wallets full, the wholesalers pay the doctors. His father and he practice together for twenty years, till the old man dies of a heart attack coming back from a home birth.

The suit wears out. The degree turns yellow and some of the ink fades away from sunlight. Wearing the hat when it is twenty years out of style he orders a new one, exactly like the old one from his tailor in the city. His hair whitens. He needs the cane Doctor Weinstein gave him decades earlier when he goes to church. At work and during the week he, an old mountain man, uses a long Irish walking stick, hand carved by a patient.

He delivers most of the women in the county and their mothers. The head in the hat is respected and the surgical instruments sharp. Fifty years does not age the edge of good steel. Fifty years makes new knowledge hard to cut through, old knowledge as sharp as a scalpel. A doctor of the hills he rides his mule through fields, hears the same bugs buzzing in weeds and views the horizon from under an old felt hat with a formally educated mind. He is for and of the mountain people, a man who sees the city, rides in a carriage to work, and comes home to his mule and a simpler life.

Take away the towns and cities, packages brought in by express on intercity trains and the new doctor continues healing. The flat land doctor, an alleopath is lost. Our family's old doctor depends on pills from New York, if they don't arrive in regular shipments he has no cures, no treatments. Growing more interdependent each year city and urban people grow to need what they cannot grow, cannot find and cannot live without. Modern Medicine, old in paradigm, fragile in application waits for the train to come, is dependant.

The new doctor, a mountain man, is independent as remain the hill people in this era. He has cures and treatments as long as the sun shines in the hollow, herbs grow and water flows from the spring. He travels the hills on a mule carrying one simple bag. If he needs a potion, ten minutes walk in the forest with a patient or patient's child and they gather it, learning an herb, it is always there when needed.

One of those things the new doctor favors is the enema. A simple treatment, older than the pyramids, if you call the new doctor odds are high that he will have water boiling purifying it for an enema at some point in his stay.

The enema given in city or hollow has the same effect, it promotes health. The same too, whether in city or hollow every child seeks to please their mother, learns to hold in the contents of their bowel and reaches a porcelain bowl or out house bench. The enema recreating the greatest of strains to hold it since the days of toddling to the potty: it bonds the patient with the enema giver as a child to a loving mother. The doctor, a kind and caring man, is associated with the enema in the soul of all his mountain patients. He has the love, honor and respect they reserve for a mother.

The mountains surrounding the new farm are steep, craggy. Mountain people are a maternal culture. They inherit their values from a mix of Scottish fathers and more Iroquois mothers than white. Among the Iroquois tribes lands, homes and hearts belong to mothers. Men hunt, fish and travel in groups. Women farm the land, work and raise the children. When mothers speak men listen.

Mountaineers are hard to reach, independent, less likely to trust city, white man's ways, more likely to use cures from the local plants, or water in a bag. Plain houses, people less rich, toilet paper uncommon, corn cobs common a different people exists down one horse trails than do on flatland highways. In the barn is one good mule. In the house is one good enema bag. Becoming familiar with enemas and other intensive care as a child under the tutelage of the new doctor, is that why Aunt Mindy becomes a nurse?

Is his influence greater than that? A doctor, he is more. Most people hear the preacher every Sunday and the doctor more intently only when needed. Aunt Mindy sees him a few times as a patient. She sees him every Sunday as their minister. A cove church, never more than 50 people in attendance, can they afford a minister? Most mountain churches have lay ministers. The mountains are beautiful, make travel hard. A small church in every valley is common. Theirs is Doctor John's. He takes over the ministry from his father as well as his practice.

One of the people, his education sets him apart. His heart binds him to them. As Jesus rode into Jerusalem on a donkey preaching God's love, Doctor John rides up the cove on a mule every Sunday to preach God's love. In politics and seminary halls religion gets complicated, trinities, angels on the head of a pin, predestination and all sorts of other interesting and perplexing things. To Doctor John and Jesus it is about love. That is all he preaches, all he applies as a doctor. Aunt Mindy sees that, hears that and follows him. She sees nursing as a way to apply God's love, as Doctor John sees doctoring as a way to apply it.

In the Piedmont did my mother every have an enema prescribed by the old doctor? In my momma's youth, it is take a dose of medicine, then grandma leaves you in your room. Getting well or dying, is much attention given either way? If you die grandma pulls the sheet over your head instead of up to it. Is momma that way too? A good momma, she cares giving me minimal attention when I am sick.

Momma gives me maximum attention when I am in trouble. Hating spankings, they are better than no attention! At least then I know momma loves me. I miss being on her knee as she reads stories to me. I miss being a little girl. Being over her knee listening to the paddle popping on my bottom is worse than listening to Uncle Remus stories. Why doesn't Momma tell me stories anymore? The only reason momma has me on her knee for years now, is for a spanking! Why can't I be a baby again and Momma love me again? I want love, holding!

Mindy is different. I see a tear on her cheek when I am paddled. One kind-eyed lady loves me for being good, loves me when I am sick and not feeling good, loves me when I am wrong and in pain. Where does Aunt Mindy's compassion come from, the farm, the new community, her soul?

"Constance, Aunt Constance taught me to love, to care," Aunt Mindy says, kissing me, putting me to bed.

Grandpa's sister comes to live with them as part of the deal on the farm. Being an old maid, my grand aunt never marries. Remembering seeing her when we visit, she is really sweet, nurturing, the kind of woman men talk about wanting. Shy, she reaches middle age living with her parents, rarely going out.

Inheriting the farm, can she run it herself? Does she have anyone to inherit it from her? Selling his farm my Grandfather agrees to take over his father's farm. As part of the deal, Aunt Constance comes to live with her brother and his family.

Working out well, Grandma is relieved. She worries about living in a house with two women. Marrying my father Momma leaves home the year before this happens, never living with Grandpa's sister. On visits to their new home she finds her Mother and Aunt compatible. Grandma runs everything. My grand aunt never has her own home and always lives with and listens to her mother and father. Acting like something between a sister and another daughter to my grandma they mesh. Being happy as stray puppy being adopted by a big loving family, my grand aunt has a whole family to take care of her now.

Aunt Constance takes care of them in new ways. She is wonderful cook and keeps an immaculate house. Suiting my Grandmother who is more at home in the fields working with my grandpa, they make a great threesome. Carrying over to health care as well Grandma doesn't have any use for sick people. My grand aunt is totally at home nursing the family.

The new doctor's recommendations of enemas and more personal care are things my grand aunt does without a quibble. This is the way she shows her love for her family. Nothing is as loving, and in the spirit of showing the kind of love talked about in the Bible, God's love, than giving a good warm enema to a sick child or adult. All the family has their enemas and other care, when needed, from their maiden aunt. When my grandmother has to have one, she fusses the most about taking it. Grandpa and the kids roll over in their beds without complaining, accepting their enemas, hot packs, soups and other treatments.

When sick, you get to stay in from working on the farm. Seeing you holding up your night shirt, bare bottomed running, or at least walking briskly to the outhouse, everyone left working in the fields knows you and Aunt Constance have been discussing the necessity of such a walk. In that discussion one minute from the beginning you are certain the walk is necessary. Aunt Constance agrees. In Aunt Constance's chapel of healing the favorite hymn is 'I gotta go!' You do not go. The 'I gotta go's' get her to close the clamp. The nozzle stays put. Your run to the outhouse happens five to fifteen minutes after she removes the nozzle. The nozzle is removed after the quivering of your calves, the bulging of your belly and sufficient lowering of the water level in the enema container satisfy Aunt Constance that you have taken a good enema. Making the trip to the outhouse singing the chorus to 'I gotta go!' at least three times a day with a full colon is expected if you are too sick to work.

Sometimes seeing a need her aunt calls one of them in from the fields in mid morning for an enema session. Getting hot as summer comes on, everyone has an adjustment time during which their bodies loose too much salt in their sweat. Adapting to the heat this problem passes for most. Others never adapt pouring out salt all summer. On those first few hot days of the year outdoor workers seek relief. Suffering headaches as the brain swells with salt depletion people suffer. Modern doctors recommend salt pills. These absorb slowly easing the pain gradually over a few hours and can upset the stomach. When these headaches strike my grandmother takes her salt pills then takes to her bed for the rest of the day. This is before they move to the mountains.

The new doctor has a better solution. A teaspoon full of salt in every quart those living on the farm with my grand aunt get from two to four quarts of this salty solution up their behinds for these headaches.

Begging her to stop, then quivering to hold the salty enema my Grandmother tries the new treatment. The warm enema, the salty water, absorbs into her blood stream and pumps through her brain, easing pain as salty waves reduce the swelling. She holds it for 15 minutes. Her headache vanishes. Running to the outhouse she walks back to the field to work in joy over the sudden and complete relief. Then she runs back to the outhouse making a few trips to expel the rest of the enema. Water and salt absorb more than ten times faster via the colon than via the stomach. The positive effects are instant with enemas and remembered. A line of patients wait for good saline enemas on those days.

Aunt Mindy notices her aunt has a visible glow after treating a rash of these headaches. To a nurse healing is the reward. Visibly in pain before the enema, the person having the enema leaves the treatment table for the outhouse smiling, pain free.

Beginning with the change of seasons in the fall and spring, colds are common. The doctor and rational health care advocates recommend large warm baking soda enemas for colds or flu. Treating the constipation that usually accompanies the beginning of a cold is not the main reason for giving enemas. Large warm baking soda enemas given during a cold do five things: The first three have to do with curing the cold by activating the immune system. A cold is not over until the immune system recognizes the disease causing virus or bacteria and destroys it. The last two are to make the patient feel better.

One: Enemas do relieve constipation, usual with a cold or flu.

Two: Enemas remove foreign proteins from the gut helping focus the immune response on the cold virus. Over 70% of the body's immune tissue surrounds the GI tract. A bowel full of toxic foreign proteins confuses the immune response. Remove the foreign proteins and the immune system can focus on the problem.

Three: Warm water, ideally at 105-107 degrees Fahrenheit, warms and activates that 70% of the immune system by inducing an artificial fever local to the colon. Doing this by enema localizes the effect to the abdomen. Being in a hot room or sauna heats the lungs and sinuses, the residence of the living viruses. If the immune system is ready to attack the virus, this is good. If the immune system is not: it is bad. Heat helps the virus and germs to spread. Heat the gut and the immune system gets to work, sends in more troops to the cooler lungs and sinuses and attacks, or scouts the attack on the disease while the disease causing organisms are cooler and less active.

Four: Using baking soda rather than salt restores the acid-base balance of the body. Tissue destruction, as with colds and flu, and most infections, causes an increase of acids in the system. Washing this out via the colon and chemically reducing it by using baking soda tremendously reduces pain and discomfort of a cold. It softens and loosens mucus, and acidic muscle aches evaporate. Use baking soda in the enema and aches ease. Don't use it and the other benefits are there, the aching, headaches and other acid caused problems linger.

Five: The rapid absorption of the water from the colon reduces the dehydration caused by fevers and illnesses and increases elimination via the kidneys.

For a more complete description please see the article on colds at http://www.lifeknox.com To be effective these enemas are given over a period of time, three or four good enemas the first day, then one a day, or more if needed to control symptoms, until the patient is better. The same positive effects are not obtained by laxatives or small chemical enemas. Small chemical enemas and laxatives may increase the problems associated with colds and flu.

One cold season Grandaunt Constance gives 15 good enemas in one day. Aunt Mindy has three. Reservations are required at the out house.

Growing up with them, enemas are routine to my Aunt. Does she remember the first time her aunt gives her a good cleaning out? She does. It is before she starts school. The memory blending through years of loving care they only end on the eve of her wedding. She holds me until I go to sleep, then excited, nervous she is constipated as are many brides and grooms to be. Aunt Constance fixes that.

On the farm, and in that time, enemas are common for many conditions. An enema given unneeded does no harm and leaves the patient relaxed and euphoric. An enema missed, when needed, is deleterious.

With ten people in the house, three of them menstruating once a month, two with chronic constipation, and all of them susceptible to colds, flu and summer heat, it is common for the enema bag to be drying in the linen closet, and a reason for a young girl to be watching when her Aunt buys a new one at the drug store. Enema bags do wear out.

Enemas, one aspect of her Aunt's labor intensive care, there are hot compresses, foot baths, soups, herbs and other natural ways of healing, not just the pills and potions my mother grew up taking.

Aunt Mindy watching and experiencing, acquires her love of caring for other people from her aunt. This lady is a big influence on my younger aunts and uncles, Mindy most of all. As the youngest she has more formative years with her aunt than any of our family except my Grandfather.

When did he start having enemas from his sister? When he was seven and she was nine. That enema from his sister is part of playing "nursey" when they don't think their mother is watching. He getting a cold enema has cramps; she getting a hot spanking has lessons.

Her mother shows her the right way to do it and says, "Ask next time!"

Aunt Constance does. Her interest and ability to care for others not deterred by the spanking grows into her being.

Aunt Constance love of nursing is contagious. Aunt Mindy catches it. Finishing high school, my aunt goes straight to nursing school, and finishes her education before she marries. Having a little hospital in our town, thinking about working there, it is a chance for her to start over, have a place of respect.

Does anyone divorce then? Being divorced makes her a failure, a failure as a woman. As a nurse she can work overcoming some of the stigma. She is ashamed going home to grandma and living among her old friends, their husbands and families. It hurts. Testing our town to see if she will fit, does she? I know she fits. Fitting with me, loving me, it is going to be the same as it was for my maiden grand aunt. I know it. She will live with us always as Aunt Constance did with my Grandfather and Grandmother. Is that what grandma plans when she sends her to us?

## Chapter 18
# THE OLD PADDLE

Daddy has a plan. Being fall, winter coming does it involves freezing? Daddy slept in a railroad car one winter when he was twelve.

"Once is plenty," he says.

Keeping enough wood to last two winters Daddy is always prepared. Borrowing a flatbed truck from the plant he carries my three brothers still at home and Ed with him. A day trip, the second that fall, they leave early, will return fully loaded with wood and maybe a deer. A rifle behind the seat, in case a deer appears, a pair of two-man saws and several axes, the woodsmen are ready.

Mining coal nearby it is cheap enough for most in our town. We use wood. What does it cost to heat our large house? Sweat and time. Using the company truck and the plant's forest is a benefit for employees. Absences excused for boys helping on firewood trips everyone recognizes the need for heating fuel. Today it's Daddy and Ed's turn. It takes two to use a two man saw. The men go in pairs. Every wood bin fills before winter. Then he goes with other men to bring wood for their families and a few widows.

Coming home tired my brothers and Daddy sleep well. Moving thousands of pounds of wood by hand is work, even though my brothers look at it as far more. In the woods, hunting some, working a lot, bears maybe it is an adventure. One trip each year, during the summer, the whole family goes. Spending the weekend sleeping in a tent Momma and I fix meals over a campfire and hunt for mushrooms and herbs. Daddy and the boys cut and load wood.

Scrub trees cut in 18 inch sections for fire wood gives us winter heat. Splitting thin the straightest pine of that first load kindling is created. Stacked longer in the heat of summer it dries more and occupies a separate wood shed. The rest of that load, and the others are split in different sizes and are in different stages of greenness, the last ones cut being harder to burn requiring planning to use.

Daddy, the great fire starter, organizes his winter wood with precision. Carrying out this plan his lieutenants, my brothers, line up their wood soldiers in neat military rows.

Daddy lectures David my nearest sibling with a twinkle in his eye, "Wood, good heat!..." He smiles and rests a minute, "heat's you twice."

The splitting mall lands hard on the wedge with a clink forcing the grain apart. Daddy slips a bigger one beside it and hits again.

David wonders dropping the blade of the axe through a smaller section splitting it with one stroke, "Heats you twice?"

Being August it is hot, not a time for imagining warmth. David tries to think cool, not hot. Cool, ice coating trees, shimmering silver, leafless, seeing your breath condense and fall to the ground, these are things worth imagining, not heat. Heat it is, water dripping off noses, shirts clinging to wet backs, beads growing then running together on foreheads sending streams of salt brine into eyes, stinging. It is not a time to focus on heat. The wood they are splitting is for the winter.

Daddy looking at him smiles, "See its making you warm isn't it?"

David's nose is dripping and his shirt completely wet. Is he warm?

Daddy says, "We'll finish these ones," pointing at a dozen chunks of wood in the drive, "and leave the rest for a cooler day. When it is cool enough you can spend an hour a two a day after school and get it done before cold sets in. The warming will feel better then!"

David understands. An old wood cutters joke he hears before when he is about eight and Daddy first works with him in the yard.

That same year, David, eight, begins making kindling with a hatchet. I, six, start making biscuits. Boys mature slower and axes are sharper than rolling pins. Taking more time to do one piece than Daddy does to do 100, he is learning, joining the men as I am the women, working. Now at 12 he is moving up. He splits logs. Can he bring the splitting mall down hard enough to move as fast as Daddy? With wedges he can cut any round of wood. A few more years and he will be able to keep pace with the old man, not yet.

Biscuits are easier, by nine I am as fast as Momma and make perfect biscuits. David's lack of size and strength in wood cutting is a handicap. My size is no disadvantage. A taller stool in the kitchen is my crutch. It takes four more years and longer heavier arms before the wedges sink into the wood for David as they do for Daddy.

Making twinkly yellow blazes, I like wood. Sitting in the living room, no lights, yellow flames, amber glows, radiant warmth on my face, cold darkness on my back it is the atmosphere. Surrounded by Momma, Daddy, my brothers and sister it is the family. Fires blaze in our fireplace at least twice a week.

Chunks of split wood disappear in our wood furnace, a few at intervals throughout cold days, a stack before dawn and before we go to bed. Tightening down the dampers on warmer days and at night, we keep the furnace going from late frost till the Spring thaw. My brothers get the fuel ready. A dumped pile of wood helter skelter off the driveway they make disappear into neatly stacked, sorted bins for easy access during the winter.

For the next two months, every afternoon after school, they work. The splitting maul and wedges clinking until they finish at least four wheel barrow loads and stack it in the wood shed. Finishing a few weeks before Christmas we are ready for winter.

Free from the hard work of chopping wood each day David has free time. Mary has free time and an idea. They get in trouble.

"Where is my paddle?" Momma says.

Grandma makes kindling too. She makes a special kindling. Searching the cabinet by the stove she finds the paddle the preacher gives Momma. It only takes her a few minutes with David's hatchet to make it into a bundle of fine kindling. She plans to use it to start the fireplace after dinner.

My mother stands with her mouth open. David and Mary smile.

"Momma!" My mother says.

"I'm sorry, Sarah," Grandma says. "I thought it best to make kindling of it. It had an aura, like something from hell needing to burn, to be in hell, to be gone."

"Momma, the preacher gave me that paddle!" My mother says.

"Wait a minute, Sarah. I brought you something. I was going to give it to you for Christmas, " Grandma says going to her room.

Returning she is carrying an old leather paddle with small bored holes.

David and Mary stop smiling. Remembering that paddle well, living with Grandma and Grandpa doesn't mean no paddlings as Mary hopes. It means paddlings as needed. Would Mary ever talk back to Momma, tell her she is a foolish old nigger woman? Doing it to Grandma is as big a mistake. Grandma doesn't paddle. Grandpa does. Is he old? Are his arms strong? Does she cry like a baby before he is done? Sitting gingerly for a full three days after Grandpa paddles her, Mary has a new respect for her grandparents, an intense respect for that paddle, and a new respect for herself.

Does she catch the next bus home? The paddling more painful, the tears more earnest, it is a thought. She stays. Why? Momma, smaller, less able to give a paddling than Grandpa, her paddlings are bad, not as bad as Grandpa's. The paddlings Momma give make her leave. The paddling Grandpa gives makes her stay.

She had been there almost a month.

"Mary, let's talk," Grandpa says. "You had a pretty rough time at home before you came to stay with us. Do you want to talk about it?"

"What is there to talk about, Grandpa? I can't go home. I miss home, my friends, my family, everything. I can't go back, Grandpa." Mary says.

"Do you want to live here, grow up on a farm, working on a farm?"

"Momma did, and Daddy did. I don't like feeding the pigs. They are dirty."

"Is that how you feel, Mary? Dirty?"

"What are you talking about, Grandpa?"

"I mean do you feel dirty. Do you feel like you need a long hot bath and just scrub and scrub and scrub?"

"Huh!"

"Do you think it washes off?"

"What do you mean, Grandpa?

"The stink, the dirt, the black in you. Don't you want to wash it off so you can go home and be like your friends, white? Date white boys, get married and have white children. Forget you are black?"

Mary does not say anything. If God would let her do that, let her take a long bath and wash the black off and go home, be what she was, that is what she wants more than anything.

"Do you think I don't feel like that sometimes?" Grandpa says.

"You feel like that? You don't want to be black?" Mary says.

"Who the hell wants to be black? I was born black. That is what I am. Because that is who I am a lot of doors are closed. I have to go along with the white man, act as if I am something I am not, or they will kill me? Do you think anyone wants to be black?"

"You feel like that. Grandpa?"

Grandma says, "We all do at times, Mary, we can't think about it. There isn't any use thinking about it. It doesn't change anything."

"I don't know about that, Darla. Sometimes we have to think about it. Mary has to think about it. She has been white her whole life, now she is a colored girl. It is new to her. She has to think about it," Grandpa says.

"I'm not a nigger! I am--- I am--- just different," Mary says.

"Maybe someday they will have another word for it, but for now we are the N word. That is what people call us on the street. That is what our people call each other. That is the only word they have for it. It has a definition. Different isn't it. The N word means less than white, not as smart, lazy, needing guidance at best, needing a white person to tell us what to do, dirt, or filth, deliberately bad at worst. Polite is colored people. If respect is used they call us colored people. It means the same thing, without the bad part, still inferior. Maybe someday things will change, but not today. Not in my lifetime, girl. We will have to live with the N word and being colored people, being second class citizens as long as I can see into the future," Grandpa says.

"But Grandpa, I don't want to be a nigger and die like Amber. I don't want to be run out of town like Sammy. I don't--- I don't want to be a nigger, a colored person, whatever, but I am!" Cried out Mary has been living with this for four years since Amber dies and Momma starts whipping it into her. A numbness, a resignation resonates in her and Grandpa's words. Grandma is right. These are things that don't change, bad things. Is there any use talking about them.

"Amber died because she loved a white boy. Sammy has to hide because a white girl loves him and he loves her. It's the way the world is. If you love a white boy and he slips around to see you at night, you are his whore, that's fine, with both the colored people and the whites. It isn't fine with me. You live with us, that is not going to happen! Our family doesn't raise whores!"

"What am I supposed to do, Grandpa? I came here because of the way this changed Momma, and because I know that. I want to be a wife and mother someday, have a home, a husband. I don't want to be a white boy's whore. I don't!" Mary says.

"The North in most ways is better than the South, but this one. Here there are fifty good Colored boys you can date, marry, have a family with and have a life. There weren't any where you lived. We know that it will work out here for you. You stay here, grow up, marry one of those nice colored boys. It's important!" Grandpa says.

"Isn't that what I have to do, Grandpa?"

"Yes, it is what you have to do to have a worthwhile life." Grandpa reaches out to hold her hand. Their hands squeeze.

"Now there are some rules. You have been here three and one half weeks. I haven't given you any rules, now we start: One, Grandma or I say, you do. You have been doing that. Doing it with a little less resistance to feeding the pigs would be good. Two, you are colored not the N word. Have you ever heard me or Grandma say the N word?

"No."

"You won't. I haven't said it except to the Klan when they were hunting a man a last year. He ran along the creek going west. When the hooded men came I said, "That nigger boy went down the creek east. They lost him in the woods, but caught him and hanged him the next day on the road. There is no place for us to run, Mary. That man had no place to run. He was running. Nothing I did helped him. I can help you. To live colored in this world there are rules. One, we have to accept our place. Act inferior. I let the white man know I know he is the man, I am the boy. Your grandmother is the girl. The white woman is the woman. We are children to them. Do that and smile that stupid grin they want to see and they will let you be. Be uppity, fight back, show off your brains, and they will bash them in. You have to play that role to survive, to live. If it is wrong, it is wrong. You have to do it."

"Grandpa--- It's wrong. I am a person. I have a mind. I'm not stupid. Only one of the white girls made better grades than me. Why do I have to act like an idiot? Can't I be me? I want to be me!"

"Do you want me to disagree with you?"

"I don't want to be a jive nigger, Grandpa. I want to be smart. I am smart."

"You are smart, that is the second part. This is the first part. If you don't do this act and follow these rules in dealing with the white man, it is running across the road without looking. What you are saying is not wrong, do it in the wrong place with the wrong person looking and it will get you killed or hurt. You are my responsibility. Mess up on this and I will blister your bottom as I would have blistered your bottom for going in the street when you were little..." Grandpa looks in her eyes to see the reaction. There is a blink, a double blink. She knows he can paddle her. "and if you think your Momma whips hard, remember I was the one that taught her how to do it. She was a good student. I am the teacher. No matter how good a student she doesn't have a man's arm or strength.

Now for part two. You are smart. You are a good person with moral values, character, plans, dreams and you are who you are. So are we. From now on, neither you nor I will use the N word. We will use colored people if we need to say it or Negro, but be sure I here the O on the end of that word. If I don't I assume it is an er, and nig is as bad as nigger. I don't hear that O, and your bottom does not sit comfortable for a while. We are what we are. We are not N word people.

"We are no better or worse than any person living on this planet because we have black skin. That goes two ways. One we are not better, we don't look on ourselves as better because of how we are born, and two, we are not worse. We reflect this in our thinking, what we say, what we do. There is nothing worse than a colored person that hates whites because they are white, except a colored person that hates colored people because she is colored."

"What, Grandpa?

"You don't want to be colored. Do you hate being colored?"

"Yes, Grandpa--- I don't know, Grandpa, can I hate myself?"

"Yep, but you can't keep doing it long. Pretty soon you have to turn it on something outside you. I see it in you. You are turning into one of those colored people that hates colored people. We are going to stop that now before it sickens in you and makes you bad. You are a beautiful colored girl, smart and my Granddaughter. You are who you are and I love you as you are! I, God willing, am not going to let this turn you sour inside."

Grandma says, "I love you too, Mary!"

"On the farm, in this house, we live with respect. We are who we are. In town, the white areas of town, we have to be something else, but here in these trees on these fields, I am Mister. Grandma is Mistress, and you are Miss. We live with what we have to too survive. We live in our own space as we are. The fact is you are growing, a child. I can shape you, make you better. Don't think your black skin is a sin, that because of it you have done or are anything wrong. It's not the mark of Cain. It is a gift of God to be who we are. We have to live where we are, at least until we can move or change it. No matter where we are we can close our eyes, go inside and respect ourselves. If you are disrespectful of yourself, me, Grandma or any person of color or non-color, I will change your attitude, not because I am mad at you. Not because you are bad, but because you have to change to have a good life filled with love and good people. Do you understand me, Mary?"

"Yes, Grandpa."

It last about three days, the anger, the demon, slips out over the pigs again.

"Grandpa, I told Grandma I don't want to feed the pigs. I don't want too. It makes me feel dirty."

"Is that what she said, Darla?"

"She said, 'If you want the pigs fed, feed them yourself. I am not going to do it. It was your job before I came, you do it.' We talked about it. She got mad at me and said, 'You are a stupid old woman. People are right, you are a foolish old nigger woman."

"Is that what you said, Mary?"

"Grandpa, I didn't mean it like that."

"You said it like that?"

"That is what you said," Grandma says.

"Ok, I said it wrong. I didn't mean Grandma is stupid because she is blacker than I am."

"Mary, do you know where you are?"

"Let's see, I am in the South, land of bole weevils and Jim Crow, right?"

"Down here, black is black. Up North, most of the time if you are fair, and act white, people will let you be white. Down here light black is black." Grandpa says.

"Do you think other people here call Grandma 'a foolish old nigger woman'? You heard it in town the other day didn't you?" Grandpa says.

Grandma and Mary listen to a white woman complaining because a store owner finishes waiting on Grandma before he waits on her.

"Yes, that was wrong, Grandpa. Grandma was there first," Mary says.

"It's wrong, Mary. What if Grandma, or you, had said something about it, looked her in the eye and said that calling Grandma a nigger was wrong, what would have happened?"

"I don't know. We would have been in trouble?"

"Grandma would never be able to shop in that store again. We get the cloth for our clothes there. There is no other store in the county that has what Grandma needs. If that white woman had connections, the Klan would come calling. They whip with bull whips. Those that survive have deep scars. Did Grandma do the right thing, saying nothing and slipping out with the cloth to make you a new dress?"

"Yes, Grandpa! It is wrong."

"Things are different here, Mary. We aren't treated with respect in town. We never have been. Do you think Grandma is a foolish old N woman, or I am too stupid to vote or go to school? The only black school was thirty miles from here then. I watched white boys and girls I played with go off to school, come home with books under their arms. I stayed home. My mother taught me how to read and do math, she didn't know any more than that, so that is what I know. Selling my beans in town Saturday a white man does all this figuring, reweighing and gives me my money. The best I can figure, it is about half what I was due. Could I say anything, do anything. He made this smirk at me like I am stupid, too stupid to know the difference. Do you think I don't feel these things?" Grandpa says.

"I'm sorry, Grandpa. It slipped out."

"It slipped out because you see us treated with disrespect. We're always treated with disrespect, as are you, but not in this house, not by our children, and not by you. Respect is important, maybe it is more important because of what we suffer when we leave this place. Others have it worse, they have no home, no land, no place where they are important, respected. In this house, on this land, we are respected. I am respected. Grandma is respected. YOU are respected!" Grandpa says.

"Grandpa I didn't mean to be disrespectful."

"You were!" He stops walks to the fireplace and puts his head down. "Do people treat you in the North like we are treated?"

"No Grandpa, people treat us pretty much like they treat everyone else. That is the way it has always been in school and with Momma when she goes to the store. A few treat us different, but if other people are around they put them in their place."

"Everyone deserves respect, Mary. It's important," Grandma says.

"I didn't mean to disrespect you, Grandma. It slipped out, I'm sorry!"

"It needs to stay slipped in, the N word stays slipped in, Mary," Grandpa says. "We treat you with respect. You treat us with respect and you respect yourself!"

"I do respect you, Grandpa, and you too, Grandma. I love you."

"We love you too," Grandma says reaching out to hold Mary's arm.

"What do you expect, Grandpa? I said I was sorry."

Grandpa goes over to a cabinet in the hall and brings that paddle back into the kitchen.

"Grandpa, I didn't mean any disrespect. I didn't!" This time there is emotion in Mary's response.

"Honey, I understand, and I'm not mad at you. Grandma's not mad at you. We know when a change has to happen, a way of thinking has to change. We respect you. We love you. We love you enough to help you change your attitude. Do you understand?"

"I understand, Grandpa. You don't have to paddle me!"

"I do. I don't want to, but I do. Bend over the table, Honey," Grandpa says.

After she is in position Grandpa says, "Mary, tell me what this paddling is for."

"Disrespecting Grandma."

"That's right, Honey. Disrespecting Grandma, but stand up. We need to talk about this. Before you ever disrespected Grandma, who did you disrespect?"

"You, Grandpa, I'm sorry!"

"I didn't hear much of that. What I hear is you disrespecting yourself through disrespecting us!"

Mary standing looks in his eyes. No cold black pupils, no anger, there is a softness a concern. It draws her.

"Who are you?"

"Just Mary."

"You are not just Mary. You are the Daughter of Sarah and Sam, two fine colored people. You are the granddaughter of Darla and Charles. Are we good colored people?"

"Yes, grandpa!"

"Your other grandmother was the daughter of a US Congressman a pretty young colored girl with kinky blond hair. Your other grandfather, a real white man, was the grandson of a Confederate General. My great—distant father, another real white man, was president of the United States. In that living room is a book written by my great great grandfather, a fine colored man. If you think you are just Mary, you are, but you are them too, what's left of them. What will be left of your mother and father, us. Are you in pain because you weren't born with blue eyes and blond hair?"

Mary doesn't answer. One of her friends from home is a big blue eyed blond. A friend that in a few years will be able to marry one of the boys Mary likes in their class.

"You are a wonderful beautiful, smart young colored girl. You thinking about someone, Mary?" Grandpa says patting his paddle.

"I have a friend, my best friend at home. She writes me. She is a blue eyed blond."

"Would you trade places with her?"

"In a heart beat, Grandpa! I'm sorry."

"Tell me about her."

Five minutes of drifting through the school yard sharing Ingrid with Grandpa, Mary almost forgets the paddle on his lap.

Grandpa finds what he is looking for in her words. "Mary, you help Ingrid with her school work, don't you?"

"Sure I help a few other kids. It's something I do."

"What do you think Ingrid feels about that? What do you think she would say if her grandpa asked her if she would trade places with you, be smart?"

"I don't know, Grandpa. Do you think being smart is better than being white?"

"I do. Do you?"

"But, I have always been smart, Grandpa. I don't notice it, like I do being colored."

"What about Ingrid? Do you think she notices being white? Does she notice you are smarter than her?

"She brings me her papers. Why would she notice being white. Everyone else except me was white. She is like everyone else."

"Mary, every person on this earth has something not as good as other people around them they see about themselves. When we are your age that is all we see. Some people see is that they are too tall, too short, their nose is too big, they're not smart… they're colored. You're colored. Is that all you should be looking at?"

"I'm short too, Grandpa."

Grandpa starts laughing. "OK you are short too. Do we need to add the S word to the list of rules, S for shrimp?"

"It doesn't bother me when people call me a shrimp."

"When you can have it not bother you so much, at least inside your soul, when people call you the N word, then you will be free to be you, Mary. It's wrong. It's wrong to be prejudice against people because of their birth. Some people are brown, some are short. Short people are discriminated against too, Mary, or is it tall people. Grandma is always asking me to get something down for her. She never asks you. Which one of us is she discriminating against?" Grandpa says.

Mary smiles, lets out a little laugh. The tension breaks.

"Mary, we have to change your thinking, change the way you are seeing yourself inside. You are colored. Nothing I can do will change that. You are short. Nothing I can do will change that. The way you feel about being short is fine. The way you feel about being colored isn't. I understand how you feel. I understand you need to accept yourself as you are, not as others see you, but as you are. You can be smart, short, a wonderful girl and colored."

"Grandpa, I don't want to be colored!"

"Does Ingrid want to be slow? You are what you are. You have to help her or someone else has to help her with her school work. You have to be colored and live with that. It is no different than crossing the street. When you mature enough and are smart enough to do it on your own, we don't need this anymore." Grandpa moves his paddle on his knee.

Mary had almost forgotten about that.

"Mary was calling Grandma the N word wrong?" Grandpa says.

"Yes, Grandpa!"

"Was thinking of Grandma as a N wrong?" Grandpa says.

"Yes, Grandpa!"

"Is thinking of yourself as a N wrong?" Grandpa says.

"Yes, Grandpa. I know it's wrong. You don't have to paddle me!"

"You need to put it in your soul, deep inside. I can help you. Those things, the way you handled them was wrong. The way you think about it is wrong. The way you took it inside and let it fester into seeing yourself as that woman in the store sees you, that has to change. Will change. I want you to see it with emotion, with regret, with a change in your heart. While I am giving you this paddling I want that to be in your mind. I want that to change. Get back in position, Mary."

Her bottom pouted up she grips the far side of the table.

"What did you do wrong, give me the things we covered."

"I used the N word. I called Grandma the N word. I thought of Grandma as the N word. I thought of myself as the N word."

The paddling generates intense pain. Mary cries. Getting up it is different.

Hugging her, Grandma and Grandpa, sandwich her, "We love you. We know you, respect you. We know you are a good girl, will make the changes you need to make to survive. Make the changes in here..." Grandpa cups the back of her head in his hand, "Be somebody, you. Don't let a word define you!"

Grandma and grandpa hold her tight between them not letting her move, each taking an ear and repeating softly, "I love you" in it until she stops crying, and hugs them back.

"I love you," Mary says.

Tears streaming down her face she looks in Grandma's eyes. She looks in Grandpa's eyes. There is no anger. There is love. She was wrong, knows she was wrong, not so much what she said or did, but what she felt. She will to do better. That is why she is paddled to help her, not hurt her. With Grandma and Grandpa is where she wants to be, where she wants to grow up and be a colored woman, a wife, a mother, a person of respect.

"Grandma, where is the slop bucket. I want to feed the pigs," Mary says. "Grandma, I'm sorry I said what I did."

"I'm sorry you thought what you did," Grandma says.

"Me too!" Mary says.

Looking at that paddle in our Momma's kitchen Mary has no idea Grandma brought it to our Momma. What if she needs it after they go back to Grandma and Grandpa's house?

Grandma says to Momma, "This one is lighter, not likely to do any harm, but as capable of giving a good paddling. You remember it don't you?"

How can Momma forget?

Wrestling matches with her brothers a constant as a little girl, one breaks out in the barn. Plowing into the brothers in the middle of a tussle and ending up on top of the pile she pants and holds down writhing legs, backs and arms. It starts that way with Daddy, a wrestling match.

Hay forks to the top of the barn. She and Daddy are covered in straw and dried grass. She looks at him resting on her pitch fork. Rippling muscles, powerful arms, the hay gliding in puffs to the top of the pile off his pitch fork he is different, or is it she that is different. She wants him in new ways, has wanted him in new ways for years. She wants to touch him. The child in her she wants to wrestle him. Why does she do it? A handful of hay, his overalls pulled back and it glides down his back to his crotch.

Dropping his pitch fork he turns on her. Their teens bring Daddy powerful arms, shoulders and muscle mass. Her teens bring her weaker arms, thinner shoulders and a thinner waist. Only broad hips, vulnerable breasts and buttock muscles that are easily pinned are new to her body armor. She picks a foe unbeatable this time. Daddy trounces her. Her cotton dress falling above her waist she grabs him in a leg lock. She tries to hold him down. Then it happens.

"You!" she says.

"You!" he says, smiling.

She squirms, no longer trying to get away.

He, his body caught between her legs pins her shoulders to the loft floor, settles his lips on hers with a quiver. He is afraid, drawn and lost in pheromones filling his nose and rubbing from her skin to his. He kisses her. She kisses him. They kiss their first kiss, her first kiss. Her weak arms and magnetic legs grip him in a lock more powerful than he has known. He surrenders. She surrenders.

It just happens. Neither of them intends to make love. Her panties tumble to her feet. His overalls fall off. Her legs relock around him. Passion, an explosion of love, they make love as they have been dreaming of doing with each other. Finished, he lifts his weight off her standing on his elbows gently kissing her. She smiles.

"I love you, Sam," Momma says.

"I love you, Sarah," Daddy says settling into her arms never wanting to get up.

Grandma comes to call them for dinner, finds them.

"Sarah, Sam, what are you doing?" she says, knowing.

"Momma!" my mother says.

In the house, her panties in place, his overalls on, they talk.

"Momma, I don't know what happened. We were pitching hay. It just happened!"

Grandpa coming in from the field for dinner gets in on the conversation.

"Charles, they were making love. I caught them in the act," Grandma says.

Grandpa blinks.

"Sam, how long have you been doing this?" Grandpa says.

"I, we've never done anything like this before. She put a wad of hay down my overalls. We were wrestling. It just happened. We didn't mean too. We didn't mean too!"

"Is that what happened, Sarah?" her father asks.

She nods.

"She could be pregnant!" Grandma says.

"Bend over the table please, Sarah," Grandpa says getting out the paddle.

Daddy says, "It was my fault. Don't paddle Sarah. Paddle me."

"I won't and I will, Sam," Grandpa says. "I'm going to paddle Sarah, then I'm going to paddle you." He lays three hard licks on Momma's bottom. "You aren't children. If you want to do what you did with her, you're going to marry her!" He raises the paddle again.

"I love you, Sam!" Momma says tears falling.

"I'll marry her," Daddy says.

"What?" Momma says.

"Say yes, Sarah," Grandpa says giving her a light swat.

"Yes!" Momma says.

She climbs over the table and grabs Daddy kissing him with passion for the second time.

"How am I supposed to whip her with her climbing around like that," Grandpa turns to Grandma. To my parents he says, "Enjoy your kiss. You're not to hold hands, kiss again or touch each other until you're married. You, Sam, no shirts off, full long sleeved shirts, underwear, and a tie with your overalls. I want you to wear a tie out of respect for Sarah until your wedding. Do you understand?"

"Yes sir!"

"Sarah, long dresses, petticoats, panties on, and Grandma's girdle from now till your wedding. Do you understand, and if I see you touch him or you have one minute alone with him until you say, 'I do' we come back and finish the paddlings." Then to Grandma, "You'd better start douching her, now."

Momma and Grandma, disappear.

After a long five days it is hot wearing all those clothes and trying to work. It is hot knowing what waits. They marry.

Now, years later, looking at that paddle how can Momma forget?

"It's for correction, not punishment, Sarah, and you are right, David and Mary need correction," Grandma says. "I know the children won't know this but you do. This paddle is a paddle of love. The last time we ever touched your bottom with a paddle it was this paddle. I'm giving it to you to use, but every time you use it I want you to remember Sam and you and the last paddling you had as a child in our home. What has been missing, Sarah, is love. It's not whether you paddle or don't paddle, it's whether you paddle with love. You listen to Sam. He loves you and the children. Listen to your heart. If you need to use it, use it. Always use it with love. Don't use it because some preacher who has never included God's love in any sermon I've ever heard, or Mary has ever heard, thinks it's a good idea.

"Now David and Mary, you sneaked out of the house and went to a movie in the night without asking. If your Mother doesn't use this paddle on you for that, then I'll finish that paddling that Grandpa started to give her more than twenty years ago. Correction is part of loving, teaching you right."

Mary smiles knowing that Momma and Daddy got in trouble for kissing before they were married and stops smiling. She knows the leather paddle hurts worse than the wooden one, and knows again. Neither she nor anyone else besides my grandparents and parents know the whole story, know that Momma is not a virgin on her wedding night.

Mary starts the change in our home. She gets up off the table her bottom on fire, tears streaming down her face and grabs Momma hugging her tight, not letting her go. "I love you, Momma!"

Momma shakes. She hugs Mary back and starts to cry, sobbing, letting out years of programming, hate, evil and sin. The paddle warm in her hand, she feels warmth on her bottom. Momma feels it. Is she in her kitchen, or Grandma's? Is she paddled or Mary? She and Mary stand hugging crying and saying, "I love you!" over and over to each other. Grandma joins them, then David. Tears flowing, they smile. Love is back in our home.

Momma bends over and picks up the paddle, touches it, looks at it. There are memories.

David stops smiling. There is one more paddling to do. He remembers and experiences a third way wood or leather can heat. The leather paddle, soft, reaches around, burns where the wooden paddle doesn't, doesn't leave bruises where a wood paddle does, gives a better, more painful, less injurious correction.

Momma takes a deep breath, and hugs him as he gets up off the table. "I love you!" Giving two paddlings at the same time is work, this time a work of love. Looking at the old paddle, one she knows well as a child, does she expect to feel it impacting holding it in her hand? It holds a special meaning to her. Can she use it and not remember love?

"Thank you, Momma," Momma says hugging her mother.

David sobs holding his bottom, less grateful to Grandma as the burning needs tears to extinguish the flames. Later learning the story of our parents marriage and the paddle helps explain Momma's lecture to Amber from long ago. The blisters hurt for two days.

That afternoon we use the Preacher's paddle as kindling to start a fire in the fireplace. The whole family, including Daddy home from work, watches. It is a lovely fire. The red glow of love twinkles into the night. A leather paddle replaces wood. New heat, a slightly different sound echoes off the pots and pans in Momma's kitchen when trials are over. It gives more pain, more tears and more love. It is a better fire, one from heaven, not hell.

Other things can be worse source of heat than wood. Grandpa tells us about the plains and the times when his granduncle rides with the Buffalo soldiers in Nebraska. Grandpa spins one of his yarns as we watch the fireplace simmer to life. Yellow flames from the preacher's paddle whip red the bottom of a pine log. It is in hell in real flames and disappears to ashes. Flames, the pain of hell, become warmth of life. Momma slides the pop corn popper onto the flames.

Growing trees is hard on the plains. No source of wood, it is mostly grass land. The people there need wood for heat and cooking. Being doubly bad, no wood, and intense cold, they have to have fuel. An alternative source, first from buffalos, and later from cows, either way it is the same, buffalo chips or cow chips--- manure! They burn manure! If I were a plains living girl, the men of the family wouldn't be gathering wood we would be piling cow manure on a truck!

Do you know me, pickly me? Imagine eating food cooked on a dried cow manure fire! Does Grandpa say it gives the food a special flavor? Special flavor!

"Here, Sharon," Aunt Mindy says passing me a bowl of pop corn.

If I lived living in the plains in pioneer days I would be eating fresh veggies and grass before I ate food cooked with that special flavor. If I were eating more fresh veggies and fruit would I avoid what happens next? A diet high in fresh vegetables is rich in vitamin C, and other things that keep you from getting sick.

The pop corn taste good. There is a good heat in our living room, a good aura.

## Chapter 19
# NURSE MINDY

Wednesday, the company truck in the yard, Ed drives it from the plant to pick up Daddy and the boys after night shift. Before dawn I hear my brothers.

"Momma, it's dark, too early to get up," David says.

"Momma, what time is it?" Tommy says.

"Momma, let me sleep!" Georges says, his voice rumbling in the basement, often being confused with our father's voice.

Momma is shaking them forcing them out of bed.

Fumbling footsteps in the hall, dragged from warm beds, boots on, clomping out the door following my father with camping gear, they are up. Breakfast simmering on the stove does Momma let anyone up and out without breakfast?

Smelling good food is waiting. I could get up to eat. I don't. Do I feel good? My nose stuffy, the aroma of Momma's food does not lead me to the kitchen. Not today. Do I smell it, and if I do, does it have appeal? It is Wednesday. Momma goes with a church group to another town for some sort of activity. Leaving later in the morning, she gets me up in time for school. Soon we will be gone leaving Aunt Mindy alone.

Begging off going with Momma she is better, less tearful, ready for time on her own. Resting, sleeping in, reading a magazine, or going down to the library for a book, no Momma watching, it is Aunt Mindy's day. A baby bird, having squawked enough in the nest and flying behind Momma, she needs a solo flight, a day without supervision.

Do I spoil her day off? By the time I get up, I don't want to get up. Having an awful cold, I want to stay in bed. Calling me down to breakfast Momma stands at the bottom of the stairs then goes back in the kitchen. When I don't come, it is Aunt Mindy that checks on me. Feeling my forehead I have a fever, am listless and sniffly. I am sick.

"I'll stay home with her," Momma says, putting her bag back in the hall closet.

Will Nurse Mindy allow that?

"Sarah, you go. I'll take care of her," my Aunt says.

Momma goes on her outing smiling. Does she want Aunt Mindy taking care of me? Momma lets her have a day, prefers that she be busy with me. A solo flight with a real baby bird in tow is best for her. My therapy is her therapy. I sniffle then smile; Aunt Mindy taking care of me. Am I going to have a whole day of her undivided attention?

It is worth having a cold! Wishing to feel better so we can enjoy it more, I am going to have a whole day to teach Aunt Mindy how to play with dolls, this time with us covered up in bed. We play with my dolls almost every day and she gets better. Talking to our favorite doll, Samantha, she opens up. A little more practice and she will understand Samantha talking too.

Looking at my doll sitting by the headboard I say, "Samantha, Aunt Mindy is staying with us!"

Her smile stitched on, Samantha is happy too.

I hear them talking before Momma leaves.

"It really is the best thing to do," Aunt Mindy says.

"All right, if you think it will help, go ahead," Momma says.

Getting on in the church bus with the rest of the ladies Momma asks Aunt Mindy, "Are you sure you don't want me to stay?"

"Have a good time, Sarah," my aunt says.

Listening to the engine wind up and lull away as the driver catches each gear, the noise is less and less then gone--- as is Momma.

I think, *This could be dangerous! Momma would give me a dose of cough syrup and make me stay in bed. What will Aunt Mindy do?*

She is a nurse and she asked Momma about something. Being on our own I smile at Aunt Mindy. What is she planning, and why does she asks Momma if it is all right? There is cough syrup in the bathroom medicine chest. Is she asking Momma where it is?

Apparently there is more to it. The first thing, she doesn't fix me any breakfast! Juices, lots and lots of juices, that is what she brings me! I admit I am not hungry. Drinking juice all day is fine. Staying covered up in bed is fine. I want to go back to sleep. Am I going to be much fun?

"Kerchew!"

If sneezing a lot is fun, I am going to be fun. Looking at Samantha, she thinks staying in bed is OK too.

"You need to rest and get better!" Aunt Mindy kisses me on my forehead then says, "I am going to give you some enemas this morning. They'll make you feel better!"

Was that what they were talking about? I don't know about that! Looking at her I love her, she knows that, but enemas? I don't blink. No reaction is the thing to do, make like I do not hear her! I know what an enema is. Most of the kids around the neighborhood get them. Not me! Momma doesn't give them. Maybe if I make like it isn't going to happen I won't have them from Aunt Mindy either!

"Do you know what an enema is?" Aunt Mindy asks.

Not giving up, she looks at me.

"Un huh. Your momma puts this hose in your bottom and fills you up with water!"

I know what an enema is! Do I want to know what an enema is personally? I see a high school girl holding an enema, running for the bathroom two weeks earlier. I am across the hall playing a card game with her sister and another nine year old when she has it.

Fumbling with my cards, I have the old maid. I try not to look at it giving away my hand. Glancing down the hall I see her mother. Is she carrying a bulging hot water bottle? The bag sways. A hose dangles below it swings down then back up to a black tip poking out between her mother's fingers.

"What is that," I ask.

"Mother is going to give April an enema," Susan says, playing a card as if her Mother were only bringing a glass of water to her sister.

Going into her older sister's room her mother says, "Are you ready?"

I can't make out the answer. It is a mumble. The door closes and catches behind her. In ten minutes, her mother comes out carrying the empty bag. A drop falls from the tip of the nozzle hitting the floor.

"April has all that water in her bottom?" I ask.

"Unhuh," Susan says. "Momma is going to get a bigger bag for her. I heard her say that this morning. I sure don't need a bigger bag!"

Susan bugs her eyes with the last sentence.

Poking her head in the door to where we are playing cards her mother says, "If anyone needs to use the bathroom, use it now, please."

I make a quick run. Hanging up to dry in the bathroom is the enema bag. I sit looking at it. Seeing it, seeing the glistening drop of water hanging from the tip it draws me. I touch the bag before washing my hands and go back to the card game.

Waiting ten minutes, her mother opens her sister's door saying, "All right, April."

Running down the hall with her nightgown held up Susan's sister makes a beeline for the bathroom. Her long hair waving, she bends, hurrying, trying to run inhibited, she squeezes her bottom together with one hand. She has no panties, only her nightgown. I see her butt.

Do I want to have to go to the bathroom that bad? Having an enema is like having the mother of all cases of diarrhea, and Aunt Mindy wants to do that to me! Maybe if I suck my thumb she will feel sorry for me and not do it!

I am interested. I am nine. Like every kid my age, controlling my bowels is important to me, very important. Watching her sister run, the look of urgency on her face and knowing that her bottom is full of water, ads to my interest. It is something to fear, nothing is as embarrassing as losing control of elimination to a nine-year-old. It is obvious that my friend's older sister (she is about 16) is barely able to hold the water in her bottom. I feel sorry for her.

"I have never had an enema," I say.

"My mother gives really GOOD enemas. They make you have to go to the bathroom, make you feel better--- and feel good!" Susan says.

Her sister takes the water into her bottom, holds it and gets it in the toilet. She is a good girl. Taking, holding and releasing a good enema in the toilet for her Momma, toilet training revisited, gives her a sense of worth, accomplishment. Something that she never talks about!

Do kids admit having enemas? Most kids have enemas, and never talk about it. Do kids make fun of other kids who have enemas? To admit having your bowels filled so full you can not hold it, is to admit human frailty, a need for cleaning, filthiness within, a political no, no.

An enema, like diarrhea, is funny when it happens to someone else, not funny when it happens to you. Enemas, a private thing, having them is interesting, exciting and feels good, having some one else know you have them is humiliating.

Susan smiles. Her big sister is her hero, and mine too. Hearing her sputtering away in the toilet makes it all right to talk about enemas for that moment in time.

"I can hold my enemas. I am a good girl for Mother when I need one," Susan says.

On hearing that, the sympathy I am feeling becomes envy. Wanting to be a good girl for mommy too, wanting my Momma to pay attention to me like that, I want Momma to give me enemas like Susan and April have. The last time Momma sees me naked with something up my bottom, it is my finger. She spanks me!

Momma was good to me about potty training and changing my diapers. My big sisters tell me. Would I love to have this part of being a loved toddler follow me growing up, like Susan and her sister? The only time Momma touches my bottom now is with a paddle. It is not fair!

Am I glad it is not me running to the bathroom, or sad it isn't me? Going to be me this time, I am afraid. What if I have an accident? I don't want to have an accident! Susan and her sister do well with enemas. Will I?

Aunt Mindy, seeing my apprehension, my eyes darting up to hers then streaking to the floor, puts my mind at ease, "You will do fine! Your friends get enemas at home don't they?"

"Uh huh," I say.

I tell her about my friend's sister getting an enema.

"You know how your head is achy, and you feel bad all over?"

That I know about! Feeling it in every joint, I want it to stop!

"After your enemas you will feel a lot better, and it helps your body fight the cold. You'll get better quicker with enemas," Aunt Mindy says.

"OK," I say.

Ok is a word, not a word, an agreement, a non-agreement, a question? What ever she says I will do! I will have them--- OK! I know she is going to do it. I am willing, not volunteering!

Giving me squeeze she sits me back looking in my eyes as she holds my shoulders in her hands, "Sharon, I want you to go to the bathroom, a number one, a number two if you can."

Not answering I do, a number one. I don't feel like doing a number two. After I am done, Aunt Mindy gets it ready for me.

Running water in the bathroom comes first. Snuggling under my covers, covering my ears, trying not to hear, I know where that water is going!

Back in my bedroom she asks, "You have never had an enema, have you?"

"No! Do I have to have one now?"

Skipping the enemas is--- OK, more than OK, yes, skipping them is good! Skipping it seems less and less likely. What if I have an accident? What if I can not hold it? I do not want to have an accident with Aunt Mindy there. My eyes avoid hers.

I think, *She will warm me up first, give me an order. Please hug me! Do something to take my mind off what you are going to do to me.*

"Ok, come with me," she holds out her hand.

Slipping off the bed I nervously grab her hand. She takes me in the bathroom.

"Little girls have their enemas in the bathroom. Since you haven't had one before, I better give you your first enema this way. When you know how to take it, we will do the others in bed, like your friend's sister. OK!"

I nod, looking at the floor, not making eye contact.

A 10 ounce red bulb with a black nozzle sits on the sink. A kitchen pot of warm water waits for me.

"Go ahead and take your panties off, Honey," she says.

I glance up. She smiles at me, looks at me, a look of love, a look of compassion. I look down, embarrassed. Drawn to her eyes I glance at them, then look away.

I take my panties off. My face gets red.

Sitting down on the toilet seat and putting the pot of water on a stool in front of her, she is ready.

My heart pounds. She puts me over her knee!

*Please, I didn't do anything wrong,* I don't say it with words. I say it with my eyes.

She smiles at me, "It's OK."

I am still over her knee!

"Honey, I want you over my knee with your bottom up."

I lose my night gown. It tumbles down to my shoulders. With my bottom straight up, naked as a jay bird, everywhere important, I tense up! Being in this position tense, my teeth begin chattering I expect pain. Is she going to spank me? Every time I am bottom up over anyone's knee it is for a spanking. Burning with a kinetic mechanical blaze from stopping a hand or paddle absorbing its energy, my bottom is on fire by this time over momma's knee.

"Aunt Mindy, please don't spank me," I say.

Stopping, holding me in a strong grip she leans over whispering in my ear, "Honey, I'm not going to spank you. I'm never going to spank you! You get spanked enough! Did you hear me?" She says.

Am I supposed to answer her?

"I want you to repeat that back to me, Sharon!" She pats my bottom.

"You're never going to spank me! Really?"

"Really, Sharon!" She says, "This enema needs to flow up inside you. That works best when you are bottom up like this. I'm not going to spank you! I don't want to ever give you pain! This enema won't hurt you. It'll make you feel better."

"I'm sorry, Aunt Mindy, everyone spanks me this way. I don't want you to ever spank me either! I'm sorry!" I still quiver, "I'm sorry!" I can't stop saying 'I'm sorry' in this position. Being a reflex, it comes out.

Holding me steadily with my bottom cheek in her hand, I feel warmth and love. Melting something in my heart, I am in love, not a sexual love. Coming later, and not with Aunt Mindy, sexual love is a few years and a large surge of hormones away. With her it is love, the love of a little girl for a special person.

I want love like a baby, not a grown up! Needing love and mothering by a grown up, Momma doesn't do it. No one does it. No one has time to love me, nurture me or hold me--- No one until Aunt Mindy. Loving me Aunt Mindy is sitting in the bathroom with me balancing over her knee ready for an enema instead of busy with housework, church or other siblings.

Wishing to be her little girl, her only child, I want to be her girl! If I am her girl and she has to spank me, I will remember being over her knee for my enema. I will remember the love, the gentleness. The spanking will cause pain. I will cry. I will feel the love over her knee having it.

It will not hurt. Hurting lasts, injures, does not correct or heal. It never happens. Aunt Mindy, true to her word, never hurts me, never spanks me. All I remember over her knee is caring motherly love, gentle, surging and feeling good.

Watching over my shoulder, upside down, I look up from the floor. Filling the bulb, flipping it straight up, pushing air out of it, then inverting it, refilling it until every bubble of air is gone, it is full to the tip with water, water for me! She coats the nozzle with Vaseline.

I watch it disappear behind my bottom. I expect imminent contact. My muscles tense. No pop, I feel her fingers at my bottom. She spreads me. I feel the nozzle. It enters. It feels good. Wiggling, penetrating, sliding in me, small, nothing like a finger, nothing, absolutely nothing, like a spanking, I startle, inhale a nip of air, relax.

As I do the base of the bulb, the part that sits on the table, rotates straight up. She crushes it. She squeezes. The round bulb collapses in folds of rubber. Its contents come in me. My eyes dilate. My buttocks tighten. The nozzle vibrates. Inside my rectum a stream of water converges into a lake of warmth. My rectum fills. I need to go. Brooks of water babbling over my valves of Houston pour deep into my colon, empty my rectum. The need passes. Water in a bulb, poised over my anus only a second ago, disappears. It flows a warm tickle swimming up my descending colon. The water keeps coming, surging, filling. She squeezes. The bulb empties.

An electric tingle, the nozzle races out of me. The water in me discovers a relaxing passage through my sigmoid colon. I feel warm. A bulb full of water gurgles high in my bowel.

The bulb dipping straight down in the pot, water races in the nozzle. She holds it, a thirsty baby fawn drinking from the pot, no force, fingers balancing, inverted, it sucks itself full. A folded piece of rubber, sides round, regain their shape; it fills, fulls out; the last dimple fades. Its thirst quenched. It is ready.

The bulb on human finger legs scampers from the pot, a drip then another falls off the nozzle onto the water surface. Waves spread. It follows the path, slick with lubricant, traveled before. It nestles in me. Another surge of water gushes, swirls, rushes. Again and again we do it. It feels good. Pouting my bottom to her, my nurse guiding the tip from the pot back and forth I forget embarrassment. I forget long years of my bottom touched only with pain. I close my eyes, concentrating on feeling, memorizing tingles, touches and good feelings. Each round with the syringe is an electric, warm, fuzzy, surging tingle.

Water repeatedly filling me, how many bulbs of enema does Aunt Mindy give me? Is she counting? I feel water swelling my rectum. I clinch my anus with urgency at the beginning of each fill. Water tumbles deeper in me. The swelling eases. This time there is no easing. Water in my rectum, keeps grappling with my anus. My valves of Houston no longer act as water falls cascading deeper into my colon. They are submerged in a flood. This bulb of enema fills my rectum. It has no deeper place to go.

"How are you doing?" She says.

"OK, I think! I have to go to the bathroom!"

"It is important to fill your colon. With a cold, if the colon is not filled, the enema is not effective. I want you to take as much as you can." Her hand slides around my right side. She massages my abdomen. As she kneads above my cecum she feels it, the rounded end of my colon full of water. "That's good we have the water around to the end of your colon. We're doing good?"

"Unhuh" What is she talking about?

"What we need to do now is stretch out your colon a little bit, not enough to be uncomfortable, but enough to make it open up and let the nooks and crannies fill and have a good cleaning."

She fills the bulb, relaxing down, pouting my bottom up, I swallowed the nozzle and feel the surge, the urge. There is no easing? This time I quiver. My calves tremble. I draw them up, a foot touching her arm. She squeezes the now familiar red bulb.

The pressure is different! Inside of me water pushes back, tries to escape. Relaxing in a warm, wet, earthly, heaven, reality comes back with watery shoulders nudging my anus, tries to get out! Tension returns. I squeeze my buttocks together gripping the nozzle. Aunt Mindy feels it. Her fingers gently pressing on the bulb she feels the pressure. My colon is pushing one way. My nurse and her bulb push the other. I breathe in shallow breaths.

"Honey, breathe all the way out. Now relax your stomach. You can keep your bottom tight and hold it in, but try to relax the rest of you. Can you do that?" Aunt Mindy rubs her hands over the goose bumps on my bottom then moves to my back.

Every muscle tense, I breathe out in little bursts--- then let go. Relaxing, expiring, she feels my back soften. I hang limp from my pelvis on her knee. The pressure eases. I let go. The bulb pushes its surge into me. My colon open; I take it. She feels my abdomen. My cecum, hard, tight, full, it stretches. I have to go now as I have never had to go! I try to breathe in. All I can take is shallow breathes. My colon is too full to move down making room for my lungs.

"Aunt Min--- dy! Can I go to the bathroom, now?"

"In a minute, honey, in a minute!" She rocks me on her knee. "This is the part that's hard. When you have an enema it is important to take as much as you can and get the colon really full. It doesn't hurt, but it is hard to take a good fill like this without someone helping you, someone that knows how to do it. Someone that is sure to get that little extra fill in to make the walls open up for cleaning and absorbing. You did well. You're a good enema patient." She keeps rocking me rubbing my back. I feel the water rocking in me. I feel urgency. I feel warm. I feel love.

True to her word, she lets me climb off her knee in 60 seconds. She getting off the toilet and lifting the lid for me, we change places. Have I ever been this glad to get my bottom on a toilet?

"The rest of your enemas it will be important to hold it for longer after I get it in so that you absorb part of it. This time it isn't because we are washing you out. The constipated stuff in you needs to be pumped out and not reabsorbed."

It feels good taking the enema, but now, embarrassed, I need to go. How can I go with Aunt Mindy right beside me? Trying to hold on and not go is hard, too hard. I can't look at her. I do, furtive glances, desperate pleas for privacy. I need to release the torrent of water now pouring into and expanding my rectum beyond its capacity.

I ask her with my eyes, *Please, can I go now?*

Smiling at me, a crinkle of approval, a hand touching my hair. "You can let it go now, Honey!"

I hold back a second more, my face burning red with embarrassment. I lay my head in her hand. My rectum relaxes. Putting out tears with my spankings in drips, this is different. I pour out my enema in gushes. Out of control, it cascades out. Spankings hurt. The enema going in and coming out tingles, feels good.

"I am sorry, Aunt Mindy." I want to hold on, not go with her in the room. My face turns pink.

"It's OK, honey. No one expects you to keep the enema in you long. They make you go. I need to stay with you so you do it right and it doesn't hurt, OK?"

"What?" What is she talking about? I know how to go to the bathroom!

"Honey, don't let it out fast, hold back a minute now."

I do. A minute later, she tells me to let go. I do.

"It won't cramp, or feel bad, if you do this, honey." she says, "If you push it out too fast, or if I give it to you too fast, an enema causes cramps."

Do I want cramps? I don't want to smell bad either. The results of enemas smell bad. I don't get cramps releasing it and holding it back as she tells me. Reaching around me to flush the toilet she eases the smell too. Is having an enema attention? Wanting attention, I look into her eyes this time not with an embarrassed glance, but a steady gaze, I feel love.

"I love you, Aunt Mindy," a single tear rolls down my cheek.

"I love you too, Sharon," she holds me as another wave of enema pours out of me.

Always feeling not good enough, not good enough for the preacher, not good enough for my teachers, not good enough for Momma, I feel good enough. Aunt Mindy loves me when I am dressed up sitting beside her at church. She loves me when I am sitting by her on a toilet pouring out the most awful stuff. She loves me.

There is a new feeling. I worked to relax as she gets the last bulb in. This time I can not stop relaxing. It sweeps over me. A profound easing of tension as the enema flows out. I go limp. It is hard to sit up I am relaxed beyond immagination. Everything bad that has ever happened to me is pouring out with the enema. I feel an emptiness, a good emptiness.

Suddenly, I start crying. Not a hurt cry, not a sad cry, a cry from deep in my soul, deeper than my bowels, deeper than anything physical it fills me and empties me more than the enema. It gushes out of my eyes as the enema gushes out of my bowels. I can hold the enema back, not the tears. They gush. Uncontrollable emotions gush from somewhere inside and keeping coming.

"Honey," Aunt Mindy holds me close to her as I sob. "Are you all right?"

Has she had a patient do this, cry with an enema before?

Aunt Mindy holds me tight, lets me cry, "It's all right, Honey. It's all right. Let it out. The enema is not hurting you, is it?"

"No! Why I am crying!"

Something old, something sad, something never expressed, something traumatic is pouring out of me. Aunt Mindy sees it working in the hospital. People hurt, frozen inside can melt with warm enemas, feel love long missing, their hearts fill as water fills their colons. They release both crying. I cry.

Enema flows out. Tears flow out. I empty. I empty filling with a euphoria that follows enemas, a filling with self love, self worth missing since my sister's death.

"I hate you. I hate you. I wish you were dead, that was the last thing I said to Amber! She said 'I love you' and left to see Albert! I never saw her again. That was the last thing I said to her!" Where does this come from? It comes out of me as Aunt Mindy holds me.

The tears burst out in a huge gush. Why am I remembering this now?

"I know you loved Amber. I know Amber loved you. She knew you didn't mean it, Sharon. You were a little girl, mad and jealous over Albert. She understood. I know she understood. She loves you. Someday you will know how much she loves you."

Aunt Mindy holds me close kissing the top of my head.

"I love her, Aunt Mindy. I love her so much. She is my sister!"

The tears keep flowing, a block of pain, a block of sin, a block of missing Amber, of what I said pours out. Aunt Mindy holds me.

Happy, with a happiness difficult to explain, I smile at her. I am not embarrassed, ashamed anymore, I am me. I have a colon. I have smelly waste. I have goodness in me. I have love. I feel love, Amber's love, Aunt Mindy's love. Amber forgives me, forgave me long ago. I am a good girl.

"Honey, I am going to leave you alone, give you some privacy. Remember don't force it out, let it flow out of you." With that she holds my shoulder, turns and starts to leave.

"Please don't go, Aunt Mindy! Hold me!"

She stays holding me, rubbing my back, talking to me.

I think years, minutes back. Sadness pours out. Embarrassment, shame ends. Our eyes meet, lock. She smiles. From the back of her eyes an invisible hose connects to the back of my eyes. Love flows from her to me filling my mind, filling my soul, as the enema flows out.

It takes me a bit, gushing, then drying up, then gushing. Soon the gushes slow to an occasional trickle and stop. I finish my first enema. Knowing it won't be my last that day, I hope for more on other days from my nurse. It is embarrassing, yes, but once beyond that, enemas feel good and touch deep.

Having an enema is special. It is special to everyone that has an enema given to them and truly feels it as it is. It isn't the same for the person giving the enema. Feeling good to me it doesn't feel like anything to the giver. Having their panties on and their colons empty, they don't feel a thing, except in their hearts, knowing how much their loving care can and does mean to their patients! For a parent or nurse to give an enema can be a chore, or it can be pure act of love and compassion.

Is it the kind of loving care that God gives us? It is the kind of love that my Aunt gives me, an unconditional love, expecting nothing in return, helping me. What do I have to do to be loved? For the preacher I have to be perfect. For Momma I have to be imperfect and repent. For Aunt Mindy I have to be me, sick, spewing waste, or well and smiling, me!

She does something for me in the privacy of the bathroom that is loving and that I, like others who have enemas, can't talk about. Spreading my bottom and putting the enema inside me, opening me filling my most private recess, opens my heart. It is not an adult feeling, or a nine-year-old feeling. Being, filling, taking, holding on for Aunt Mindy, a nurse, is toilet training. It is being loved as a two-year old. Holding, releasing it is going in the potty chair to have her say, "Good Girl!" As a two year old, a child immersed in total love, learning to do for themselves to please Momma is that what I am missing?

Giving enemas in the hospital, it is a job for Aunt Mindy. It is a chore to most nurses. They don't feel it. They don't get anything out of it themselves. Properly given patients do. Enemas open far more than the bowels when filled with love.

Aunt Mindy does something that feels good and is good for me. Nothing I give or can give her in return compensates. I am full, my colon bulges. I take it. I benefit from it. It is about me. She does the giving. I do the taking. I smile. She smiles. Aunt Mindy feels good about taking care of me. I smile a thank you, knowing it is enough for her, for God.

God smiles when he does something nice for us. Giving an enema is good for us and helps us. Enemas are most often given to children with no thought of payment in return. Doing nothing for God other than smile he takes my offering as payment in full. He loves me! Like my relationship with God, can I give anything to Aunt Mindy for the good she does for me? I smile, a child having nothing to give him or her. God smiles. Aunt Mindy smiles. All God expects of me is to take his love. When the opportunity comes to let that love pass through me to others, he expects me to love as he loves me. When I grow up I am going to give my children love and enemas like Aunt Mindy gives me.

Loving me and caring for me because she loves me! I see a view of God and what it means to be like God in her face. God is love. Aunt Mindy loves. I see God's love in her.

For my next enema, she carries in a towel, a jar of Vaseline, and a bulging hot water bottle with a hose and small black nozzle on it, like the one I saw two weeks ago.

"Please hold me first, Aunt Mindy."

I nestle in her arms. She smiles.

"Take off your panties, honey," She says. "We don't want your enema to get cold."

I take them off. She has me pull up my nightgown and puts a towel under me. The next thing I know I am on my side. Aunt Mindy is spreading my bottom. Feeling the little nozzle sliding in, tingling, I relax into it. Feeling good, I enjoy it, but not as much as the bulb's nozzle. One quick tingle and it is over, in.

"Are you ready?" She opens the clamp.

Never answering, I feel water surging in my bottom. I sigh as she lifts the bag. Going in me, this time it never stops! My eyes dilate. I am having another enema! Holding Teddy close to me I have to work to keep it in me.

"Breathe deep now, honey, and let it in," she says.

Wanting to go, it is funny. I feel funny about telling someone else I have to go, even when she is giving me an enema.

"You feel like you need to go, don't you?"

"Un huh!" seems an appropriate answer for my first word during the enema.

"Hold on! If you feel like you can't hold it, tell me and we can stop for a minute."

I don't answer her. I am typical. Almost everyone, when they have an enema, gets quiet and holds on. It has something to do with needing to go. It is something to be quiet about.

Building in waves, I have to go, then don't. Aunt Mindy keeps pouring it in me, senses when I am having trouble. She stops the enema two or three times as she gives it to me. After a while, the times when I don't need to go become less and less. My aunt clicks the clamp closed and rubs my back. She keeps doing this until finally I think I am going to pop. I am so full of enema there is no place in me left to fill. Quivering, my legs say what I am thinking.

"Aunt Mindy---!"

"Unhuh!" gently mimicking me, she pats me on the back! Stopping the flow and reaching around she rubs my abdomen. It is tight— and full!

"Do you feel full yet?"

I nod my head "YES!" then add, "Are we done?"

Aunt Mindy lifts up the bag and clicks the clamp open, "Not yet, honey, a little more!"

The water lowering only a little in the bag, I begin to quiver.

"Well, it is up to you! How much more do you think you can take?"

"No more, Aunt Mindy, NO MORE!" I am sure.

"I thought you might say that." My aunt closes the clamp and lowers the bag.

"You've taken a good enema— You are doing fine with enemas!" She smiles as she pulls the nozzle out of me.

Sighing, I wanted it, not wanted it. Now I have an enema in me. I know what it feels like. It is OK in political correctese. It feels good in English. Panicky about needing to go, I feel good. Accomplishing something, working with Aunt Mindy to get it into me, it is something we do together. How can I explain it? Holding it I want it out. Releasing it, I want it back in.

The friend that I visited, whose sister had an enema while we played cards has a little brother. A two-year old his momma is potty training him. She makes a big deal out of it when he goes potty in his potty chair. I feel like the expression I see on his face when he goes potty. Is it like that? He goes potty when he is supposed to, his momma gives him loves. He is happy. He did it. I do it too. I want to please Aunt Mindy. I want to please momma, the preacher and my teachers at school. Working together to get the enema in me, I am holding it to please her. I am a good girl! The way she smiles, I know she is happy with me. This makes me happy.

I have to hold it for ten minutes. Ten minutes is a long time to a girl with a big enema in them. First, she covers me up. Sitting down on the bed behind me rubbing my back she pampers me the whole time. Not saying anything, I love it. Does Momma ever have time to do anything like this for me? The feel of Aunt Mindy's hands on my back as the water surges in my bottom washes and rubs away a little web of insecurity that niggles me. I feel mothered. Aunt Mindy gives me mothering.

As I get to know Aunt Mindy and my family better, it is the same with her. Her aunt is the one that nurtures her as Aunt Mindy is doing for me. I cry, I feel so loved. Hugging Teddy then Samantha I pass the love to my babies. Teddy looks at me with one glass eye. He feels the love too.

When she lets me up to go potty, she tells me to go really slowly. I do. It doesn't hurt me in the least. I never have a cramp during or as I release the enemas. Feeling better as soon as I start to let it out, I have to run to the toilet three more times before it is completely gone.

Snuggling back in my bed with the covers up to my ears I feel warm. She is right. I feel better. I sleep. When she brings the enema bag back it is almost noon. This time I am ready and want it.

Taking more water, at the end, when she is ready to stop, I asked her, "Can you wait a minute? If you can give me a minute, maybe I can take a little more."

She waits rocking me. Taking almost another pint I quiver.

"What do you think? Can you take any more?"

"Do you want me to take more?"

I am struggling.

"It is important to take as much enema as you can hold, Honey," my aunt says. "The more you take, the better the effect."

I try. I can't.

"I'm sorry, Aunt Mindy."

"Honey, you did really well. You are the best enema patient your age I have ever had! You're a GOOD girl!"

Beaming my biggest and most sincere smile at her, I am a GOOD girl! Covering me up, she sits down beside me on the bed and brushes my hair out of my face.

"I love you, Aunt Mindy!"

Would Momma ever do anything like this for me? Not like Aunt Mindy. Momma's love is distant. Aunt Mindy is gentle. Wanting her to take care of me forever, I have three enemas the first day, and one each the next two days. Loving each one more than the last, Aunt Mindy plays games with me, reads to me, touches me and fills me with love. I watch her thinking how wonderful it would be to be her girl. Her children are going to be lucky to have her for their momma when she has them.

## Chapter 20
# NEVER SAYING GOOD BY

Forever is boredom on a rainy morning rain drops multiplying on a window pane. Minutes expanding exponentially, become hours, then days, then years, then infinity in time. All years plus one is infinity, forever. Heaven is forever being with Aunt Mindy. Do I see a year ahead, plus one, plus 2, plus 4 or plus 16? Do I see graduation from high school, marriage, a family of my own? Do I see being grown, middle age or old, a life with no Momma, no Aunt Mindy

Looking at Aunt Mindy across the room talking to my mother I whisper to my doll, Samantha, "Aunt Mindy is going to live with us forever!"

Aunt Mindy and momma talk about it, about Aunt Mindy being a nurse working at the hospital, living with us. They need registered nurses. It is going to happen. Aunt Mindy is going to work at the hospital. Aunt Mindy is going to live with us, be with me forever!

The happiness in me too great to hold in I expel it through my feet, bouncing.

My teacher says, "Sharon, you may be the smallest girl in my class, but half the time you are the tallest because you are constantly bouncing." Then she rubs my head, "Tomorrow I want you to settle down."

Trying to stay on the ground the next day I can't! My feet won't stick. Are there springs that go off in my toes every time I think about Aunt Mindy staying with us? My heart is hers. I am going to grow up with Aunt Mindy sleeping in the next room, reading to me, playing with my dolls, playing with me, maybe giving me a few more enemas, and never, never spanking me! Why? Because I am her GOOD girl! Why? Because she loves me!

Starting the first day and for the whole time she is here, do I get in trouble? Not once! I do my chores before momma asks! I don't talk in class! I never write on a wet concrete sidewalk again, ever, not in my whole life!

Reading me stories at night before I go to sleep does she think I am her baby? OK, so it is not the three bears. Aunt Mindy checks out books at the library and reads them to read me. Being classic literature, her choice of reading material is better for a ten-year old. She gets books with big words, books she says are good for my mind. Books that make her keep a dictionary beside my bed in case she doesn't know what a word means. Most girls learn to sleep with a hairbrush that way they can wake up and make themselves pretty. I wake up with my hair sticking ever which way and look up words. Momma wakes up with her Bible on her night stand and reads verses. With Aunt Mindy reading, it is her job to look up words.

"What does that mean?" I say every few sentences with some books.

Aunt Mindy starts reading me old romance classics. She reads me *Little Women*. She likes it. It is about girls, but girls liking boys. Boys, dirty, smelly things that they are, why does anyone want to talk about or write about boys? She is the one that likes to talk about boys, men actually. I am not ready for boys, yuck. Will I ever like boys? She does, but older boys, sometimes with gray hair.

Samuel Clements has gray hair in the pictures on his book. Some gray haired men are interesting to read about. Others write well. You may know him as Mark Twain. Does he write well? Do I like Mark

Twain best, even if he does write about boys? Listening to her I wish I were a boy and could run away with Aunt Mindy down the Mississippi river like Huck Finn and Jim.

Reading not being enough, she helps me with my homework, then ads to it. We go to the library and get books on far away places, about scientist and their discoveries, about great men and their lives. She even buys me a book about great Black men for my birthday and reads it to me. The library doesn't have anything about black people except *Little Black Sambo,* and *Uncle Tom's Cabin.* I didn't know the ancient Egyptians were black or that there were any great black people. There was even a Roman Emperor that was black and one book says that Jesus must have been more black than white.

I am learning. Aunt Mindy is my teacher. Learning is fun with Aunt Mindy. Daddy at work thinks of things to teach us on Sunday. She, not working, thinks of things to teach every day when we come home from school. By spring we have read two dozen books as I go to sleep, and more while I am awake.

Our teachers are not sure what to do with us. David and I learn so much more than our classes, they talk of skipping us a year ahead. Momma looks at us. Aunt Mindy looks at us. Small for our ages, not any more mature than any other nine or eleven year olds, they think we had better stay with our age groups. Aunt Mindy's teaching does not advancing our school work as much as broadening our reading and thinking. I don't get bored in school nor does David. It is different stuff. No one ever tests us on Black heroes or important black people and Aunt Mindy is interested in Africa. We read every book about Africa in the county library. In my years of schooling I remember about one chapter on Africa in one book. I made an A+ on that quiz.

She lets me snuggle listening to her read. Smart girls snuggle too. She misses the years since my birth loving me as a baby. I miss the years since Amber's death, the affection I had and lost. My Aunt is my sister, the sister I miss every day of my childhood. Aunt Mindy is what Momma is before the preacher helps her. Aunt Mindy is what Amber was, only more intent. Amber looks forward with Albert to a life without me. With Albert she will have her own family. Aunt Mindy looks forward through her life seeing me, seeing me with her until I am ready to have a family of my own, seeing me as her only child.

We play. We talk. We bond. She is my best friend, the adult that fills needs long denied, lost in lonely years and dried to dust. I cry with her holding me when I have the enema, not from pain, from love.

As Aunt Mindy reads I doze off. In a dream I am five.

Amber asks Momma, "Momma, I need to see Albert."

I feel love watching Amber go.

I shout it after her. "Amber, I love you!"

"I love you too, Sharon!" She says.

I feel the love that night when Momma tells me a story before Albert and Nathan walk in the door. When they do, worried, afraid, without Amber, I wonder. Why can't they find her? She is right there!

Amber stands behind Albert. Her dress is dirty. She has a bad bruise on her head. She says, "Albert, I love you! Find me!" Then she looks at me, "I will come home, little sister, Albert will find me. I know you love me. I love you!"

Then when I look away and look back she is gone. I wake up.

Lying awake thinking, I wonder, where is Amber? No one ever found her. They say she is dead, but wouldn't we be able to find her if she is dead? I never believe she is dead. Albert will find her. Drifting back to sleep in the darkness I am only awake long enough to remember the dream.

The enema, being held, the reading and the dream create tears of love falling on dry emotions. Moist, dryness in my heart lives, beats. With each day of rain, precipitation from Aunt Mindy's love, I grow inside, withered feelings flesh out and breathe. She loves me. In that love I become me.

I am her baby girl! The one she wants, the one she expects to have, and doesn't until she has me. She needs me, needs a child, is as inseparable from me as I am from her, is a woman, never to be a mother, mothering another's child. We stick together. Sticking to her I am a little girl that loses her mother's love then finds it. Aunt Mindy has me. She is keeping me. To be sure she does not go away like Amber I keep her under close surveillance.

Am I a pest to Aunt Mindy? It is Saturday morning, raining. I stay with her all day then sit outside the bathroom on the floor waiting for her to come out. Not rushing her, I am patient. She has time to both wipe and wash her hands.

Momma hears the crash.

"I'm sorry, Aunt Mindy," I get out before Momma gets up the stairs.

"Are you all right, Mindy," Momma says, then scolds me saying, "Let Mindy have a minute's peace, Sharon!"

"Sharon's no bother. It was an accident, my fault. Nothing is broken! Maybe if you could get me a little ice and something to wrap it, I'll put that on my head," Aunt Mindy says.

I look at her. She has a bruise in the same place as Amber, but not as bad.

Emerging from the bathroom falling over me Aunt Mindy breaks nothing. The bruise from hitting the wall heals.

Momma says, holding the cold pack on Aunt Mindy's head, "Wait down stairs or in my room if Aunt Mindy has to go to the bathroom, or needs a few seconds privacy."

I think Momma means minutes, but that is a long time for a nine-year-old. I am glad she says seconds. How can I be away from Aunt Mindy that long and be in the same house?

Is Aunt Mindy as happy with everything as she is with me? I wish. Being older than any of the other single women at church or in our community, and divorced, she is unhappy. I am her only friend other than my mother, and Ed. Having trouble finding her place in the community is a problem I don't expect. Hating being divorced and wanting her husband and a family is hard for her!

Can't she marry Ed? I think she needs to marry Ed. That solves the problem. She doesn't want to marry Ed. He is nice, but the more she is with him, the more she feels the same. No love is growing. On the other hand, she loves me and like a daughter, an only child. We both need that!

Can I get her a husband, or babies of her own? No, but I am a daughter to her. For my Aunt Mindy I will be her little girl, plant flowers with her, be hers! She will take care of me always, live with us forever.

Then my plans go up in smoke. Do I see her heart? I see the part extending to me, what about the other parts, the grown up parts? Wanting to stay with me is in her heart, but she doesn't think she will like working in the hospital.

What about nights? I am a child sleeping ten hours a night. She sleeps seven. In those three hours without me she talks to Momma, but the conversations end. Putting on her night gown climbing in bed she is alone missing Uncle Jim. This part of her heart I, nor Momma nor any friend, unloved in that way, can fill.

Receiving a letter it turns out she has applied to the Navy. She is going to be a navy nurse and see the world— and sailors. Is this something she has to do?

Beginning to hope, Ed has given her the confidence to look.

Looking for a man is hard. To look a girl has to look, and not look. She will look, they will look. The key thing is position. Is our town a good position? Two eligible single men does not a good position make. Is a pond with two fish a good place to plan a fish fry? A navy base is a good position: a sea is full of single men in white fish uniforms. Can she smell a good one sizzling in the pan?

She is sure enough of herself to sit in front of the men's room door and see what falls over her then hook him and reel him in. Does it matter if men trip over her and break something? Being a nurse she can fix them. Men will be fall for her in the Navy. Feeling that she will find someone to love her in the navy she will. We both know it.

My problem is simple. She might find another man to love in the navy. Where will I find another Aunt Mindy? Can I live without her? I love her! Taking it well until the day before she goes, I come apart!

Chattering like a squirrel in class the next day, but not before I have a crying jag, the teacher tries to comfort me! She doesn't spank me, nor does she send a note to momma! Pulling Janet's hair and yelling at her, I am being a bad girl! Taking me aside, my teacher tells me to behave, nothing more! Writing a note my teacher puts it in a sealed envelope for momma. Now I will get attention! I will need Aunt Mindy to stay with me, hold me while I cry and help me be a better girl. Carrying it straight home after school and giving it to Momma while Aunt Mindy is standing beside her; this will show them how important it is for Aunt Mindy to stay! Momma gets this soft look in her eyes and hugs me! What is the matter with my Momma?

"Momma— aren't you going to paddle me?" I say, "I've been a bad girl!"

Momma shakes her head and gives me the note to read. Mrs. Cole says I am upset about my aunt leaving and need some special love! She doesn't say anything about me being bad!

"But, Momma, I was bad," I add, looking to the cabinet where she keeps the paddle.

"I am not going to spank you, honey! I do want you to be the girl you have been while Aunt Mindy has been here. I know you are upset that she is leaving. I know you love her, and I know you are a good girl!"

I look at Aunt Mindy, "Please don't leave. Please don't leave! I'll be a good girl, Aunt Mindy. How can I be a better girl? I don't want you to leave? Please!"

Beginning to cry, I know it is my fault! If I am a better girl, my Aunt Mindy will stay. I'm not a good enough girl for her to stay with me!

"I'm sorry, Aunt Mindy! I'm sorry! Please stay! I will be a better girl! I'm sorry!"

I am sobbing, irrational. She can't go. It is my fault she is going! I am sure! I grab her and crying tell her, "Please, please don't go, Aunt Mindy! Please! Stay with us! Please stay with us!" She hugs me, and looks me in the eyes. Is she crying too?

"I don't want to leave you, Honey! I love you. You are the baby girl I never had! I love you! But don't you see, I don't belong here! I need to be where there are other single people, where maybe I can meet Mr. Right, and have a life, Honey. IT IS NOT YOU," she sobs as she holds me! "Honey, I'm never going to leave you! We can write. I'll write you when I get settled; you can write me! We'll be pen pals!--- Honey, I'm never going to leave you! I have you right here in my heart! We can have a sign! Every spring, the Jonquils bloom. Every time you see a Jonquil bloom--- Know that I love you!" She holds her hand over her heart. "I know you have me in your heart!" She puts her hand over mine. Then she says, "Some day when I have a little girl, I want her to be like you. Until then you will be my only little girl, my baby— if your momma doesn't mind?" She looks at Momma.

Momma has a soft look to her, nodding her head. She is crying too. She doesn't mind. I am Aunt Mindy's little girl!

The woman I love so much leaves the next day while I am at school. We never say goodbye!

This happens over a two or three day period. She doesn't call Ed to tell him she is going. What can she say to him? Knowing he cares for her, she doesn't care for him in the same way. Thinking it is best for her to disappear Aunt Mindy's chooses to avoid saying good by to him. Momma doesn't agree, doesn't interfere.

Aunt Mindy and I write. Writing her a long letter every day for a month, Momma sees how much she means to me. Loving Aunt Mindy fills my heart, my mind, writing makes her real to me, makes her with me. Aunt Mindy is the adult that makes me feel love, helps me love myself. In those days that she takes care of me she is my friend, my idol, the one I look to, to see myself, my reflection in her eyes.

In the time she is in our home she changes me. Talking about me with Momma, Momma seeing us together changes Momma. Before Aunt Mindy leaves I stop seeking care and comfort with Momma seeking it from Aunt Mindy. Momma's arms open I pass by them going to Aunt Mindy. In my joy do I see Momma changing, wanting to hold me, wanting to be my friend?

Ignored she sits stringing beans alone one day when I come home from school. Aunt Mindy is at her interview at the hospital. Ordering me to come to her I do. Is she going to paddle me?

"I love you, Sharon," she says.

Smiling she lets me go.

Pulling up my chair and taking a bowl of beans to string, "Momma---." I start to say something, but it doesn't come out.

I don't know what to say, then Aunt Mindy comes home. After the work is done Aunt Mindy and I leave to play with my dolls. Do I notice the sad look in Momma's eyes?

After Aunt Mindy leaves, I notice the change. Why is Momma hugging me all the time? Every time I come home from school she hugs me, tells me I am a good girl, asks about school and all sorts of things. She is almost like Aunt Mindy. Almost, she still paddles me, Aunt Mindy wouldn't do that, but even that is not the same.

If she spanks me, she holds me afterwards and strokes my hair until I am done crying telling me, "You are a good girl. I know that. You made a mistake. It's all right."

The spankings once common become rare. It only happens three more times then stops. Is the preacher unhappy about this? If he is, it is his problem. Momma is listening to another voice louder, more passionate, more filled with God's love. Momma hears Aunt Mindy from half way around the world clearer than shouts in her ear on Sunday morning. I do too. Picking up my pen I write her another letter.

Closing my eyes I see Aunt Mindy telling me, "Sharon, you are a good girl!"

Knowing she loves me and wants me to be a good girl for her, I am.

Having to do school work and help Momma it is hard to write every day; it is hard for Aunt Mindy too. Does the navy want her to work? Writing me is not part of her duties. I write her every week: it is my Tuesday evening routine. Does she write back? At least once, usually twice a week there is a letter for me from Aunt Mindy.

Writing her about school, my projects, friends, church and nice things I see and feel, Momma says I am never the same after Aunt Mindy. I almost never get in trouble at school. My grades go up and everyone says what a GOOD girl I am.

Writing me about the places she is going and sees, it is strange and different, special too. Jagged mountains rising straight from the sea, black sand beaches, volcanoes and ocean waves high as houses, she is stationed in Hawaii. No one in our family has seen a place like Hawaii. Getting cold at home, in Hawaii it is always summer. I wear a jacket to school. What is Aunt Mindy wearing? Loving the beach Aunt Mindy goes swimming every day wearing a flower pattern swim suit! Every day is summer in Hawaii, never requiring a coat. Hawaii is the most beautiful place she has seen, and so she describes it in every word. Wanting us to see it, she sends us pictures in her letters. It is beautiful.

Meeting a sailor, she starts keeping time with him and writes me about him, "Paul is a cook, and fixes the best Cajun food I have ever tasted. I'm afraid he's going to get me fat!"

Writing the next day, "Paul is gone. I hope he will be back soon. The scuttlebutt is that they are out for two weeks and will be back by the end of the month. Last night he took me to a nice Japanese restaurant, we had sushi, raw fish. Have you ever eaten raw fish?"

I cringe, my nose turning up. No one eats raw fish. Fish is meant to be eaten well done, cooked in a skillet. Now she eats raw fish. She is supposed to be catching a good one and fry him.

She continues, "Then Paul took me to Waikiki. We walked down the beach our feet sinking in the sand then down to the waves and let them lick over our feet. The moon lit his face so sweetly I had to kiss him. Do you know what he did next?"

Why would she ask me? It takes a month to ask then get an answer back, by then we will both forget what we are talking about? What did he do next?

She keeps right on writing, good Aunt Mindy!

"He got down on his knees in the sand and asked me, 'Mindy, Will you marry me?'" Do you know what I said," she asks then puts some dashes and--- "continued."

A continued! How can she put continued? Aunt Mindy how can you do this? What did you say? Looking down the page I see a little notation, "over"--- the tease!

"I said, 'yes,'" writes Aunt Mindy!

## *Chapter 21*
# PEARL HARBOR

She says "Yes!" Happiness comes through Aunt Mindy's letter. She and Paul are getting married! Bouncing up and down when I read it, am I bouncing like a kangaroo? Momma says I am. Happiness for Aunt Mindy percolates through our family.

Writing her, as does Momma and the rest of the relatives, does it take a sea plane to carry her mail that week? We want to know everything. Wanting to be her flower girl, can I be her flower girl? Disappointing, Hawaii is too far. A Hawaiian wedding, it sounds wonderful. Thinking they will marry there, Hawaii becomes to my Aunt Mindy the tropical paradise it is in dreams to others. Half way around the world, too far to go for anything, Aunt Mindy will marry surrounded by new friends, nurses from the base and men from Paul's ship.

All this happiness makes a letter I wrote to her weigh on my mind. I don't know why I write it. Depressed, lonely, I miss her. A rainy gloomy day why isn't she here to tell me a story, talk to me? Knowing I shouldn't do it the minute I do, I do anyway. I send her a letter asking her to come home telling her how much I need her. It is partly her fault; she sends me a letter telling me everything is not sunshine in Hawaii. I am not there. She misses me. Reading her letter I miss her. I write her.

She meets a few interesting men when she arrives in Hawaii. Young, they are never married and yet to have children. Knowing they want children makes her withdraw. Breaking down with the doctor, she tells him about Jim, about their wonderful marriage, about losing him because she does not have a baby. Jim loves her, waits years for her to give him a baby, then there is so much hurt, so much pain. She never wants to go through that again.

"Mindy, who have you seen about this?" The surgeon asks.

"No one, Sir, I just don't seem to get pregnant."

"You're a nurse. This is stupid," he says.

Walking her to the appointment desk he says, "Schedule her for a complete GYN examination. Everything we can do. Every test. Every procedure, ASAP. Send the results and reports to me personally."

"Aye, Aye, Captain," The yeoman says.

The doctor walks away without answering.

Aunt Mindy stands in front of the yeoman as he gives her appointment after appointment.

A week of various tests, she hopes. An appointment to go over the results, a three hour wait, and the doctor sits Aunt Mindy down.

"Mindy, the tests are conclusive. You'll never have a baby…" the doctor says, going on for another fifteen minutes explaining what is wrong.

Aunt Mindy, a nurse, understands what he is saying, but never hears anything after that second sentence, "You'll never have a baby!" An adult, a military person, she sits at attention repeating over and over in her mind, *You'll never have a baby*. When he puts his hand on her shoulder tears start dripping from her expressionless face yet she remains at attention unmoving.

"Yes sir," she says.

"I'll leave you for a while. Take the time you need. I'm sorry," the doctor says.

Breaking down after he leaves she sobs. A quiet day at the hospital another patient in the waiting room hears through the open transom.

"Jim!" One word, a call to the other side of the world, she wants Jim, to have his baby, to be his wife, to die. "Oh, Jim!" Only sobs follow.

The emotion, not new, not unexpected the doctor knows her history, knows about Jim, knows another man, a Navy man, one of us, a man he likes.

Is the delay seeing the doctor an accident?

"I'm sorry," he says explaining that he is delayed by an emergency, something believable for a surgeon.

For three hours she and a tall, handsome man with twelve years of service and first class chevrons on his sleeves sit in the waiting room. At first meeting expecting the stay to be minutes they are silent. Finding out it is to be hours they are both ordered to wait. Alone, nervous, Aunt Mindy fearing what the doctor will say, talks. The man listens.

"Unhuh," he listens more than shares as she spills out her life.

More than any other topic in that four hours waiting for her diagnosis she talks about me. He smiles telling her about his nieces and nephews. One of them, a boy, is going to college. The sailor is paying for it. He understands loving other people's children.

"Why don't you have children of your own?" Aunt Mindy says.

Why doesn't he? He is handsome enough to be a movie star. What woman wouldn't want him for a husband, in her bed, making babies with her?

He smiles, puts his head down and says, "I just don't." His deep base voice rumbles, settles through the floor.

The doctor eventually calls her into his office leaving him sitting in the waiting room. The "Oh Jim!" a cry for help the sailor, knowing she is alone, goes to her, opening the door.

"Are you OK?" The petty officer asks.

Embarrassed, her face a mess, steaks of tears undried down her ckeeks, Aunt Mindy says, "I'm OK. I'm sorry."

At this point the doctor comes back, "Mindy, you shouldn't be alone today." Then to the man he says, "Paul, can you stay with her today and bring her back tonight. I want to keep her over night, but there is no reason for her to be in the hospital today. Take her into town, go visit the Queen's palace, a movie or something. Get her out of here and bring her back at 8 PM."

"But sir, I am due back on the ship at 2 PM," Paul says.

"Don't worry, I'll call and tell them I am pulling you off duty for the rest of the day."

This is how Aunt Mindy and Paul meet.

Paul, a special patient of the doctor's, cooks for the hospital for six years before transferring to a ship. The doctor knows him well, knows of not one but four of his sister's children that Paul puts through college. He is a good man. Mindy, the doctor works with, a nurse on his staff, he likes her too. Like my Momma the old surgeon has a plan and like Momma has the power to give orders and make things happen.

Paul, the perfect gentleman, walks with Aunt Mindy and listens to her as she makes conversation. She never reveals the horrible truth about herself she learns that day. Nor does Paul say much more than he already has about himself. He talks navy, about his job, about serving, traveling, the places he has seen, the places he will see and friends. The diversion ends her tears, is the cure she needs.

8 PM sharp she is back in the hospital. Paul goes to his ship. Missing me, Aunt Mindy, gets a sheet of paper and writes me twenty minutes after being assigned her hospital bed. She wants me with her more than ever. There never will be a baby girl like me for my Aunt Mindy, only me.

I feel the sadness through the page as I read her letter.

"I'm sorry, Aunt Mindy!"

I wish she could hear me, but then even more than now letters take time. It is about two weeks from the time she writes before I receive her letter. Two more weeks pass before she gets my response. Can a lot happen in a month? It can. It does. What ever we were talking about is a month passed before we know what the other has thought. Being a difficult way to communicate, I love letters, but hate them too. We are a month behind in everything.

Writing, being hopeless, I can tell she is coming home. Committed for one enlistment, are we going to have a steamer trunk full of letters over the next four years, then have her sleeping in the bedroom beside me?

Another problem is Uncle Jim. She cries out for Jim. Are any of the sailors Uncle Jim, or like Uncle Jim? Is there anyone except Uncle Jim to Aunt Mindy? Is he is the only one she can love? What ever she says or thinks I know replacing her Jim is impossible. As in the hospital and in any crisis it is his name she calls out. Adoring him she never wants to live without him.

Aunt Mindy can not know, I do not know--- Daddy suspects. Uncle Jim has Daddy fix and deliver cars for him; he sees him. Jim has a son, a healthy baby boy, another baby due in three months and an unhappy marriage. Not talking to Momma about this, it is too soon, Daddy plans to tell my mother after Christmas--- IF Uncle Jim gives him the go ahead. Does my Uncle want his wife back? After this baby is born will he take a vacation in Hawaii? Walk on the beach with Aunt Mindy, get her out of the military, bring her home?

I think Aunt Mindy is coming home until the first letter about Paul. I am happy and surprised. Daddy remains silent about what he knows and silent about what he doesn't know, telling neither us about Jim nor Jim about Aunt Mindy's impending marriage.

Sunday is cold. We go to church then stay for winter festival. It is an ordinary December day. There is no mail. Two weeks and four days till Christmas, I have another ten days of school. Helping Momma fix Sunday dinner, then eating until sleepy is my main activity. Is Daddy going to play basketball with my brothers? He gets out his gym shorts and slips them under long pants. He puts on his coat. I put on my coat. Walking we start to the high school. Running our neighbor is yelling, screaming at everyone on the street, telling people at their windows.

"Sam, turn on your radio quick. The President is talking," he yells to my daddy then gallops down the street shouting to others. The radio on, we listen. President Roosevelt is talking. Did the Japanese attack Pearl Harbor? They what? They can't do that! They can't! What if something happens to Aunt Mindy's Paul? Spending the day in shock I know she is taking care of hurt people. The news is dark, cold. The streets empty. No one shows up for the basket ball game. Everyone listens to the radio. We are at war! No personal news, not much news of the battle, there is an attack. It happens at dawn. Nothing else from Hawaii! My brothers talk of enlisting. Commissioned a lieutenant in the army last spring Sammy is stationed in New York.

Momma cries, worries, tells them, "No, stay home. There will be plenty of young men for the service. Don't go!"

She is as pitiable as I am when Aunt Mindy goes in service, and more afraid. Aunt Mindy is not in combat. The young men leaving are different. Many of them will never return, some dying fighting Japan, others dying fighting Germany. It is a big thing this war. None of our lives will be the same. Chaos, everything is in upheaval.

Getting a letter from Aunt Mindy the next day, it talks about her new husband to be, and how wonderful he is. Then it says they are going to be married in January, on a beautiful day in Hawaii. Then in the spring when the Jonquils are blooming, they plan to take leave and come home. Aunt Mindy is coming home with her new husband. She is going to bring him to see me! OK, maybe it will be delayed because of the war, but she is bringing her husband home to see me. Happiness exudes!

Going back to school, everyone is talking about the war. Knowing my Aunt Mindy is in the military, and at Pearl Harbor, questions about her are constant.

"What was it like, the bombing?" "Did she see any fighting?" "How many hurt soldiers did she treat?"

Needing her next letter, I need to know what to say and if Paul is OK? I know she will tell me, us, about it, about the people she helps in the next letter. Will it come next month? I know the mail is delayed. I know she is the Florence Nightingale of this war. I am proud of her, my aunt in the navy. She is doing her part in the service of our country.

That night Ed comes by, "Sarah, what do you hear from Mindy."

He wants to be sure she is OK. We are sure she is. Stationed at the hospital, it has bright red crosses on it. The Japanese won't attack the hospitals.

Momma tells him, "Ed, I am sure she is all right. We haven't heard anything. I'll tell you as soon as I know."

Does Momma tell him about the letters and Aunt Mindy's cook? Needing time Ed will forget her, at least that is what Momma thinks. She will tell him how Aunt Mindy feels when his love fades, when he is ready.

When I get home the first day of school following my Christmas break, momma is crying. What is wrong? Momma doesn't cry often. Making me sit down, with tears streaming down her face, she looks at me.

"Honey— Paul, Aunt Mindy's husband-to-be was a cook on a ship. With their wedding coming up, he invited Aunt Mindy for Sunday breakfast on his ship. We know she left nurse's quarters before daybreak to go there, to meet him, to be there while he was getting breakfast for her, and the crew. He wanted her to meet the men he works with and his commander.

"Honey, Aunt Mindy, your Aunt Mindy, Mindy, my baby sister Mindy— Honey, Mindy was on the ship when the bombing started. The ship sank. No one has seen her since then. Grandma called, they got the telegram today! The navy believes she is dead, along with Paul and all the other people on that ship!"

Momma burst into tears.

I sit looking at her. Is she crazy? Aunt Mindy isn't dead! I know she is all right, taking care of everyone else. Then what she says hits!

Getting up I scream, "NO! NO! NO! It's not true! She's fine! She will write me another letter and tell us it is a mistake! She is OK--- She's alive! Aunt Mindy is alive, helping other people!"

Leaving the table I run. Running to my place in the woods where Aunt Mindy sits and listens to me talk, I keep saying, "No! No! No!" She can't be dead. She is alive in my heart. She is alive! She is coming back to see me. She is going to bring her Paul and we are all going to be family! Not true! It isn't true! A light snow falls. Darkness creeps into the woods. Thomas comes to get me.

Not believing it, I do not believe it then! I do not believe it when they have her funeral! There is no casket. There is a huge beautiful headstone with an angel and border. Knowing it cost a lot of money, no one and everyone knows who pays for it. A few days later someone sees a gold Cadillac and a man, kneeling, crying, holding the headstone. The next week Grandma gets a letter. There are now three full scholarships at the nursing school Aunt Mindy attended. In her name those scholarships will go on forever funded by a trust.

What is this? This is foolishness. She is not dead. She is in Hawaii and fine! I know it. She will write me. I look in the mailbox every day. She can not die or leave me, without letting me say goodbye! Why would I accept this? Keeping the faith that she is alive, that she is coming to see me in the spring, as she promises, I do not give up!

Going to church the next Sunday, the preacher announces that our beloved Mindy was killed in the attack on Pearl Harbor, Momma crying. We hear a painful wailing. Coming from the choir it is Ed.

Completely forgetting about Ed and his love for her, that is how he finds out she is dead. He sobs. He stumbles out of the choir loft and makes his way outside. Following him, forgetting him we don't even think about him! Stopping, he is sitting with his face buried in his hands on the church steps. Why didn't any of us appreciate how much he loves her, have the courtesy to tell him?

Momma sits down beside him trying to comfort him, trying to tell him Aunt Mindy loves him, "Ed, she, Mindy, Mindy loves---." Choking up the words don't come out, aren't true.

"I love her," he says.

Ed goes. Never seeing him again, we hear that he is down at the Marine Corps recruiting office the next day signing up. Saying he is old the recruiter is about to turn him down, then Ed takes off his shirt and challenges the recruiter to try him out if he thinks he is tough enough.

Taking one look, the recruiter smiles and says, "Sign here!"

Ed doesn't want to wait. They have him on the next bus after they do his physical.

Months go by. Knowing Aunt Mindy will come back to me, I know she won't leave me. I develop a cold spot in my heart, as the adult that shows so much love never writes, never makes any contact. In time, it is a wound in my tree of life that grows over. Being invisible, doesn't mean the wound heals. It stays as fresh as the day momma tells me she is dead.

I pray for her every night. Writing her every day I put her letters in the mailbox. Momma waiting until I am gone to school gets my letters out, saves every one of them.

Never crying, I never admitted she is dead. I can't! It is my fault. I tripped her, made her fall and hit her head. It is my fault that she doesn't stay with us. I am bad. I must be bad! That is the reason that she is not here with us now! Is that the reason Amber left too, because of me? Amber loved me. Aunt Mindy loved me. Did both of them die because of me?

I tell this to Momma.

Hugging me tight she won't let me go, "Honey, the only reason Aunt Mindy thought of staying is because she loved you. You are the reason she wanted to live. Don't you know that? Amber too, Amber loved you very much. She didn't die because she loved you! Don't think that! It's not true!"

Aunt Mindy says it is because she needs to have a new life that she has to go, says she will always love me, that she is coming home to me. In my mind I feel that if I were a better girl she would be here. It is my fault. I tried to be a good girl. If I am a better girl she will turn up, write me and tell me it is a mistake! She is all right! She and her sailor are coming to see me in the spring when the Jonquils bloom again. I never stopping believing in her, I believe she is alive and loves me.

Then in the spring, I make my daily stop by the mailbox. Inside is a letter from Aunt Mindy. THERE IS A LETTER FROM AUNT MINDY! I quiver. I open it.

> *December 6, 1941,*
> *Sharon, My Dear Sharon,*
> *You are not a bad girl! You are the most wonderful girl, my girl! I love you. I will never leave you! I have you in my heart and in my mind every time I close my eyes.*
>
> *Sharon, I am so happy. I want you to know. Now there is Paul. I love him too. Be our flower girl! I know you can't come to Hawaii now. When we come home in the spring I want you to find some Jonquils for us and we will have you for our flower girl there.*
>
> *Honey, Paul and I will never have a daughter like you. You see there is something special about Paul. I went in the service to get away because I couldn't be a mother. Paul had mumps when he was a young man, was very much in love with his sweet heart and about to be married. He still loves her, as I love your Uncle Jim, but neither of us can or could give our life partners what they need, children. He has been cooking in the navy for the last twelve years, happy enough, among men, doing service. This is what I am doing being a navy nurse.*
>
> *We met at the doctor's office, he took me to a nice restaurant, but before we even finished the salad he was telling me he couldn't have children expecting it to be a nice dinner, then a good by, or let's be friends kind of thing. You should have seen the look on his face when I told him I couldn't either! Maybe that look was more*

*because I started crying so hard we didn't get a chance to try the main course, but it started something.*

*I will always love him, but not like Uncle Jim, and he won't love me like his Mary either, but we are good company, and get along well. He needs a wife, a woman in his life, and I need a man in mine. We will be happy, although, always childless. Like other couples who cannot have children, we want them. We want you. Most families have a couple or two like us, childless aunts and uncles. I always wanted a little girl like you, now I know there will never be another girl like you. You will always be my girl, my only girl.*

*Paul and I have talked and I talked to your mother before I left. I want you to be my child, or at least partly mine. Your mother agreed that you could come visit me and spend some time in the summers if I had a place.*

*Paul and I will have a place in married base housing next year. You can come visit us over the summers. It is a beautiful place, we can go swimming in the ocean every day. Paul and I would be so happy to have you with us! Come to Hawaii with us, Sharon!*

*We love you!*
*Aunt Mindy*

*PS, Remember, when the Jonquils bloom again, know that I love you.*
*I will write you more tomorrow. I must sign off now. I have an early morning. I am going for breakfast on Paul's ship to meet the men he works with and his commander.*
*Love*
*Mindy*

Reading it, I read it over and over. Never knowing where the letter comes from, it is lost, found and mailed. Someone sends it along, never realizing how much it will mean to me. As I read it, I almost cry. Welling up in my eyes are tears. Stopping them, holding the letter close to my heart, I run to my special place.

Starting to go in and sit down, I see them! I haven't been there for a few days. My special place is surrounded by a double row of Jonquils! Their yellow heads bob above a snow patch each of them beautiful. How does she know? Why does her letter arrive then, when the Jonquils are blooming?

Falling on my knees in the moist wood's earth, a yellow Jonquil bounces kisses my face. Something hurts my knee. A sharp little pain I move then try to find the pebble with my hand. It is not a pebble, it's a ring, a ring on a thin gold chain, Amber's ring!

I remember Amber's words, "This ring symbolizes Albert's and my love. Wearing it means I am his, always his. There is a ring in my heart for you little sister. I will always love you too. Ok, this ring seeing it, when you see it know that I love you, OK?"

Is *Aunt Mindy in heaven in a cloud watching over me? I, a clove, a flower, embedded in the ground of life live. Does she live? Clouds and flowers living above me guide me. Flowers past in the soil feed me. Breaking ground, poking green tendrils through a pile of snowflakes I take my place on the earth. In a year or three I blossom, become a woman, experience the love of a flower. For now my immature leaves reach for the sun. Holding me are Aunt Mindy, Amber, Momma, Daddy, brothers, sisters, a world of Jonquils.*

*The beginning*

Albert is in Hawaii behind a stack of sandbags his machine gun looking out over the Pacific. Will he find Amber. When will I meet my husband, love him? Will I see Aunt Mindy again, talk to her again?

*The stories continued in:*
*When The Jonquils Bloom Again*
*books 2, 3 and 4*
*to be available soon.*

Send a post card to:
PTL Publishing
PO Box 65130
Vancouver, WA 98665

To be advised of publication dates. As well, this book will be reedited and included in a series publication later. Free copies will be given to those we view as providing us with meaningful editing. If you see any errors or things that you think should be improved send us your comments.

Thanks

J G Knox

## About the Author

J. G. Knox, a fiction writer, one who loves, one who shares love and life in words. What else is important about J. G. Knox? Are writer's credentials significant? Credentials matter in nonfiction. Eloquence does not substitute for knowledge in a text book. Fiction is for enjoying. Fiction is fiction, not reality. Joy and enlightenment matter in fiction. Did you come away from reading this book with empathy for Sharon and her family? Did you come away with a better understanding of yourself and others? If so, then recommend this book to others.

Printed in the United States
116459LV00003B/43-66/P